T0323376

Soho at Work

What is it like to work in a place that is both a thriving and close-knit community and a globally recognized part of the commercial sex industry? London's Soho has always been a place of complexity, contrast and change throughout its colourful history, yet urban branding, local community initiatives and licensing regulations have combined to 'clean up' Soho, arguably to the point of sanitization, and commercial over-development remains a continuing threat. In spite of all this, Soho retains its edge and remains a unique place to live, work and consume. Based on a ten-year ethnographic study of working in Soho's sex shops, combining archival material, literary sources, photographic materials and interviews with men and women employed there, Tyler draws together insights from history, geography and cultural studies to tell the unseen story of this fascinating workplace.

Melissa Tyler is a professor of Work and Organization Studies at the University of Essex. Her work on emotional, sexualized and aesthetic labour, on gender, sexuality and the body, and on place, space and workplace setting has been published in a range of international journals, authored books and edited collections.

Soho at Work

Pleasure and Place in Contemporary London

Melissa Tyler

University of Essex

CAMBRIDGE
UNIVERSITY PRESS

University Printing House, Cambridge CB2 8BS, United Kingdom

One Liberty Plaza, 20th Floor, New York, NY 10006, USA

477 Williamstown Road, Port Melbourne, VIC 3207, Australia

314–321, 3rd Floor, Plot 3, Splendor Forum, Jasola District Centre, New Delhi – 110025, India

79 Anson Road, #06–04/06, Singapore 079906

Cambridge University Press is part of the University of Cambridge.

It furthers the University's mission by disseminating knowledge in the pursuit of education, learning, and research at the highest international levels of excellence.

www.cambridge.org
Information on this title: www.cambridge.org/9781107182738
DOI: 10.1017/9781316875704

First published 2020

Printed in the United Kingdom by TJ International Ltd, Padstow Cornwall

A catalogue record for this publication is available from the British Library.

Library of Congress Cataloging-in-Publication Data
Names: Tyler, Melissa, 1971– author.
Title: Soho at work : pleasure and place in contemporary London / Melissa Tyler.
Description: [New York] : Cambridge University Press, [2019] | Includes bibliographical references and index.
Identifiers: LCCN 2019037649 (print) | LCCN 2019037650 (ebook) | ISBN 9781107182738 (hardback) | ISBN 9781316875704 (ebook)
Subjects: LCSH: Sex workers – England – London – Social conditions – 21st century. | Sex-oriented businesses – England – London. | Gentrification – England – London. | Place attachment – England – London. | Ethnology – England – London. | Soho (London, England) – Social conditions – 21st century. | Soho (London, England) – Economic conditions – 21st century.
Classification: LCC HQ186.L66 T88 2019 (print) | LCC HQ186.L66 (ebook) | DDC 338.4/7306709421–dc23
LC record available at https://lccn.loc.gov/2019037649
LC ebook record available at https://lccn.loc.gov/2019037650

ISBN 978-1-107-18273-8 Hardback
ISBN 978-1-316-63559-9 Paperback

Cambridge University Press has no responsibility for the persistence or accuracy of URLs for external or third-party internet websites referred to in this publication and does not guarantee that any content on such websites is, or will remain, accurate or appropriate.

For Philip, Ellis and William. My greatest pleasure and place is wherever you are. By a happy coincidence, that is quite often in Soho.

Contents

Illustrations

Preface: Working Soho

Writing in 1901, temperance reformer and politician Arthur Sherwell observed that 'so far as the more intimate facts of its moral and social life are concerned, Soho remains to a very large extent a terra incognita to the outsider'.[1] Drawing on invaluable insights from the many cultural historians who have written about Soho, as well as first-hand accounts of those who work there today, this book's aim, as far as possible, is to get to know Soho, to 'place it' at work.

Somewhat paradoxically, given the decidedly adult nature of the area, it was at a vaguely recalled point during my childhood that I first contracted 'Sohoitis'.[2] As so many others have written about, it is the sound, smell and feel of being in Soho that I remember most poignantly. In particular, I can still sense the excitement of arriving in Soho early on a Sunday morning, ready for a day out in London with my family. My father had been a student in London in the 1960s. He knew a car park in Soho (on Brewer Street) and a family-run local cafe where we could start our day with breakfast, before exploring Covent Garden market and the West End's relatively deserted streets and parks. To beat the (practically non-existent) traffic, we would arrive early, park and head straight into the heart of Soho. The sounds and smells of coffee machines, the (then) exoticism of freshly baked croissants and hand-pressed orange juice, and the excitement, to my childlike understanding, of so many people, dressed in feathers, sequins and leather, being up and about so early in the morning left a lasting impression. Of course, with hindsight, it was more likely that the still exuberant revellers that surrounded our quaint family gathering were not early risers at all but were at the tail end of the kind of nights out described by cultural historian Judith Walkowitz. But many were probably exhausted workers coming in for much-needed sustenance before heading to bed, having been busy in Soho's many bars, restaurants, clubs and brothels throughout the night. The atmosphere was warm, noisy, cosy and incredibly friendly. Of course I overly romanticize (this is one of the more obvious, and troubling, symptoms of Sohoitis), but those experiences, in those cafes, are among my fondest childhood memories.

Feeling simultaneously part of something, somehow in the thick of it, but also on the periphery, and quietly soaking in everything going on around you is both comforting and unsettling, whether you are a child in awe of a world that seems like one big party or an adult ethnographer with a notebook, camera and recorder. These Sunday morning trips to London, but particularly to Soho, were something I looked forward to more and more. To my child's eyes, they gave a glimpse into a different world. But in some ways they provided a window on a way of life that was not so far removed from the small village I grew up in. Indeed, for many who have written about Soho, it is this sense of Soho as both a close-knit community and a place 'on the edge', a small village in which everyone knows everyone else's business, in the heart of one of the world's largest and most vibrant cities, that makes Soho so compelling.

Like historical author Mike Hutton, I realized that I had been seduced by Soho from an early age. He recalls in his book *The Story of Soho* how family visits left him with a similar sense that Soho was a place of stark contradictions:

Somewhere to have fun, and yet to remain wary. Sometimes warm and welcoming, yet also mean and threatening. It walks a fine line between the exhilarating and the sordid.[3]

My fascination with the extremes Hutton describes, and with Soho as 'an island of entertainment and temptation',[4] continued throughout my childhood and then waned as I moved on and moved away from my family home. It was as a young adult in the early 1990s that I rediscovered Soho, visiting again for the first time some fifteen or so years since those early encounters with Soho's partygoers, street workers and cafes. My initial sense was that Soho had changed beyond recognition; gone were many of the cafes and family-run businesses I remembered; fading was the variety of shop fronts and names. In their place, commercial sex was ubiquitous. It may well be of course that the latter was there in abundance throughout my childhood. At this point Soho was somewhere to visit for me, not a place to study. Perhaps I hadn't noticed the plethora of neon signage, plastic curtains and paper-covered windows, or the endless racks of PVC underwear and sex toys, the cards in phone boxes advertising 'models' or in doors to stairwells inviting customers in for a 'French polish'.

When I gradually began to visit Soho more and more another ten or so years later, in the mid-2000s, the place seemed to have moved on again. Sex shops and the industry more generally no longer seemed to dominate.

This role had now been taken on by high-street chains and brand names familiar on retail parks or in shopping centres in many other towns and cities across the United Kingdom and elsewhere. But, throughout all of these changes, something remained that made Soho the place it was. And it is this 'something' that is the focus of this book and of my ongoing love-hate relationship with Soho. I have tried to convey this in the book's title, *Soho at Work*, to emphasize that, for me at least, and for the cultural historians, geographers and sociologists whose ideas I draw on, as well as in the first-hand accounts I weave into the narrative, this 'something' is largely associated with the combined effects of Soho's working communities and the place itself – Soho is not a passive backdrop against which social action takes place: as a character in its own narrative, it *does* something.

As an academic researcher with a particular interest in emotional, aesthetic and sexualized forms of work; in gender, sexuality and the body; in sales-service work and in organizational spaces and places, I became increasingly fascinated with Soho as a workplace. It was on a cold January day in 2008, while asking for directions in one of the licensed sex shops on the edge of Soho, that I started chatting to a man called Michael who had worked there for several years. He seemed as interested in Soho as I am, and we continued a thread of email and face-to-face discussions over several weeks and then months until, prompted by him and the themes recurring in our conversations, I decided to make my interest in Soho official and embark on an ethnographic study.

And so, initially through my conversations with Michael and others he put me in touch with, I started out on a study of Soho that lasted from roughly 2009 until the present and remains ongoing. Every time I think I am 'done' with Soho, I am somehow drawn back to it. For the research on which this book is based, I undertook a series of interviews with people who work in Soho's sex shops[5]; I observed them and their customers in the shops, and I walked the streets, watching, looking and listening, and photographing as I went. Without thinking about it consciously at the time, I drew in this sense on a well-established tradition of London writers, from Charles Dickens to Ian Sinclair, who have walked its streets in order to get to know its character, inspired by Parisian flâneurs and psycho-geographers. All of this combined to give me an ethnographic 'snapshot' of what it is like to work in this particular place, at this particular point in its history, in a sector of work for which the area continues to have a reputation well beyond its own geographical boundaries.

Soho at Work is the outcome of that study. It tells the story of contemporary Soho through its focus on this specific group of workers, in this very distinctive setting. The story is told largely in their own words and mine, but with strong echoes of and references to the work of others along the way, especially sociologists, historians and cultural geographers. I am grateful to other writers who have produced meticulously researched accounts of Soho and its neighbouring areas on which I have been able to draw – most notably Judith Summers, whose *Soho and Its History* has been a constant source of insight and inspiration. I have also drawn heavily on Carol Walkowitz's *Nights Out: Life in Cosmopolitan London*, which explores how Soho's distinctive character has evolved through the history of its people and places, against a backdrop of theories of urban cosmopolitanism. Another invaluable source was Frank Mort's *Capital Affairs*. Focusing on London and the making of the permissive society, Mort inevitably hones in on Soho, drawing in incredible detail on the area's history and mapping out changes and continuities in what makes Soho the 'edgy' place that it was and, many argue, still is (or at least might be again). Peter Speiser's (2017) *Soho: The Heart of Bohemian London* provided a rich overview of key developments and characters in Soho's colourful past, telling the tale of 'one of London's most famous, cosmopolitan, colourful and notorious neighborhoods'.[6] Walking his reader through Soho's streets and squares, considering those who have made (and squandered) their living there, including through the worlds of art and entertainment, Speiser's narrative is a compelling starting point for anyone who wants to get to know the area and to consider the contemporary legacy of Soho's chequered past.

Mort in particular has emphasized that the 'porousness of London's sexual cultures was encouraged by the city's extremely compressed urban layout'.[7] But others have highlighted the significance of this too: Walkowitz begins *Nights Out* by noting how, from the late eighteenth and early twentieth centuries, Soho's porous geographic identity and borderlands, not to mention its doubtful commerce, politics and population, all contributed to its pre-eminence as London's cosmopolis.[8]

Aligning itself with this view, the account of Soho that will be given here tries to connect its history, geography, culture and economy to understand what makes Soho 'work' as a dynamic nexus of its materiality and the meanings with which it is associated. My hope is to show, in the pages that follow, how this combination is what makes Soho work the way it does and has, throughout its colourful history. Soho may not be perfect, but, as a working and residential community with a long and unique history, it is precious. And, as the following chapters explain, in the face of constant attempts to clean it up or to clean up on it, it is nothing if not persistent; long may it continue to be so.

Acknowledgements

As someone who enjoys sharing ideas and learning from others, single authoring is not my preferred way of working. However, many people have helped me over the course of writing this book, so that it has never really felt like a solo endeavour. This means that there are many people to thank.

First and foremost, I would like the men and women working in Soho's sex shops to know how extremely grateful I am to them for so generously sharing their time, thoughts and experiences with me. I recall many interviews undertaken at sales counters in the shops, often with hard-core porn films playing next to us as we talked. On numerous occasions I had to apologize to the transcriber for the sounds that were audible in the background of the recordings. Many of the interviews also took place in local cafes and bars; some happened in Soho Square and others on benches in St Anne's churchyard, while participants shared their lunch break, and often also their lunch, with me. A whole network of people welcomed me into their working lives and community, and without their generosity and openness I would have been adrift.

I remember doing interviews while helping to unpack stock and with participants who 'walked and talked' me around their store, and the streets around their workplace, making suggestions about what I should photograph and make notes on. I recall one particular interview, on a very rainy Monday morning, when one participant, Jason, spotted me in a cafe on Old Compton Street and invited me to have a coffee with him in the small office at the back of his shop. As we talked, and he explained why working in Soho was so important to him, his red setter dog curled up by our feet (admittedly blocking what heat was coming from the small radiator). To be recognized and welcomed in this way was greatly appreciated. As each batch of interviews and observations drew to a close, I always felt somewhat regretful at the prospect of not spending time in Soho for a while. Not only did participants share their work time and space with me; many also introduced me to people working in other shops, and for this I am also very grateful.

But I also remember how unnerved I felt the first time I interviewed Andy, when he cleaned out his nails with a Stanley knife blade throughout the hour or so in which we talked in a very quiet shop down quite a secluded alleyway. I also recall phoning my daughter's school to find out if she was having a good day, simply to reconnect, after my interview with Richard in the shop in which he worked, an unlicensed (and now closed) shop that specialized in school-girl– and 'barely legal'–themed hard-core magazines and films. As will be emphasized in the chapters throughout this book, Soho is a place of extremes, and of complexity and contradiction, welcoming and off-putting in equal measure.

My aim in writing this book was to convey some of this through the narratives of the men and women who work in its sex shops, and to produce an account of their work, and of Soho, in which they would recognize themselves; I apologize in advance to anyone for whom this isn't the case. One of the many things that, for me, makes Soho such a fascinating place is that, within its compact geography, it is multilayered and constantly changing. This makes it difficult (some might say laughably naive), to try to 'capture' this in a single study or text. And at the end of the day, the book is my own account of the myriad stories and commentaries I have encountered over a ten-year period.

As well as those who work in Soho's sex shops, many in its cafes, bars and restaurants have welcomed me as my laptop and I have spent many happy hours (alas not of the 'two-for-one' cocktail kind) writing up notes and drafting chapters. Worthy of a special mention are Bar Italia and Balans for their kindness and patience. There are many Soho 'institutions' that are not connected to the sex industry there, or at least not directly so. Two of many such places are the Algerian Coffee Stores and Gerry's Wines and Spirits, both on Old Compton Street, both of which have provided welcome comestibles at either end of the working day.

The Soho Society generously shared materials and updates and invited me to attend planning meetings, AGMs, social events and Soho Society annual fairs. This gave invaluable insight into Soho as a thriving and vibrant residential community, as well as a greater understanding of the constant struggles over planning and commercial development there. The British Library, The Photographer's Gallery, The Museum of Soho, Soho Radio, Westminster City Archives, and the planning, licensing and enforcement teams at Westminster City Council were also important sources of information and understanding. I was grateful to be consulted over the Council's review of Licensing Conditions for Sex

Establishment Venues (SEVs) 2012 and to be able to feed some of the concerns of those who work in Soho's licensed sex shops into this consultation process. I am also very grateful to Champagne Charlie, who kindly shared his thoughts on the importance of Soho's LGBTQ history and venues and who offered a performer's perspective on the implications of its current commercial development (as well as many fine evenings of entertainment when publisher's deadlines were the last thing on my mind).

Over the years in which I have been working on the book, many academic colleagues and friends have generously shared ideas, experiences and suggestions or have provided very welcome opportunities for me to talk about my research on Soho. My first thanks must go to Ruth Simpson and Natasha Slutskaya, whose ESRC seminar series on dirty work provided the initial opportunity for me to start thinking and writing about Soho back in 2008. Philip Hubbard very generously shared materials and insights with me in the early stages, and his work has been a constant reference point in the years since and continues to be so. There are many others to thank for their interest in the project and for their insight, in person and through their work, but of particular note are: Joanna Brewis, Dawn Lyon, Kathleen Riach, Katie O'Sullivan, Torkild Thanem, David Knights, Alison Pullen, Karen Dale, Gibson Burrell, Martin Parker and Irena Grugulis, as well as many other colleagues at the universities of Loughborough and Essex and at the various universities where I have presented my research on Soho, including Bristol, Brunel, Keele, Kent and Lancaster. Special thanks go to the Gender and Diversity Studies group at Radboud University, particularly to Yvonne Benschop. I am also grateful to doctoral students, particularly those in my 'Advanced Qualitative Research Methods' course at the University of Essex, for their patience over the years in putting up with constant examples from my Soho research. I am especially grateful to Alison Clarke, Sophie Hales and Louise Nash for being a source of constant inspiration and such a pleasure to work with.

I am hugely grateful to Valerie Appleby at Cambridge University Press, for her commitment to the project and for her enthusiasm for its ethnographic orientation, and to Toby Ginsberg, for his expertise and guidance, particularly on the images. Wade Guyitt, whose thoughts on the manuscript in its final stages were very welcome, was the most diligent copy editor anyone could hope to work with.

My final thanks go to my family. Ellis and William have been patient and encouraging throughout. Ellis has kindly shared my interest in Soho. A week of work experience at the Prince Edward Theatre there gave her a glimpse into Soho's working community, and her own ideas and insights have been very welcome. Philip has always been a source of support and inspiration, generously making time for me to work and sending source materials my way. Everything he does for me, at work and at home, is appreciated more than I can say.

As I said, this has never been a solo project, and I am very grateful to everyone whose contributions have been invaluable along the way.

Introduction
Pleasure and Place in Soho

'Soho is not always pleasant, but it is never dull.'[1]

This is a book about working in a particular place, a place 'built around enjoyment and entertainment'[2] as well as exploitation and excess. It is about how that place 'works' to shape the experiences and identities of those based there. Occupying less than a square mile, London's Soho is something of a simultaneously global and local space. With its golden squares, red lights, black markets, pink neon, blue films and, most recently, rainbow flags, Soho has, throughout its history, been a colourful place in which to live, work and consume. Described rather affectionately by cultural historian Judith Walkowitz as a 'land of lost causes',[3] and by author Nigel Richardson, who experienced Soho bohemianism in the 1950s first-hand, as both 'bad and beautiful', it is a place of 'backstreet industry and below-stairs debauchery', where those who want to stand out can and those who want to blend in can become invisible.[4] 'By reputation the most exciting and tempting part of London'[5], Soho has been at the heart of the capital's sex industry throughout its history.[6] In his substantial biography of London, Peter Ackroyd highlights how sex in the city has commonly been 'associated with dirt and disease; if not with these, then with trade'.[7] In Soho these three elements are definitively, even doggedly, intertwined.

Despite considerable changes in recent years, Soho continues to have an international reputation for commercial sex in all its many forms. An urban village in the heart of one of the busiest cities in the world, Soho is 'both homely village and red-light district', as Judith Summers puts it.[8] A magnet for consumers, it is also a vibrant workplace and a thriving residential community. Throughout its history, Soho has welcomed outsiders, and, as Figure 1 illustrates, those who live and work there today are keen to emphasize that this is still very much the case.

In *Nights Out: Life in Cosmopolitan London*, Judith Walkowitz notes how Soho has 'long been a storied place'.[9] Legends abounding in Soho credit the area with the unique ability to continually reinvent itself as a bohemian enclave, sustained for over three centuries; others claim that Soho is no longer what it was, having caved in to gentrification and

Figure 1 'Outsiders Welcome', waiter's apron, Old Compton Street

sanitization or, at the very least, a 'blandification' of its character.[10] Walkowitz challenges both interpretations, and I follow in her footsteps, arguing that Soho is neither timeless beauty nor terminal disease, but a little of both, and more. What makes Soho what it is as a working community is its capacity to thrive in the most adverse of circumstances. And this distinctive character, I will argue here, sustains its ability to continually evolve through reinvention and recitation, often of its own historical and cultural reference points. In this sense, Soho is the outcome of a dynamic combination of meaning and materiality through which social and material processes collide in order to produce this distinctive, somehow excessive and irrepressible, sector, setting and space. Soho's pleasure markets of food, theatre, fashion, music and sex interlink with the specifics of the area's history, location and urban geography to enable Soho to literally 'take place'.

Yet although much has been written about the area, little is known about the work experiences of those employed in the many sex shops for which this very particular place has a global reputation. How does Soho's global association with commercial sex impact upon the work experiences of those employed there? What is it like to work in one of Soho's many sex shops? What are the emotional, aesthetic and sexual demands of the role, and how are these demands shaped by the place itself? How does the constantly 'changing face' of Soho shape the experiences of those who work there?

Drawing on an ethnographic study of sales-service work in Soho's sex shops, this book aims to respond to questions such as these by emphasizing that *place matters*; in other words, place is not a neutral backdrop but plays an active role in shaping the ways in which work is perceived and experienced. In this sense, the book aims to convey a strong sense of what it feels like to work in this particular place, at this particular point in its history.

Soho at Work has four specific aims. First, it seeks to provide a rich, detailed account of Soho as a place of work at this point in its evolution. In this respect, the aim is to offer both a contemporary and historical account of Soho as a working community, by situating current experiences in their historical context, and with reference to the accumulated meanings and associations that are materialized in Soho's commercial sex industry. Second, *the books* draws on the findings of ethnographic research to document the working lives of some of the many men and women who are employed in Soho's sex shops. Extracts from interviews, excerpts from field notes and vignettes will be woven into each chapter to bring the place and its characters to life and to convey the themes considered in each chapter through rich, ethnographic detail. As Peter Speiser has written in his history of Soho, 'there are so many sides to Soho and so many things going on that it is difficult to know where to begin'.[11] Although much has been said and written about Soho, the area is as fascinating as ever, arguably more so at this particular point in its history than it has been for some time, as it seems to be (once again) on the cusp of a resplendent re-emergence, or of going down all together, depending on whose point of view is being expressed. One of the aims of this book is to explain why these different views abound and to consider what impact they have on those who work there, with reference to Soho's reputation for sleaze, style and shabby sophistication.

Conveying something of Soho's many layers, historical and contemporary, and depicting the multiple traces of its past in its present and possible future is an important aim that underpinned the ethnographic approach taken to the research. With this in mind, the third aim of the book is to develop a conceptual and theoretical analysis of the significance of place to understanding lived experiences of work, mapping out the analytical potential of an organizational geography for studying and understanding the relationship between sector and setting in interactive service environments. Drawing on observational, photographic and interview data, the book aims to provide a detailed analysis of the emotional, aesthetic and sexualized labour performed by men and women working in Soho, teasing out some of the distinctions as well as the overlaps in how these different aspects of interactive sales-service work are experienced in and through the particularities of their work setting.

Finally, and on this basis, the book strives to make an interesting contribution to research on 'dirty work', work that is associated with multiple physical, social and/or moral taints, by focusing on lived experiences of abject labour or forms of work that provoke a simultaneous sense of fascination and repulsion for those who perform them. In its discussion of the latter, the book aims to emphasize the significance of place to understanding how abject forms of work, and abject work *places*, are experienced, perceived and made sense of.

What remains of this Introduction will try to set the scene for the rest of the book, providing an overview of current issues shaping lived experiences and perceptions of Soho. The complexity of the place now, and historically, makes it impossible to reflect the full range of these, but I hope to 'conjure up' a feeling for the place and to be able to convey a strong sense of the lived experiences of those who work there, in the sex industry, at this particular point in time. With this in mind, the discussion will focus on three key themes: (i) the changing commercial culture and character of Soho; (ii) current issues shaping the regulation and licensing of Soho's many remaining sex shops and entertainment venues, and finally; (iii) current concerns and debates regarding the gentrification, urban rebranding and sanitization of Soho.

Judith Walkowitz asks in her account of cosmopolitan London, '[H]ow did this tiny space … become a potent incubator of metropolitan change?'[12] To find answers to this question – and there are many – Walkowitz considers the commercial economies that connect Soho to its peripheries and to the world beyond, charting how these economies enabled Soho to 'gain fame as a relaxed zone of freedom and toleration, [as a place] … where the usual rules did not apply, while also producing a social scene marked by segregation, tensions, and inequalities'.[13] In addition to considering this contextual focus, the aim is to map out the main chapters of the book, explaining their respective focus and outlining how the chapters connect together in order to meet the aims just described. But first we need to give some thought to where, and what, Soho is.

The Name, the Place and the Experience

As Daniel Farson puts it in his book *Soho in the Fifties*, 'Soho has always been a state of mind rather than a boundary',[14] a sentiment that is captured in the details of the origins of its name.[15] As literary critic Alec Waugh wrote in 1920, Soho epitomizes the idea that 'certain words and certain names seem to contain within them the very essence of the things and places which they designate'. He goes on: '[T]here is a glamour about the word: it is crude and rough.'[16] Thought to be an exclamatory Anglo-French call originating in the mid-sixteenth century when Henry VIII acquired hunting fields following the dissolution of the English monasteries,[17] Summers notes how the term 'So-hoe!' seems to have been used specifically to signal the discovery of a hare. *Brewer's Dictionary of Phrase and Fable* adds that the name most likely evolved as a localized synonym for 'tally-ho!'.[18] It is perhaps apt that these predatory associations continue to the present day, as the name has come to mean something well beyond the hunting ground to which it originally referred. One of the earliest recordings of the term 'Soho' originates from 1562, when the Lord Mayor of London and his retinue hunted and feasted in the area after undertaking a formal inspection of the conduits, which brought water into the City. This combination of business and pleasure has been another enduring (if not always endearing) characteristic of Soho ever since.

The place itself, as a geographical location, is bound roughly to the north by Oxford Street, to the west by Regent Street, to the east by Charing Cross Road (formerly 'Hog Lane', immortalized by Hogarth – see later in this chapter) and to the south by Shaftesbury Avenue. Cross any of these boundaries and the change is palpable. Step into Soho and one immediately, even now, can feel a sense of being somewhere distinctive in the heart of a bustling metropolis. Part of the reason for this, and a contributing factor to much of Soho's history throughout the twentieth century, is that no public transport runs, or ever has run, through its streets. Indeed, the imminent arrival of London's Crossrail network has caused some concern that the accessibility the development is likely to bring to this part of London's West End might threaten Soho's relatively geographically 'protected' status. Speaking on the ITV News in February 2017, actor and presenter Stephen Fry explained why he had launched a petition to 'save' Soho from the transport scheme, saying that Crossrail posed a threat to Soho's 'authentic soul':

Soho is not just a metropolitan enclave . . . [I]t is a focus, a magnet for the young, creative and open-minded around the country. I believe and hope that this petition will do a great deal to focus public awareness and understanding of the dangerous waters lapping up against Soho and the very real and exciting possibilities that arise from retaining the area's spirit.[19]

As this evocation of Soho as a 'magnet for the ... open-minded' empha-sizes, the place is much more than simply a name or a geographical location. Many commentators have described Soho primarily as a sensory experi-ence. As Summers puts it when she evokes the place's distinctive aroma:

Soho smells by turn of soy sauce, dust, exhaust fumes, lust, strong coffee and cheap perfume, good wine and old beer, urine, ripe melons and rotting cabbage leaves[20].

Richardson similarly describes the place's distinctive smells and chro-matics when he recalls his bohemian adventures in 1950s Soho:

There were smells that rotated me through the compass points of Europe and beyond – Polish cabbage and Russian tobacco, French bread and Italian sausage, Swiss cheese and Turkish coffee ... Miraculously, while the rest of Europe nursed a monochrome post-war hangover, Soho had colour.[21]

Added to this, for those who work in Soho's sex shops – especially those located, as many of them are, in the basements of 'lifestyle' stores or remainder bookshops – Soho's distinctive odour is one of Victorian drains and latex. On damp days especially, the smell can become so overwhelm-ing that (between bursts of customers), cans of air freshener will be liberally sprayed at regular intervals, to avoid the smell becoming 'too off-putting', as one sex shop worker explained to me on a particularly rainy Sunday afternoon.

Indeed its olfactory distinction signals some of the ways in which Soho has, throughout its history, been a series of contradictions and conun-drums. Again Summers sums this up when she says: 'Soho is always acrid, often dirty and sometimes sordid, yet it is never intimidating. It is a humane place, built on a human scale'.[22] While many would take issue with this rather romanticized view, Summers' sense that the dis-tinctive 'spirit of Soho', the area's 'authentic soul' as Stephen Fry describes it, is a humanitarian one is widely shared, as is her emphasis on Soho's characteristic generosity in providing shelter, hope and oppor-tunity to generations of immigrants, all of whom have added to its skills, tastes and flavour.[23] This way of thinking about Soho has a long history. Thomas Burke's *Nights in London Town* (1915) describes Soho as 'the heart of Bohemian London' where 'every street is a song'.[24]

Writing at the end of the 1980s, Summers puts particular emphasis on Soho as a place where there is no pressure on people to conform or to homogenize; rather, 'Soho is Cosmopolis, and its residents are cosmopo-litan by birth and in outlook.'[25] Above all, the people of Soho are working people, so much so that – more than its name, or its geographical loca-tion – the place *is* its working community. As Summers puts it:

Soho is a tired chef having a quick smoke in an open doorway. A shop window hung with a lethal display of kitchen knives. A black leather harness studded with steel, better suited to a horse than a person . . . A woman in thick make-up and thin clothes enticing a man to come down to some dimly-lit cellar staircase. Ronnie Scott's Jazz Club at any time of the night. A Chinese nun saying a prayer in St Patrick's church. School gates sandwiched between a kebab restaurant and a hostess bar[26].

As Summers also emphasizes, in the composition of its workforce, Soho is infinitely varied. But as she also notes, throughout its history Soho has had a hard life, kicking off with delusions of Georgian grandeur, from which it soon moved on in order to get on with the more mundane tasks of making a living and sustaining a community.

As a workplace and a home for 'artists, con-artists, artistes and artisans', as Summers put it,[27] there is no other district in London, arguably in the world, like Soho. The skills brought to England by French Huguenots following the repeal of the Edict of Nantes in 1685 resulted in the proliferation of literally hundreds of workshops within Soho's borders. By the middle of the seventeenth century, almost every street contained the premises of a master clockmaker, jeweller, toymaker, silver- or goldsmith. Soho has been a magnet for artists and writers ever since. Yet, by the end of the eighteenth century, wealthy Londoners had deserted the area almost in their entirety, making for more affluent areas such as Mayfair, abandoning Soho to its migrant populations. Large family houses were broken up, particularly in and around Soho Square, and the freeholds were sold off to landlords who subdivided them into cheap tenement rooms. The area fell into decay, and – although the number of houses stayed fairly constant – by the end of the 1800s Soho's population soared and over-crowding became a significant social problem.

As the backdrop to many of Hogarth's satirical engravings, the streets of the West End of London have always been a place of vivid contrasts, of elegance and squalor, indulgence and destitution. Hogarth's *Noon*, produced in 1738, depicting a mixed group of parishioners leaving the French (originally Greek) church in Hog Lane (now Charing Cross Road) shows this most clearly, with the people spilling out into the space between the church and tavern.

But Soho is not only a place of contrasts within its own boundaries. Separated off as it is between expansive Georgian boulevards designed for display, Soho constitutes the 'back stage' of West End life, serving as 'a back region of sweated labour, artisan production, and street prostitution for the front stages of pleasure along the boulevards' and in the neighbouring corridors of power.[28] Surrounded by these commercial theatres of increasingly conspicuous consumption, Soho 'became the dark, industrial back region that serviced the spectacular front stage of the West End', its 'plebian world of industrial labour and toil' constituting a vital but unsightly backstage.[29] Architect John Nash recognized the stark division between neighbouring Mayfair and Soho when drawing up his plans for a new road to connect Marylebone Park with Carlton House, the home of the Prince Regent in the early nineteenth century. Regent Street was designed to provide a complete separation between the spaces occupied by the leisured nobility and the narrower streets inhabited by the West End's working poor. Commenting on this contrast in *The Condition of the Working Class in England*, Frederick Engels wrote of Soho:

It is in the midst of the most populous part of town, surrounded by broad, splendid avenues in which the gay world of London idles about ... It is a disorderly collection of tall, three or four-storied houses, with narrow crooked, filthy streets, in which there is quite as much life as in the great thoroughfares of the town, except that, here, people of the working-class only are to be seen ... Here live the poorest of the poor, the worst paid workers ... [in] the whirlpool of moral ruin that surrounds them.[30]

Noting the especially foul smells emanating from the fruit and vegetable market and fish stalls ('naturally all bad and hardly fit to use'), Engels writes of the houses in Soho that 'their appearance is such that no human being could possibly wish to live in them'. It was the dwellings in the narrow courts and alleyways between the main streets that Engels was particularly horrified by, noting how their 'filth and tottering ruin surpass all description'. It is the inhabitants of these places that Engels found to be 'losing daily ... their power to resist the demoralizing influence of want, filth, and evil surroundings'.[31] Charles Dickens wrote similarly in *Nicholas Nickleby* of Soho's Golden Square as a once grand but now 'bygone, faded, tumble-down street'. A widely cited illustration of the squalor that characterized Soho at this point in its history is that Dr John Snow traced the source of a cholera outbreak to a water pump in Broad Street, attributed to waste from nearby stable blocks that was found to be contaminating the water supply.

Yet Nash's desire to separate Soho from wealthier parts of the West End has also served Soho well, enabling the area to retain its identity as London's 'oldest village' long after other areas lost any sense of distinction. And Soho's proximity to wealthier parts of the West End meant that, particularly during the Victorian era, it was harder to ignore the social problems festering there than, say, the equally poverty-stricken and overcrowded East End. Consequently, Soho became something of a 'project' for middle-class philanthropists during the nineteenth and early twentieth centuries (in the same way that it would later, for councillors and politicians concerned to 'clean' it up in more recent decades). In the second half of the 1800s alone, six hospitals were set up to tackle Soho's health problems, as were a number of missionary organizations, including soup kitchens and temporary housing shelters. One notable example of these institutions was the Soho Club and Home for Working Girls, established in 1884. Open each evening, the Club provided classes in drawing, singing, needlework, music, mathematics and gymnastics specifically for girls and women working in the sex trade. As Summers describes it, the Club also had a library, canteen, bank and low-cost medical dispensary for its members.[32] But despite the efforts of philanthropists and social reformers, the living and working conditions for Soho's population deteriorated throughout much of the nineteenth and early twentieth centuries. Although later periods, including the present, brought their own problems, as Summers concludes, the Victorian and Edwardian eras were among Soho's darkest times, when poverty, child prostitution and exploitation thrived.

Soho's proximity to wealthier and more powerful areas of the West End not only made it harder to ignore than its East End neighbour, however. It also meant that Soho took on the role of the West End's backstage workshop. And this meant performing the part of central London's 'Other'. Arthur Sherwell, of the West London Mission, wrote in his *Life in West London* (1892) that in practice this positioned Soho as 'outcast London', located in the heart of the West End geographically but marginalized politically, socially and economically. Sherwell equated the weak, enervated bodies of Soho's workforce with the area's industrial character, arguing that the root causes of Soho's distress were its proximity to the luxury tastes and wasteful excesses of the West End. The expansion of the pleasure and leisure industries in Soho's neighbouring areas had resulted, on the one hand, in increasing demand for the goods and services provided there. Yet, on the other, this expansion had resulted in the development of warehouses and workshops in the area, contracting available space for housing stock and raising rents due to the increasing value of available property. As wages remained low in Soho's industrial economy, this resulted in overcrowding and in impoverished living and working conditions. As Walkowitz documents, Sherwell identified a second weakness in Soho's economy: as no one particular industry predominated, the area lacked industrial coherence and bargaining power, thereby accentuating the vulnerability of its workforce. Sherwell deemed the growing sex trade to be an outcome, rather than a cause, of Soho's precarious economy and of its proximity to the West End's 'front stage'. As many households struggled to make ends meet, men and women increasingly found their way into commercial sex as the only viable way to make a living. Again, Soho's proximity to London's centres of commercial and political power was significant, constituting an accessible and available market.[33]

However, it would be inaccurate to claim that the nineteenth and early twentieth centuries were a period of complete destitution for Soho. Soho Square continued to be a relatively thriving space of commerce and social activity. By the late 1800s, local food manufacturer Crosse and Blackwell had moved to a large factory on the north-east corner of the Square, where it remained until the 1920s. As early as 1816, London's first department store also opened in Soho Square, located just off Oxford Street, in the form of the Soho Bazaar. Added to this growth in industry and retail, Soho has always been renowned for its connections to the worlds of music, theatre and entertainment, not least because of its proximity to the heart of London's theatre land, with Shaftesbury Avenue forming its southern border. As well as the exploitation referred to already, this provided the basis for an emerging cultural economy in Soho and for its growing reputation as the heart of London's creative industries. As Alec Waugh put it, writing in 1920, as a working community Soho was 'a place of infinitely varied occupations'.[34]

It was Reverend Cardwell, the vicar of St Anne's, who convened a meeting in November 1895 to consider the impact of the growing sex industry on Soho society. Not least, he and members of his parish were concerned that landlords were discovering that higher rents could be charged to brothel keepers than to residential tenants or other workers. This, Summers notes, marked one of the earliest of Soho's 'clean-up' campaigns, as the Parish tried to place restrictions on the numbers of properties that could be rented to 'traders in vice'. In 1911, *Twenty Years in Soho* reported its views on Soho's reputation for commercial sex:

It is an unsavoury subject, but the story of the last twenty years in Soho would not be complete without some mention of the crusade against 'disorderly houses' ... which has been carried on with a considerable amount of success ... [T]he result is that Soho, though by no means perfect, is a cleaner and purer place than it once was.[35]

During this first clean-up campaign, Cardwell became a dedicated supporter of Soho and its people. Summers describes an exchange between him and Metropolitan Police Inspector Mackay reporting to a Royal Commission in 1906 that illustrates this well. Mackay claimed that Greek Street, in the heart of Soho, was one of the worst streets he had ever had to deal with, as 'some of the vilest reptiles in London live there or frequent it'. Cardwell defended Soho against what he saw as slanderous accusations against his community, perhaps over-emphasizing the case somewhat by claiming that 'not a single disreputable character' lived or worked not only in Greek Street but in the whole of Soho.[36]

Consecrated in 1686 by Bishop Henry Compton,[37] St Anne's church has a long history of being socially inclusive and of being a focal point for the area's diverse and ever-changing community. One of the clergy, Ken Leech, started the London-based charity for young homeless people 'Centrepoint' out of St Anne's. It was three members of the church vestry who set up the first parish school in Soho in 1699. The Churchyard, St Anne's Gardens, was leased to the City Council in 1894, having been closed to burials forty years earlier. This closure was largely as a result of one sexton illegally dumping bodies in the ground having sold their coffins for firewood and because the churchyards of London were full. It is believed that, in addition to the essayist William Hazlitt, about 80,000 bodies are buried there. This explains why the ground is so high above the entrance on Wardour Street, something that the many people who sit there eating sandwiches on sunny summer lunchtimes are probably quite unaware of but which, it strikes me, is entirely characteristic of Soho's history and character.

The Soho community that Cardwell was so defensive of was a rich mix of ordinary working people, many of whom served the fashion and entertainment industries that Soho sits at the heart of. In the nineteenth and early to mid-twentieth centuries, their number included tailors, pressers, seamstresses, bakers, patissiers, waiters, musical instrument makers, chefs and shop assistants. Many were Protestant; others were Catholics or were Russian or Polish Jews. In the decades to come, French and Italian people, and a growing Chinese and Malaysian population, followed. In Summers' words,

With the local English population, they formed as diverse, as culturally rich and as cosmopolitan a group of individuals as have ever lived together in any part of London, at any time.[38]

As many commentators have since noted, these different communities tended to live alongside each other, mostly harmoniously but without any obvious signs of integration or assimilation. This multiplicity of cultures, religions and languages, not to mention cuisines, living together, in such a compact geographical space, is what has made Soho such an international community, comprising 'London's most varied and colourful streets', as Summers put it.[39]

Soho's cosmopolitanism is a theme that has been written about extensively, particularly by Frank Mort, in his book *Capital Affairs*, and by

Judith Walkowitz, in *Nights Out: Life in Cosmopolitan London*. The latter emphasizes how, between 1890 and 1945, Soho's porous geography 'not to mention its doubtful commerce, politics, and population contributed to the place's pre-eminence as London's "cosmopolis".[40] For Walkowitz, part of Soho's fascination lies in the juxtaposition of, on the one hand, its 'debased condition of transgression, displacement and degeneration' and, on the other, its intimate connections to major sectors of London's global economy. As she puts it, by the first decade of the twentieth century, Soho's cosmopolitan pleasures centred on its nightlife, fashion and food cultures so that 'its seedy environs served as a strategic location for the brokering of transnational goods, bodily display, politics and appetites'.[41]

Drawing inspiration from this fascinating combination, and from accounts such as these, my aim in this book is to think about where and what Soho is now, in the early twenty-first century, through the lens of where and what it has been, and what kind of place is might become, focusing on the commercial sex industry with which Soho has always had something of a love-hate relationship.

The number of licences granted to sex shops in Soho is now strictly controlled by Westminster City Council; any new applications provoke considerable debate, with some Soho residents and local businesses objecting on the basis that sex shops continue to lower the tone of the area, encouraging undesirable people to hang around, including late at night. Others seek to protect, even preserve, the presence of sex shops as a distinctive feature of the area's history and character and as a valuable counter to the creeping presence of high-street chains and consumer brands there.[42] Love them or loathe them, Soho's sex shops remain a significant feature of the area's commercial and cultural landscape, albeit in an increasingly historical form, as they – like many aspects of Soho's 'seedy' past – come under the scrutiny of civic regulation and corporate redevelopment.

Recent examples of Soho closures that have provided a discursive focal point for these debates to revolve around include the case of Madame Jojo's and the Windmill Theatre, two clubs renowned for their stage shows. The latter closed after undercover investigators claimed performers routinely flouted 'no touching' conditions in the venue's licence. Councillors were urged to shut the club down after evidence gathered by retired detectives suggested that the dancers had broken the Sexual Entertainment Venue licensing conditions that ban physical contact between dancers and customers (apart from placing notes in the garter on a dancer's leg). On further investigation, the Council's licensing inspectors drew on CCTV footage to argue against the club's licence being renewed on the basis that 'in excess of 50 per cent of the dancers' breached the 'no touch' licensing conditions'.[43] Revoking the club's licence, Westminster City Council Leader Nickie Aiken said that there was a 'thin line between seedy and bohemian' and added that what was happening at the Windmill was 'crossing that line'.[44] Much of what goes on in Soho, now and throughout its history, has occupied the complex and compelling 'thin' ground between seedy and bohemian.

Madame Jojo's is another case in point – the club lost its licence after what was reported as a violent altercation on its premises and closed in November 2014. Journalist Peter Clark summed up the feeling of many when he wrote that this particular closure of a club renowned as an (albeit commercial) haven for outsiders signalled the 'slow death of Soho', as he bid a fond farewell to 'London's most sleazy neighbourhood'.[45] The closure prompted Stephen Fry and others to mobilize, largely via social media, around a 'Save Soho' campaign, citing the closure of Madame Jojo's, one of London's LGBTQ venues notorious for its drag acts, as another sign of the area's demise.[46] In an open letter to government,[47] Fry and local singer/songwriter Tim Arnold wrote: '[T]he square mile and its surrounds is the most creative in the world. In its way, it is at least as important as the square mile in the City.'[48]

Attempts to defend the sector, and the area, as a working community have taken other forms. In 2015, artist and ex-stripper Lucy Sparrow created Madame Roxy's Erotic Emporium, a pop-up sex shop located in Soho's Greene Court, made entirely from felt. The shop sold hand-stitched felt condoms, dildos, butt plugs, porn magazines and S&M equipment. Sparrow created the shop to challenge censorship laws and defend the rights of sex workers by exhibiting products that it would be illegal to sell in an unlicensed shop if they were not made from felt. She said, '[I]t's a celebration of what Soho used to be, and in some ways still is, but is quickly disappearing.'[49]

To understand the rich multiplicity and complexity of the place, and of the 'thin lines' that shape the sector of work considered here, *Soho at Work* draws on a range of sources. These include historical and contemporary secondary sources such as memoirs, fiction, visual art and other artefacts, public records and archives, as well as published academic research. The book also draws extensively from ethnographic research involving the collation of photographic material and fieldnotes, as well as a series of interviews, conducted over the course of some ten years or so with people who work in Soho's sex shops. As with all such sources of data, these accounts (historical and contemporary, secondary and primary) are based on situated perception – in many instances they represent not an external, factual 'reality' but reflect the nature of things, of lived experiences, and of the circumstances that shape them as they are seen and sensed by those involved – from 'street level', as Michel de Certeau put it in his discussion of the extent to which, in order to understand a place, we need to be 'clasped' by it.[50] In many instances, they may reflect a particular vision and intent. Woven together, they provide a rich, detailed, immersive account of what it is like to work in a sex shop in Soho at this particular point in its history. In this sense, the book strives to be both a cultural geography – a sociological account of a particular work*place* – and a narrative history, given that so much of the subject matter discussed is produced through varied forms of storytelling. Some voices are historical, others contemporary, and added to the mix is, of course, my own.

The opening chapter considers Soho's interweaving history, geography and culture, before moving on to thinking, in Chapter 2, about place as an assemblage of meanings and materialities. Chapter 3 explores the lived experiences of men and women employed in Soho's sex shops, focusing on the ways in which their work is encoded, embedded and enacted in/ through the sector and setting. Through the conceptual lens of 'abject labour', the discussion in Chapter 4 highlights the extent to which the multiple taints attached to working in a sex shop, in Soho, simultaneously attract and repulse those who work there. It also considers the place as both the source of these taints and as a community-based resource on which people draw in coping with the more abject aspects of their work and workplace. Thinking about what it is that particularly attracts sex shop workers to Soho leads into a discussion, in Chapter 5, of the sector and setting as both hyper-heteronormative, as persistently, hegemonically masculine, at the same time as opening up possibilities for 'doing something different' with sexuality and gender, effectively undoing its constraints and normalizing effects, as one participant, Julie phrased it. The book concludes by engaging with current concerns about gentrification, commercial over-development and sanitization, considering what the future might hold for Soho's commercial sex industry and for its long-standing and complex associations with the business of pleasure in this very particular place, at this point in its history.

1 Soho
London's Gilded Gutter

'Sex sells and Soho sells sex.'[1]

As a place that 'plays to all the senses',[2] Soho has, throughout its history, been something of an abject space, maintaining a long-standing appeal as simultaneously alluring and threatening, exploiting many of those who work and consume there, while at the same time carefully nurturing its reputation as a place of bohemian indulgence, offering a warm embrace and a sense of belonging in the heart of an otherwise relatively anonymous urban environment. In his Foreword to Bernie Katz's book *Soho Society*, Stephen Fry emphasizes this, highlighting how the area has always offered 'outsiders' a chance to be themselves: 'Soho's public face of drugs, prostitution and seedy Bohemia ... has always hidden a private soul of family, neighbourhood, kindness, warmth and connection, and those qualities shine through doggedly.' Yet Soho also has an enduring reputation for violence and exploitation. Even Fry, one of its most vociferous defenders, is quick to warn us against being sentimental about Soho, for 'suffering, failure, sickness, despair and loneliness'[3] are also found there in abundance as some of London's most vulnerable people either gravitate to the area or are drawn there by other means, often combining desperation with market forces.

A place of complexity and contrast, Soho's most recent renaissance means that it is now associated as much with high specification ICT and post-production media, and a vibrant restaurant and bar industry, as it is with commercial sex.[4] Urban branding, local community initiatives, and the introduction and enforcement of licensing regulations have combined to 'clean up' Soho, as the twin processes of gentrification and corporatization have arguably sanitized the area beyond recognition – and certainly well beyond the accounts of Soho provided by artists and writers of the mid-twentieth century, a loosely knit group with a reputation for hedonistic living,[5] in a time cited by many as Soho's 'golden age' of bohemia.[6] But as a place to live, work and consume, Soho retains an 'edge' to it that can still be discerned only just beneath its increasingly corporate surface.

A hybrid place, shaped by a number of intersecting yet differential histories, Soho is home to a range of spiritual and political groups, many of which take an active involvement in maintaining the place's ethical openness and sexual eclecticism. In this respect alone, Soho is vulnerable not only to periodic attempts to 'clean up' what is often regarded as its seedier side; its character and location mean that it is also particularly at risk from a more commercial co-optation or corporate rebranding of its radical associations. This chapter explores all of these issues and the ways in which they shape Soho as a working community, particularly for those who work in the many sex shops for which Soho continues to have a global reputation. Behind its ever-changing façade, Soho's streets and shops continue to hold secrets; digging not too deeply beneath its surface reveals a fascinating series of intersecting histories, cultures and working lives that are considered here.

Historical Soho

The beginnings of London's West End can be traced back to the sixteenth century. Many of the streets that are familiar today can be found on maps and plans dating back to the 1600s, and the layout of Soho's central streets has altered relatively little in the last 400 years or so. In the first decades after the Fire of London in 1666, developers were keen to build on any available land, ignoring Elizabeth I's proclamation of 1582 precluding building tenements within three miles of the City. Speculators bought up land in the Soho Fields, an area between the royal palaces to the west, the City of London to the east and the Forest of Middlesex further north.

As Peter Speiser has described it in his account of Soho as 'the heart of Bohemian London', the area has attracted many remarkable inhabitants and visitors throughout its history. While twentieth-century and contemporary Soho might be thought of as the hang-out of artists, actors and the aristocracy, this association has a long history. The story largely begins in the seventeenth century, when the Duke of Monmouth, James Scott, who was the illegitimate son of Charles II, made Soho his home. Briefly residing at Monmouth House in Soho Square,[7] he is regarded by historians as being largely responsible for Soho's fashionable origins as early as the 1680s. One of Soho's most notorious historical figures is Theresa Cornelys, one-time lover of Casanova, and Soho's first society hostess who reputedly transformed the nature of evening entertainment in London. Under the auspices of the 'Society of Soho Square', the opulence of her masked balls was legendary, attracting nobility and gentry in abundance. As novelist Fanny Burney, another Soho resident (and later

Mrs D'Ablay, after whom the street is believed to be named), wrote in 1770: '[T]the magnificence of the rooms, splendour of the illuminations and embellishments, and the brilliant appearance of the company exceeded anything I ever saw before.'[8] Soho's association with London's fashionable elite was further confirmed in the first half of the eighteenth century, when the sons of both George I and II took up residence at Leicester House, transforming what is now Leicester Square (then Fields) into the focal point of London's social scene. Other renowned residents in the 1700s included the much-written-about Chevalier/Chevaliere d'Eon, the originator of the term 'eonism', and from whom the contemporary 'Beaufort Society', which provides support to trans people and their partners, takes its name.

Yet as has been equally well documented, Soho's reputation started to decline steadily towards the end of the eighteenth century, as London's social elite began to relocate to the larger mansions of nearby Mayfair. Increasingly downtrodden and decaying, Soho evolved into a late Georgian/early Victorian concentration of cheap lodging houses that attracted poverty-stricken residents from other parts of London and further afield, as portrayed in Charles Dickens' (1838) account of Golden Square in *Nicholas Nickleby*. The intensity of Soho's insanitary living conditions was brought home by Dr John Snow's tracing of the devastating cholera outbreak of 1854, which claimed over 500 lives in just ten days, to a water pump in the heart of Soho. Snow made a detailed map of its incidence in the area, thus identifying the polluted pump in Broad (now Broadwick) Street as the source. A recently reinstated monument as well as the John Snow pub, both on Lexington Street, commemorate his decision to have the handle of the pump removed, thereby savings hundreds if not thousands more lives by precluding residents from accessing its water, thought to have been contaminated with excrement from nearby stable blocks. This is the Soho where exiled revolutionaries such as Karl Marx lived in overcrowded rooms in dilapidated tenements, the latter causing widespread premature death and disease. Speiser reports how by 1851 there were an average of 327 inhabitants per acre in Soho, a figure that was higher than in almost any other part of London.[9]

The cheap rents, combined with its reputation as a welcoming and tolerant community, meant that Soho was something of a haven for anarchists such as Marx who were in search of a safe place to live and work. Unable to pay their bills, Marx and his family left the German Hotel on Soho's Lisle Street in 1851 and moved to two small, overcrowded rooms at 28 Dean Street, where they lived for the next five years. It was here that the family's desperate financial situation and insanitary living conditions most likely led to the death of two of their children. Marx's wife, Jenny, was reduced to begging, initially from neighbours and then from an uncle, to cover the burial costs for one of their children. As a further sign of the times (and the setting), while she was away Marx added to their problems by fathering another child with the family maid, Helen Demuth. Marx, Demuth and Friedrich Engels all agreed to cover this up in order to preserve the Marx's marriage, with all involved pretending for the rest of their lives that Engels was the child's father, until the latter finally confessed the truth to Marx's daughter shortly before he died. It was while living and working in Soho that Marx and Engels drafted *The Communist Manifesto* in the upstairs room of the Red Lion pub on Soho's Great Windmill Street.

In his book *The Rookeries of London*,[10] written in 1850, clergyman Thomas Beames describes the St Giles area that covered much of Soho during this period as one of London's most notorious rookeries. He writes, '[A] dirtier or more wretched place I have never seen. The street was very narrow and muddy, and the air was impregnated with filthy odours.'[11] Peter Ackroyd devotes a whole chapter of his biography of London to St Giles, describing it as 'the haunt of the poor and the outcast'[12]. It was here, the location of one of London's largest leper hospitals, founded in 1101 by Matilda, wife of Henry I, that the Great Plague that devastated London first broke out in the last weeks of 1664.

Beames' aim in writing his book about the rookeries was to raise awareness of the need for a new act of parliament to protect those with little choice but to live in places like St Giles, as well as (in true 'philanthropic' style) to contain the 'malignant spirit' that he warned would inevitably emerge from the inhumane living conditions to which families in St Giles and other London rookeries were subject.[13] This was a sentiment graphically emphasized by Hogarth in his famous depiction of 'Gin Lane' – a comment on the squalid life both encouraged and relieved by cheap drink, set against the backdrop of St Giles, looking towards the 'elevated' spire of St George's, Bloomsbury. Dickens also sought to raise awareness of the plight of families living in some of London's most notorious slums. In his Preface to the 1850 publication of *Oliver Twist*, he highlights the implications of living in London's rookeries for the many children condemned to do so. Referring to the fictionally named but otherwise all too real 'Jacob's Island', Dickens describes the poverty and powerlessness experienced by those living in 'the filthiest, the strangest, the most extraordinary of the many localities that are hidden in London'.[14]

Dismal though it was, the poverty and desperation that characterized St Giles was only one part of nineteenth-century Soho life. Ever complex and contradictory, the mid-Victorian era was also a period in which Soho flourished, and not simply by exploiting London's most needy and vulnerable. Increasing immigration brought with it cultural and religious variety, with various groups of craftspeople living and working alongside each other. From the early 1700s, a small-scale business and manufacturing sector began to establish itself in Soho as a diverse but distinctive working community; by the mid-nineteenth century this was thriving, largely as a result of successive waves of skilled migrant workers settling there. Hutton (2012) describes how, by the first quarter of the eighteenth century, less than half of Soho's residential population were English, and this declined steadily over the next 100 or so years as the area became more culturally cosmopolitan.[15]

The presence of its immigrant communities has continued to transform Soho throughout its history, but especially so in the late nineteenth and early twentieth centuries. Soho's history is inextricably connected with, and indebted to, migration into the area. As many historians and cultural commentators have noted, successive waves and generations of French Huguenots, Italians, Russian and Polish Jews, Germans, Greeks and Swiss, and Chinese people have made Soho their place of work and home, all contributing in different ways to Soho's eclectic and enduring character. French settlement in particular has spanned several centuries. It was said that, in the late 1800s, organ grinders on Soho streets could make more money from playing the *Marseillaise* than any other tune.[16] A tympanum above the entrance to the French Protestant church on the northwest side of Soho Square depicts Edward VI extending a welcome and a Charter of Privileges to Huguenots who settled there after fleeing mounting persecution in the 1550s. The number of settlers increased considerably following the revocation of the Edict of Nantes by Louis XIV in 1685, and with them came skills in silk weaving, clockmaking, engraving and silverwork, as well as culinary inventiveness. Oxtail soup and saveloy sausages, now English 'staples', are both thought to be Huguenot imports. In 1711, the parish council of St Anne's estimated the total population of Soho to be just over 8,100, of whom some 40 per cent were believed to be French.[17] Alongside Soho's significant number of French family-owned and -run businesses, a wide variety of restaurants, bars and cafes flourished with each incoming migrant group, as did social and religious institutions serving the needs of Soho's increasingly diverse community of workers and residents.

The Clergy of St Anne's and parish workers compiled what is undoubtedly one of the most detailed commentaries on Soho's historical narrative, published in the form of *Two Centuries of Soho* in 1898.[18] This fascinating account documents what is perhaps the first attempt to clean up Soho's streets, described in the *London Chronicle* in 1752. Referring to the plan to pave the City and Liberties of Westminster, the text stipulates that:

All sorts of dirt and ashes, oyster shells, and the offal of dead poultry and other animals, will no longer be suffered to be thrown into the streets, but must be kept until the dustman comes; nor will the annoyance created by coach makers be permitted; and when a house is pulled down, the rubbish must be carried to a proper place, and not left in the streets.[19]

In his Preface to *Two Centuries*, Walter Besant describes Soho as 'one of the most interesting districts of London' and as a place 'known to the fullest extent only by those who work there'.[20] Responding to concerns about Soho's growing reputation for sleaze at the time, the book documents Soho's businesses, social and religious institutions, and amusements over the course of the eighteenth and nineteenth centuries. In a similar vein to Beames' *Rookeries of London* published fifty or so years earlier, *Two Centuries* was something of a 'call to alms', the aim of which was to stir up parochial patriotism, particularly among local business owners, philanthropists and civic authorities. As a work of local history, it capitalized on Victorian social reform and paternalism. One particularly interesting illustration of this is the account given of how, in December 1849, the old Greek-Huguenot Church was 'in danger of being turned into a dancing saloon and music hall' when the Reverend Nugent Wade, rector of St. Anne's at the time, bought it for £1,500 and arranged for it to be consecrated by the Church of England. Given the name St Mary's, it was to be used as a chapel of ease (a church building within the bounds of a parish used by parishioners unable to attend the main church, either because it is too far or, more likely in this case, because it is too full). It is the south side of this church that features in Hogarth's 1738 representation of Hog Lane, 'Noon'. A symbolic gutter runs through the middle of this image segregating the decorous worshippers, Soho's aristocrats and hard-working artisans from the seedy squalor and chaos of their neighbours spilling out of the public house in the left-hand side of the image; taken together these two groups embody the proximity of Soho's extremes, then and since. The gutter was most likely a wry comment on Hogarth's part on how these extremes were inexorably intertwined in Soho then, as now.

Of particular note is the emphasis placed in *Two Centuries*, and echoed in Hogarth's work, on the various reforming institutions associated with the church and other philanthropic parish organizations. The West London Mission, located at Lincoln House on Greek Street, is described in some detail, with emphasis on how the Mission's leaders 'take a liberal and enlightened view of their work ... Improving the lot of the people, their aim is to show sympathy with the poor in their struggles and difficulties, and to help them wisely and well.'[21] This reflects earlier work undertaken by the founders of the Westminster General Dispensary located on Gerrard Street. At the time Cardwell and his associates were writing, there still hung on the wall of the Dispensary, behind a chair that legend asserts to have been Dr Johnson's, a framed copy of the *Evening Post* dated 19–21 September 1774, in which the founders are reported as committing '[t]o render the Advantages of this Society extensively useful, and to give the Generous and Humane an opportunity of doing much Good ... with Care, Attention and Humanity'.[22] The progressive nature of much of this work is also documented in the formation of the Hospital for Women, situated in Soho Square. Founded by Dr Protheroe Smith, Assistant Lecturer on Midwifery and Diseases of Women at St Bartholomew's School of Medicine in 1842, with the Prince of Wales as its Patron and the Duke of Westminster its President, this was believed to be the first women's hospital in the world.

The Soho institutions covered by *Two Centuries* include its religious centres such as the Protestant St Anne's church and schools, the Catholic St Patrick's, the French church of Notre Dame, and the French Protestant church, as well as halls, missions and parochial institutions in the area. Also documented are Soho's various medical centres: the Westminster General Dispensary; ear, heart and skin hospitals; the Hospital for Women; and the London Lock Hospital. Various charities and societies (such as the Royal Society for Musicians) are also described, as are the range of social clubs and unions for girls, boys, and working men and women, such as the *Societa Italiana Cuochi-Camerieri* catering for the area's growing community of Italian chefs and waiters.

The Soho Club and Home for Working Girls, established in 1880 by Maude Stanley at 59 Greek Street, Soho Square, deserves a particular mention. The Club's annual report for 1896 shows that 198 girls and young women were admitted that year, with an average nightly attendance of 47. The clubhouse provided recreation facilities and included a library and dispensary, with access to free medicines and a female doctor for all members. The reformist character of the Club is summed up in Cardwell's description:

If it were no more than a strong counter attraction to the course and low pleasures of the Music Halls and Dancing Rooms and a preservative from the temptation to lounge about the streets, it would be an institution of great value. But it is far more than this. It promotes good fellowship amongst our women toilers, it brings about a sympathy between one class and another, and affords an opening for all kinds of friendly ministration to those who have little to cheer and brighten their lives[23].

Some two-thirds of *Two Centuries* is dedicated to documenting the wide range of skilled craft firms situated in Soho at the end of the late nineteenth century. It is the range of artisanal businesses that is particularly fascinating and illustrative of Soho's emerging reputation as the workshop of London's West End. Amongst those described are: artists' colour manufacturers; auctioneers; billiard ball and table manufacturers; black lead makers; booksellers, binders and printers; curriers, leather makers and saddlers; furniture manufacturers and sellers; glass dealers and stained glass artists; livery stables; milliners; musical instrumental makers; print sellers and picture framers; sheet music printers and dealers; silversmiths; solicitors; taverns and tin-plate workers.

Considerable emphasis is placed on the significance of the Soho Bazaar, a successful commercial and social enterprise which opened at 4–6 Soho Square on 1 February 1816 'to encourage female and domestic industry'.[24] Believed to be the first department store in the United Kingdom, the Bazaar's success is credited with its stated aims: 'to encourage home work by getting the best price for it; to provide small business opportunities for those most in need of them', and 'to abolish the middle man, and put manufacturer in immediate touch with the consumer'. In its heyday, the average daily attendance of the Bazaar was reputedly in excess of 2,500 people, and there were often as many as 200 stallholders at any one time. Subsidized refreshments were provided for workers along fifty-foot refectory-style tables.

Cardwell et al. attribute the Bazaar's success, at least in part, to the restrictions it placed on the characters and appearance of its sellers. The latter 'had to produce testimony as to their respectability, moral character and good temper'. Any potential sellers deemed to be 'meanly or dirtily dressed' would be denied entry.[25] Hinting at the gendered nature of the aesthetic economy to come, particularly in the retail sector,[26] Cardwell et al. note the complete absence of male stallholders: 'many of the young ladies are young, and fair to look upon'. The Bazaar became such a Soho institution that, as it began to decline after eighty or so years of trading, one commentator noted: 'one feels as if one were almost about to say good-bye to an old friend'.[27]

A relatively short but significant passage in the section on the 'Institutions of Soho' in *Two Centuries* focuses on growing concerns about the presence of 'disorderly houses' in the area. Frequent references are made to Vestry minutes and to petitions to Parliament asking for special legislation on the subject. With growing concern that the Parish was 'sinking by the ever-increasing invasion of vice',[28] a Committee was formed to deal with the matter, the result being that Cardwell reports on fourteen convictions being obtained, twenty-four disorderly houses being closed and a further seventy notices being served on landlords running houses of 'ill repute'. The discursive terms of this clean-up are as much in evidence today as they were in 1898:

> Apart from the moral aspects of the question, we believe that unless the Vestry had embarked in these energetic measures, a large number of our working people would have been driven from the Parish because they are unable to afford the bigger rents, which vice can pay.[29]

The last, comparatively brief section of *Two Centuries* is dedicated to 'Soho Amusements', describing the growing number of theatres as having a 'demoralizing' effect on the area but, at the same time, emphasizing from the outset Soho's significance as London's 'centre of pleasure'[30]. The notorious history of Carlisle House is described, as is the growing array of visitor attractions in and around Leicester Square, but (not surprisingly, given its reformist tone) it is on Soho 'at the fall of the curtain' that the discussion focuses most of its attention. A somewhat stoical position is taken on the implications of Soho's location at the heart of London's pleasure zone, with the latter being described as a mixed blessing. Echoing the issues noted earlier in this chapter, rising rates are of particular concern, especially in relation to their implications for Soho's working poor, whose trade compelled them to live near their place of work:

> A suitable site for a Theatre or Music Hall will always fetch, in mid-London, an enormous sum; rents are consequently rushing up every day and dwellings where respectable artisans might live are being continually pulled down.[31]

This discourse of protective paternalism invokes concerns not just about class but also gender, with the especially harmful influence of 'that which is vile' on girls and young women being noted. These concerns notwith-standing, it is Soho's reputation as a place in which appetites of all kinds could be indulged that carried the area into the next century.

Twentieth-Century Soho

As Walkowitz (2012) describes it in her discussion of the area's cosmo-politan cuisine,[32] Soho had begun to self-consciously market itself as a cultural destination dedicated to food and drink and to catering for sophisticated bohemian palates by the beginning of the twentieth century. A seven-part series of the *Caterer and Hotel-Keeper* trade magazine focusing on 'Soho and its Restaurants' in 1906 illustrates this, constituting something of a culinary travelogue of the area.[33] Although Soho's 'darker social problems' were acknowledged to be 'more complicated and difficult than in any other district', these were set aside as being of less importance than the place's hybrid cuisine and culture. As Speiser notes, the decline in the number of domestic servants employed in the period after the First World War led to an increase in dining out as a social activity, especially in the capital, which also contributed to Soho's reputation for affordable gastronomy.[34] As Walkowitz reflects, what was interesting about Soho becoming a place known for its culturally eclectic food and drink was that its culinary mix reflects the place's history, culture and politics, the result being 'a hybrid cuisine, neither the ordinary peasant fare previously consumed by culinary workers in their native land, nor the international French cuisine available in grand hotels across Europe and in the West End'. As in so many aspects of its fare, then and since, Soho offered something discernibly different that reflected its character and history as a working community.[35]

Further, this highly marketable version of Soho's cosmopolitanism 'ratified London's capacity to master and contain unsettling multiplicity within a specialized enclave'.[36] This enabled Soho as a distinctive place, and as a working community, to reach out beyond its relatively bounded setting *at the same time* as serving to contain its radical edge in an easily (literally) digestible form. Like Cardwell's earlier account of Soho's craftsmen and -women, Soho workers were once again cast as the heroes of its rich and diverse biography, the 'honest counterpoints', as Walkowitz puts it, to the area's gangs, anarchists and growing number of pornographers. The cosmopolitanism this mix brought to the area came to mark Soho's reputation as a place of both pleasure and peril characterized by a romantic blend of familiarity and adventure.

Perhaps nowhere is this romanticization of Soho at this particular point in its history more apparent than in Arthur Ransome's semi-fictional, semi-autobiographical book *Bohemia in London*, published in 1907, which proffers Soho as a haven of bohemian sociality. Ransome describes Soho as being as much a 'tint in the spectacles' as a physical setting. Maps, he argued, fail to capture the way that Soho is experienced, simultaneously, as something 'strange, tense, joyful and despairing, hopeful and sordid'.[37] As Walkowitz notes, however, where Ransome and the *Caterer* depart from Cardwell's closing notes of dismay is in the emphasis the former especially placed on the creative potential of Soho's growing commodity culture. For Ransome, hinting at the shape of things to come for Soho throughout the twentieth century and since, what made Soho distinctive was its stimulating atmosphere:

> Ambience, décor, conversation, seeing and being seen – these were the cultural attractions of dining out in Soho, rather than the gastronomy itself . . . [I]t was the atmospherics of dining, not physical consumption or taste, that stimulated the imagination.[38]

Contrasting with the promotional efforts of the *Caterer* and with Ransome's rose-tinted romanticism were more pithy accounts of Soho as a place of sleaze, scandal and secrecy. In *The Secret Agent*, also published in 1907, Joseph Conrad portrayed these themes in his novel about political anarchists that serves as an antidote to the privileged bohemia celebrated by Ransome and the *Caterer*. Here the pornography shop owned by the central character Verloc is described as a trap for gullible customers, the 'special atmosphere' of which exudes a culture of fraud. The latter serves as a vehicle through which to question the political convictions and interpersonal loyalties of the self-proclaimed revolutionaries who congregate there; the shadow world that they occupy is materialized in the shop's appearance and is signified by its shady wares. The 'evil freedom' depicted is set against the isolated and fragmented identities of those who live, work and meet there. As Walkowitz has put it, the Soho of *The Secret Agent* is 'a bleak wasteland of unimproved London'.[39] Indeed, as she goes on to note, stripped away entirely are the well-meaning social reformers, artisans and philanthropic employers that Cardwell was so keen to champion, as well as the adventurous diners celebrated by the *Caterer* and Ransome. Conrad replaces the wondrous sense of community these characters embody with more fleeting descriptions of Verloc's shop and the 'strange fish' who frequent it. Through Conrad's depiction of the pornography shop in particular, Soho becomes a place of deceit and degradation and of ambivalent, suggestive meanings: 'it is both a home and shop; it sells two kinds of "shady" wares, political newspapers and sexual commodities'.[40] And the shop attracts two distinct kinds of customers: novices, who are duped into buying overpriced, substandard goods, and more mature men, who turn out to be Verloc's anarchist comrades. We are told that Verloc's young wife Winnie, who serves in the shop, produces 'rage in the heart' of the younger customers. In Conrad's hands, Soho encourages a culture of 'evil freedom', fraudulent and detached from the wider social context.

In combination with Stevenson's earlier account of Soho as the setting for *The Strange Tale of Dr. Jekyll and Mr. Hyde*, *Bohemia in London* and *The Secret Agent*, at least in literary terms, 'cemented Soho's legendary status as a site of seedy pleasures and bohemian camaraderie'.[41] Conrad and Stevenson's Soho is a 'bleak wasteland' divested of social reformers, industrious artisans, exotic bohemians and neighbourly community; it is also a place heavily coded with masculinity, a theme to which we will return in Chapter 5. Hyde resides in 'the dismal quarter of Soho', the perfect setting for him, with its 'muddy ways, and slatternly passages'. Compared to the warm, welcoming glow of his own place of residence, Soho seemed, to the upstanding lawyer, Mr Utterson, 'like … a nightmare.'[42] Combined with the blurred identities and moralities signified by its 'muddy ways', Stevenson's account of Hyde's Soho emphasizes the latter as a place of 'premature twilight', underneath which its dark and dingy streets contain the capacity to envelope a man bent on concealing his duplicity.[43] Soho's 'darkness' was not just metaphorical however. In 1910, Westminster Council commissioned the Gas Light and Coke Company to install 1,800- and 3,000-candlepower lamps along the streets that bordered Soho. In contrast, the lamp-posts in Soho were fitted with only 90-candlepower lights[44] – once again, Soho's reputation for darkness was both meaningful and material.

As Stevenson also hints, however, towards the end of the novel when Hyde's circumstances and motivations are elaborated upon, Soho's shade also provides a protective cover to those who need it (signified by Hyde's own cloak, perhaps). Its reputation as an anchor point for those who need to hide, and where the unconventional can be themselves, was also firmly established by the early twentieth century. Mort (2010) describes, for example, how the first floor of the famous Lyons' Corner House that opened in 1909 on Coventry Street, on the southern edge of Soho, became an important meeting point for gay men that came to be known as the Lilypond.[45] Other historically important venues such as Kettner's (frequented by Oscar Wilde) and the Chat Noir on Old Compton Street, haunt of Quentin Crisp and his associates,[46] were a significant part of Soho in the early twentieth century and remain so today, if only by reputation or in narrative rather than material form.[47]

Soho's sex industry grew considerably in the early years of the twentieth century, especially during World War I. Its dark corners and narrow streets relative to other parts of London's West End enabled late-night entertainment venues to mushroom, creating 'an atmosphere conducive to transgressive practices and cross-class erotic encounters'.[48] It is the area's historical association with entertainment, much of which challenged or at least played with social norms, that gave Soho its alluring notoriety and which increasingly brought customers into these venues. Walkowitz notes the significance of the role played by restaurateurs in this process, as the renting out of upper rooms enabled sex workers to have a place to go with clients solicited in the restaurants and cafes and on the streets below. As Arnold outlines, this inter-relationship was not new. The Metropolitan Police Act of 1850 had made loitering an offence, while, from 1858, any house from which more than one sex worker operated was deemed to be a 'disorderly house', and the landlady could be prosecuted. In practice, this meant that publicans often developed a mutually beneficial relationship with sex workers, as they brought in trade for each other, either side of their respective transactions.[49]

In the interwar years Soho's other markets thrived. Walkowitz describes how, in an illustration in a London travel guide, an image of Berwick Street market from above captures how extraordinarily compressed, almost 'bazaar like' the space is. Between 1893 and 1930, Berwick Street market grew from thirty-two stalls to 158, many of them selling women's clothing.[50] The market has long occupied an important commercial and social space in Soho – its messy, crowded layout prevents the free flow of pedestrian traffic that characterizes the West End's wide boulevards, most notably Nash's Regent Street.[51] As one of Britain's oldest markets (yet currently under threat from redevelopment of the space it occupies), Berwick Street market has historically been a 'liminal, carnivalesque' place.[52] Sepia-tinged photographs tend to obscure its dynamism and are better supplemented by the many surviving first-hand accounts of working and shopping there. In the 1920s, Berwick Street market became a fashionable retail space to those 'in the know', selling ready-to-wear clothing (in itself still relatively cutting edge) at a fraction of the cost of garments in the more fashionable shops along Oxford and Regent Streets. This direct selling did two important things: it brought the customer closer to the working conditions of those who produced the garments on sale, and it revealed something of the profit margins attached to the short distance between Soho workshops and the West End retailers. In this sense, because it was so open and explicit, with a vibrant atmosphere[53], the Market quickly became something of a tourist attraction[54].

The 'ready to wear' fashion produced by largely Jewish tailors along Berwick Street in the 1920s and 30s were relatively shapeless, tubular style dresses that could be worn by a variety of sizes. While not quite embodying the self-assurance of the flapper, these clothes, and the women selling them, materialized an emerging self-confidence and modern style that set them apart from previous generations of women, and which captured the spirit of Soho at the time. Walkowitz suggests that many of the Market's best customers were local sex workers who were an important source of revenue for local traders who supplied them with hats, dresses and accessories. As Speiser notes, although technically part

of Soho's night-time economy, the sex trade in this sense alone is intimately, and importantly, linked to its daytime business[55] – a theme we
return to in Chapters 3 and 4.

The blurring of Soho's temporal economies and of these neighbouring
areas is characterized by a dynamic and complex interplay between
Soho's function as central London's workshop and its service to the
pleasure zones of West End retail boulevards and theatres and to centres
of political, legal and financial power only slightly further afield. The
theatres established a firm connection to Soho after the creation of
Cambridge Circus, Charing Cross Road and Shaftesbury Avenue, forming Soho's eastern and southern borders in the 1880s, effectively creating
London's 'theatreland', sometimes simply referred to as the 'West End'.
This blurring is also defined by Soho's proximity to the centres of politics
occupied formally by Parliament and by the myriad gentleman's clubs in
and around neighbouring St James. Soho's proximity to the latter has
geographical significance to the area in a way that intertwines with its
history of immigration, a connection that is important to note in any
account of the area as a working community. As skilled craftsmen and -
women migrated to London from Russia, Eastern Europe, France, Italy
and China, the combination of cheap rents and being close enough for
'runners' to move quickly between Soho's backstreet workshops and the
finer gentlemen's tailors in St James's was what led many migrant families
to settle in the area. Gerry Black, who grew up in Soho, describes these
interconnections as follows:

The men's trade used jacket makers, trouser makers and waistcoat makers, each
of which was a separate trade. They in turn would use pressers, buttonhole and
felling hands … Pressers lived precarious lives and worked terrible hours. If
a garment was finished at 7pm and had to be delivered at 9am the
following day, the pressers would have to work through the night to finish it in
time … Tailors needed trimmings and within a few streets there were at least nine
trimmings shops all of which prospered … The work had to be taken to shop (it
was always called 'shop') three times for fittings and brought back to be worked on
and finished. *Hence the importance of being close by.*[56]

Referring to family members who were employed by the Thomas
Burberry company that took premises in the Haymarket, west of Soho
in 1901, Black goes on to explain how this proximal necessity connected
to patterns of migration in the growth of Soho's working population:

My father was a gentlemen's tailor as were all our *landsleit*.[57] We had about fifty
cousins, second cousins, third cousins and fourth cousins and nearly everyone was
in the trade working for Savile Row. That is why we all lived around Berwick
Street and Broadwick Street and D'Arblay Street [in the heart of Soho] …
because we had to be near to Savile Row.[58]

The 1891 London Tailors' Strike resulted in an influx of Jewish tailors from Whitechapel in the East End. Many of them specialized in making waistcoats supplied to upmarket tailors on Savile Row and shirts for Jermyn Street stores in the heart of St James's on the other side of Regent Street. By the start of World War I in 1914, there were seventy tailors in the Golden Square area of Soho alone, mostly in attic workshops that were relatively cheap to rent and (partly because of the number of people crammed into the space) to keep warm enough to work. As Gerry Black describes in his detailed history of Jewish life in London's West End, it was the combination of trade opportunities and cheap rents that attracted craftspeople to the area.[59] As he says, supporting the tailors were cutters, pressers and buttonholers. These workshops provided 'an industrial hinterland' for the tailors and retailers to the north of Soho, along Oxford Street, and to the west, along Regent Street and into St James's.[60] An important feature of this was that Soho's population was largely made up of different ethnic communities who, while not necessarily integrated, lived and worked relatively harmoniously alongside each other. The primarily home-based family-run businesses they operated were all small scale and specialist, complementing rather than competing with each other (a theme we return to later). This contributed significantly to the area's character, but it also meant that Soho did not have a distinctive ethnic or industrial identity or support structure to protect working conditions or workers' rights; some belonged to the Workers Union founded in 1898 and joined the 1912 tailors' strike, but many did not. Soho's growing status as a working community also meant that the increasing number of workshops in the area in the late nineteenth and early twentieth centuries exacerbated the declining housing stock and further increased rents, stretching the resources of Soho's working poor even more.

Perhaps no Soho institution epitomizes this complex interplay between the area's residential and working communities, its distinctive intertwining of geography, history and industry, and its connections to the sex industry more than the Windmill Theatre. Located on Soho's southern border, adjacent to the theatre district of Shaftesbury Avenue and Leicester Square, the Windmill was significant (and arguably so successful) because its ability to transgress borders was not simply physical but also cultural and sexual. Leicester Square has long since been regarded as the commercial heart of the West End's pleasure zone. The significance of the Windmill's location and its contribution to Soho's notoriety in the early to mid-twentieth century, largely due to the storm created by its public displays of nudity, should not be underestimated.[61] As Mort has put it,

The Windmill occupied a transitional space: a point where traditions of cultural bohemianism and sexual trespass met the wider world of West End mass entertainment and organized leisure.[62]

In 1931, the widow of a wealthy jute merchant, Mrs. Laura Henderson, bought what was then the Palais de Luxe cinema in Great Windmill Street. Often portrayed as a sexually and commercially naive elderly lady, Laura Henderson was in reality (if biographical accounts of her are anything to go by) extremely well connected to London's social elite, an astute investor, and patron of many London charities. With echoes of another well-known social enterprise some hundred or so years earlier, the Soho Bazaar, Mort describes how Henderson's aim in establishing the Windmill was broadly (if profitably) philanthropic: to help with national post-Depression recovery, specifically by employing out-of-work British theatrical performers, whose employment prospects had been severely dented by the growing popularity of cinema (as an aside, the Odeon in nearby Leicester Square was the first cinema in Britain to install a wide screen, in 1953). The Windmill's (equally famous) manager from 1938 to 1955, Vivian Van Damm, brought to fruition their shared vision of tastefully performed erotic entertainment in a theatrical staging focusing on visual display of the female body. Censorship legislation governing the latter meant that women could stand on stage but must not move whilst naked. The professionalism of the Windmill girls, and the commitment of the Theatre's management to the adage 'the show must go on', meant that, famously, the Windmill stayed continually open throughout the bomb raids on the West End during World War II, capitalizing on its achievement in the form of posters proclaiming 'We Never Clothed!'

Indeed, throughout the war Soho became a focal point of entertainment for troops passing through, particularly for the thousands of American GIs based at the nearby Rainbow Corner, a US Red Cross club situated on the corner of Denman Street and Shaftesbury Avenue. One of Mort's illustrations features Windmill girl 'Pat' on the front cover of *London Life* magazine on 19 October 1940, resplendent in stockings, tin hat and Alpine style costume, smiling and knitting. This saucy postcard-style image, a cheeky but ultimately wholesome dedication to the war effort, characterized the culture of the Windmill throughout its formative years and helps to explain both its success and its later downfall. By the 1960s, sexual entertainment in Soho had become much more explicit compared to the relatively quaint erotic tableaux for which the Windmill was known. This was largely brought about by legislative changes and by property development in the area, as well as changing social attitudes towards sex and nudity to which we return in due course.

In their zeal for post-war redevelopment, Westminster City Council published the City of Westminster Plan in 1946. The Plan called for the demolition of much of Soho's built environment, seemingly regarding Soho as 'matter out of place', to borrow from anthropologist Mary Douglas.[63] Soho's narrow, crowded streets, its alleyways and courts, were seen as an impediment to further development of the cleaner West End thoroughfares and boulevards; its remaining industrial dwellings, small-scale retail outlets and artisanal workshops were deemed anachronistic in an urban environment dedicated to consumption and pleasure and to retail on an increasingly mass scale. Many commentators speculated that this signalled the end of Soho.[64] Even though several detective memoirs at the time, such as Robert Fabian's *London after Dark*, fuelled a popular image of Soho as 'London's square mile of vice',[65] many leapt to the area's defence, with the London Correspondent emphasizing that the existence of a thriving residential community, schools and places of workshop, along with over 1,000 small workshops, did not constitute evidence of Soho's descent into dereliction. The Plan's narrow vision of Soho as a route to somewhere else was firmly rejected and its 'double edged cosmopolitanism' reaffirmed, with its heady mix of sights, sounds, smells and styles, its dark and sinister streets and shady people, its very unseemliness, being recognized as its appeal.[66] Although it was not implemented, the Plan highlighted, however, that Soho was under the planners' spotlight as a dangerous slum ripe for urban redevelopment. Yet (in another sign of things to come), in doing so, it also brought to the fore the strength of feeling, and organizational capability, of those who sought to defend its character.

At the same time as a discourse about Soho as dangerous and decrepit gathered momentum, media culture demonized Soho as a 'claustrophobic world of underworld dens, dingy old alleyways and streets' existing solely to provide a place in which perverts, prostitutes and pimps could prosper.[67] Fabian's aforementioned *London after Dark* epitomized the latter, emphasizing that what he called 'the square mile of vice' was less a geographical area that could be easily marked out and more an unsavoury 'atmosphere' pervading this particular part of the West End of London. Acknowledging that Soho's vices were more intriguing and alluring than wholly corrupt, Fabian explained his emphasis on Soho's appeal with reference to its location. As many other writers have done, Fabian attributed the area's charismatic pull to its proximity to the heart of London's power bases, notably its shared borders with more glamorous parts of the capital frequented by social and political elites.[68]

To offset the negative impact of these combined (and sometimes confusing) perceptions of Soho, local business owners and residents developed their own initiatives championing the area's cosmopolitanism. Perhaps the most notable example of this was the weeklong (and recently resurrected) Soho Fair, held annually between 1955 and 1959.[69] As Frank Mort has put it, by the early 1950s Soho was in dire need of a publicity boost. The Soho Restaurant Association, as the main organizer and sponsor of the Fair, capitalized on the area's reputation for culinary and cultural diversity, with publicity referring to Soho as 'Little Europe'. Rather than ignoring or playing down Soho's association with sex, the Fairs repackaged and rebranded it. Through waiters' races, fashion shows, talent competitions and erotic displays, the Fair celebrated the 'fleshy delights' of post-war Soho.[70] Citing the 'Soho Fair Official Programme', produced for the 1957 fair by the Soho Association, Mort notes an emphasis on two elements as forming the centrepiece of Soho's environmental distinctiveness: sex and food. As Mort describes it, the fairs were hailed as a collective expression of the area's sense of community and diversity, mixing together 'the traditions of the English carnival with [the] wide variety of hybrid and mimetic forms of European culture' that epitomized Soho's cosmopolitanism.[71] Drawing on anthropologist Frank Manning, Mort describes the fairs as a performative spectacle that brought a particular version of Soho into being in the popular consciousness, capitalizing on the area's cultural diversity to 'create an idiosyncratic mood of celebration that could be marketed to local and national audiences via the media and entertainment industries'.[72] Emphasizing the cultural eclecticism of the setting and event, taking centre stage in Pathé news coverage of the 1959 fair 'All's Fair in Soho'[73] are features of semi-naked women which, if the footage is anything to go by, were particularly popular with the assembled crowds. Mort sums this up when he describes how

Soho's carnival girls projected a distinctive erotic style that was assertive, mobile and visually charged, and their performances confirmed a link between sex and Soho's cosmopolitan cultures.[74]

In this sense, as Glinert notes, if Soho in the 1940s provided some comfort from the realities of war, Soho in the 1950s became an escape from post-war austerity:

The war over, Soho, with its potent mix of loose women, foreign foods, shabby narrow streets and exotic attitudes, came into its own. In a grey era of austerity, conformity, rationing and increasing state involvement, *Soho meant louche, loose, licentious living.*[75]

Indeed, many cultural commentators at the time and since see the 1950s as Soho's heyday, in the twentieth century at least. At a time when British society was at pains to reinstate convention, Soho's inherent bohemianism continued to offer 'the unconventional, the eccentric, the rebellious and the merely different a chance to be themselves'.[76] For the young especially, Daniel Farson wrote in *Soho in the Fifties*, 'Soho is irresistible, for it offers a sort of freedom.'[77] Jazz and blues musician George Melly emphasized this evocation in his introduction to Farson's book, in which he describes the fifties in Soho as 'a dreamlike decade when everything seemed possible' in that 'dodgy never-never land'.[78] Echoing the sentiments of many other commentators before and since, Farson insisted that Soho was as much a 'state of mind' as a physical location, evoking the area as an island in the country's post-war, grey malaise, 'as lively as Isherwood's Berlin, the Parisian left bank and New York's Greenwich Village'.[79] While, as Mort notes, Farson's account drew heavily (and nostalgically) on the romanticism of Arthur Ransome's earlier *Bohemia in London*, it provides an important historical snapshot of Soho at this point in its narrative and an insight into the cultural context at the time.

In particular, Farson's influential account emphasized the social importance of a group of British artists and writers associated with Soho's pubs, clubs and restaurants, notably the York Minster (known as the French House, or just 'the French') and the Colony Club. Attracted by Soho's sleazy reputation and shabby aesthetic, the place appealed to those who hovered on the fridges of polite society and whose work largely depended on it. This group included Robert Colquhoun, Frank Auerbach, Lucien Freud, John Minton and, perhaps most notoriously, Francis Bacon. The much-written-about Muriel Belcher owned the Colony Club. When Francis Bacon signed the membership list on its opening day, the story goes that he agreed to lure some of his famous friends to the club in exchange for a £10-a-week retainer and, most importantly, free drinks.

Bacon and his associates were attracted to Soho's air of sexual excitement and bohemian cosmopolitanism and the extent to which 'many things considered illegal or morally reprehensible were perfectly acceptable in Soho'.[80] As Bacon's biographers have emphasized, it is highly likely that his time in Soho provided sustenance for the artist's conviction that, rather than stimulate the intellect, art should be an assault on the senses.[81] As Ed Glinert describes it, Soho's decadent, licentious hedonism made it 'the perfect backdrop for someone who wanted to remain on the edge of society'[82] and on the margins of the artistic academy. In Soho 'was an entire community geared not just to pleasure, but to pleasure with ... an edge'.[83]

Speiser cites cultural historian Roy Porter's summation of the excitement associated with Soho at this point in its history. Worth citing in full, Porter emphasizes the area's capacity to bring together artists, writers and radical intelligentsia, highlighting not just what Soho meant to them but also vice versa:

A culture materialized that was irreverent, offbeat, creative, novel. Politically idealistic and un-dogmatically left-wing, it broke through class barriers and captured and transformed many of the better elements of traditional London: its cosmopolitanism and openness, its village quality, its closeness, its cocktail of talent, wealth and eccentricity.[84]

Christine Stansell's account of the cultural and political significance of New York City's Greenwich Village makes similar points to Farson's story of mid-twentieth-century Soho and Porter's more recent reflections. She notes how, like Soho, Greenwich Village projected a particular geography of the imagination as an intensive, compressed social and sexual environment associated with experimentation and acceptance, attracting creative people from all walks of life, who in turn left their mark on the place itself.[85] Stansell writes about the Village as a place where the radical ideals of modernity became embedded within a particular locale. However, unlike Soho, those who experienced the Village as a bohemian enclave were largely removed from the sweatshops and tenements where migrants to the area lived and worked. As she puts it,

Greenwich Village, as it came to be celebrated, did not refer to an actual neighborhood so much as to a fictive community. It was a selective vision of city life that installed some people in the foreground as protagonists and shunted others to the background or offstage altogether.[86]

Although more sprawling than London's Soho, the relatively compact nature of the Village's layout made for a distilled cultural experience and set of associations. Yet, as Stansell notes, the area was more of a conscious, even tactical, construction (at a time when LGBTQ people were struggling for a place, physically and politically, in US society) rather than a distinctive setting. While this contrasts with Soho, there is one important similarly between the two places that relates to the interrelationship between geography and sociability: in contrast to the wide boulevards of their respective surrounding areas, particularly the block layout in Manhattan, Stansell emphasizes how 'the twists and turns of the streets fostered a kind of purposeful sauntering', just as Soho's courts and alleys, in contrast to its neighbouring streets and boulevards, influence a particular sociability. As suggested at the outset of this chapter and in the previous section, it is this dialectical relationship between the social and the material, between the people and the place, that makes Soho *work* in the way that it does. Whether revellers or refugees, as Speiser has put it, it is Soho's unique personalities that 'lie at the heart of the area's enduring popularity across the globe'.[87] But, more so, it is the ways in which the people who live, work and consume there intersect with the area's histories, geographies and economies that constitute Soho's character as a distinctive place in a way that arguably distinguishes it from similar areas such as Greenwich Village.

The mid- to late twentieth century is a particular period in its history that illustrates this well; it is a time that has been widely written about and much romanticized, so much so that it is 'almost a legend'.[88] To the hero of Colin MacInnes' *Absolute Beginners*, Soho is the place where 'all the things they say happen, do'[89]; he argues that it is 'the most authentic' of all London quarters, a place where 'vice of every kink' can be found. Contrasting the vivacious life of Soho with neighbouring Leicester Square, 'You don't go into Soho to see films', he says, 'because Soho is a film.'

The masculine character of this period is not lost on Frank Mort, who notes how Soho became something of a social and sexual odyssey, particularly for young men. Judith Walkowitz emphasizes that what undoubtedly compelled the latter was Soho's notoriety as 'a wide open place'.[90] Memorably satirized by Tony Hancock in his 1960 film *The Rebel* and portrayed more authentically in the 1959 film *Beat Girl*, it was the coffeeshop culture that formed the basis of Soho's music scene in the 1950s, with the 2i's coffee bar on Old Compton Street claiming to be the starting point for rock and roll music in the United Kingdom. Named after the original proprietors, Freddie and Sammy Irani, the 2i's had a tiny stage in the basement that undoubtedly played a major role in the emergence of the British music scene.

If it was aristocrats who made Soho fashionable in the seventeenth century, and artisans and their cuisine in the nineteenth and early twentieth centuries, by the mid-1950s it was Soho's artists who made it such a desirable place to be, and much of this attraction revolved around Soho's many bars, restaurants and coffee shops. Hutton cites a 1951 edition of *The Soho Guide* that refers to over 400 restaurants in Soho at the time.[91] The first Gaggia espresso machine came to Britain in 1952, to a coffee shop on Frith Street, launching the fashion for Italian coffee and culture, food and fashion. As Mort describes it, Soho was systematically marketed as a special place in the 1950s, with 'the district's double character as dangerous and compelling' combined with its reputation for sexual excitement being incorporated into media treatments that promoted Soho as an eccentric and enticing part of the capital's culture.[92] The *Soho Guide* cited by Hutton refers to the various groups of people who populated Soho at the time and to its simultaneously shady and seductive qualities:

Agents, publishers, song-pluggers, crooners and band leaders talking about pick-ing up royalties for broadcasts on air. There are barrow boys with wads of cash and the Greyhound Express, movie men from Wardour Street with loud ties and cigars, small time prize fighters with their managers, racecourse touts, waiters, beggars, drinking clubs, rehearsal rooms and the sound of Le Jazz Hot . . . book-shops with thinly veneered pornography, postcards in windows that somehow manage to hint at immorality and perversion in the most innocent of phrases. *This is the Latin Quarter of London, vice ridden, glamorous, dirty and yet romantic, where the streets are shady on both sides of the road.*[93]

As well as an area (and a time) in which to see and be seen, Hutton's *Story of Soho* emphasizes that Soho in the fifties was very much a working community. Contrary to the popular belief that it was inhabited solely by writers, artists, musicians and so on, as he puts it, '[T]here was a more mundane side populated by ordinary people trying to make a living.'[94] Among them were the hundreds of people who worked in Soho's many bars, restaurants, cafes, delis and shops. Many of the area's food stores specialized in bread, cheese, sausage or coffee. Again, Soho's geography served as a contrast to other forms of retail emerging in London at the time; the fast pace of self-service supermarkets did not suit Soho, where customers took their time to savour the aromas of its small-scale shops, to interact with proprietors as goods were weighed and measured in the same way that they had been for hundreds of years, and 'to take in all that was going on around them', as Hutton describes it.[95]

Alongside these family-owned stores were other more specialist shops that proliferated in Soho in the 1950s and early 1960s as part of the area's burgeoning sex industry. The Irving Theatre became Soho's first non-stop striptease show when it opened its doors to members in 1957. Licensing regulations at the time required a minimum forty-eight-hour waiting period between a member joining and being permitted access. However, the owner of The Irving, a London Barrister named Dhurjati Chaudhuri, found a pragmatic solution: he paid the regularly imposed £100 fine, easily covered by the profits that quickly accrued. Hutton describes how nightly queues to join the 'Members only, licensed bar' that the sign outside advertised 'snaked around the street'.[96] Competitor clubs, more explicit than the Irving, quickly opened up, including the Nell

Gwynne on Meard Street in the former premises of the fashionable Gargoyle Club. By the end of the 1950s, there were over a dozen strip clubs in Soho, with a combined membership of around 200,000 and annual box office takings believed to be in excess of £2.5 million; as Hutton succinctly puts it, hinting at the scale of the emerging sex market in Soho, 'the profit margins were immense'.[97]

By the 1960s, Soho's Carnaby Street became the focal point of so-called Swinging London, with the opening of John Stephen's various shops and the music and fashion scene that revolved around it acting as an important cultural catalyst. As Speiser has emphasized, Soho's edgy history, its growing commercialism and its emerging youth culture combined to produce 'an atmosphere not to be found anywhere else'.[98] For a relatively brief period, one of the most run-down streets in interwar Soho became the fashion and retail centre of the world; Soho was an integral part of Britain's youth culture, just as the latter became central to Soho, with its growing number of clothes shops, coffee bars and nightclubs.

It is these kinds of cultural depictions and associations that have been vital to Soho's capacity to continually reinvent itself. Judith Walkowitz notes how media depictions of Soho in the 1960s have been crucial to advancing the commercial appeal of the distinct, and Frank Mort has highlighted how successive waves of publicists, artists and writers have repackaged Soho for new habitués, almost invariably drawing on the area's historical inter-connections[99].

But like all romanticized legends, Soho has its dark side. Even amongst the relatively privileged circle of Daniel Farson and his associates, Soho lifestyle took its toll in the form of alcoholism, suicide, early death and wasted talents. By the 1970s, Soho was once again 'in the grip of vice', as Summers puts it, with its sex industry entering a new, aggressive phase[100]. Throughout the 1970s and 1980s, pornography, prostitution and live erotic entertainment, much of it staged in clubs owned or controlled by Paul Raymond, were defining features of Soho's sexual culture in what was an extremely concentrated market environment. Many have argued that in the 1970s and 1980s, commercial sex effectively took over Soho. Long-time Soho resident and film producer Colin Vaines somewhat nostalgically describes the atmosphere of Soho during these decades:

Dirty, smelly, noisy Soho was an unbelievably exciting mixture of pubs, restaurants, cafes and markets. And the people! Spotty, chain-smoking youths wheeling handcarts piled high with film cans narrowly avoided being hit by taxis as the most multinational and multicultural mix of people I'd ever seen surged around the streets. But let's face it, for a teenage boy, Soho had one other key attraction: it was very, very naughty. Red lights were everywhere and every other entrance seemed to be a strip club, massage parlour, sex cinema or sex shop selling magazines and 8mm home movies. Displays inside and outside the shops, sometimes plastered on entire walls of buildings, were as graphic as the law – or rather, the notoriously corrupt 'porn squad' of the time – would allow.[101]

And the area's global reputation as a hotbed of vice lingers on. Since the mid-twentieth century, Soho has maintained a reputation as being one of the most famous red-light districts in the United Kingdom and one of the best-known areas of concentrated commercial sex in the world. The area became increasingly synonymous with the porn trade in the 1960s and with the commercial sex business that grew up in and around the Raymond Revuebar. Located in a seedy alleyway called Walker's Court (currently under redevelopment), the bar formed the basis of Raymond's growing neon-lit business empire. Fully aware that Soho has always walked a fine line between the erotic and the sleazy, many of Soho's biographers have argued that Raymond's era marked a period in its history in which its reputation tipped into that of the tawdry and tatty. As Ed Glinert has put it:

Despite the whiff of glamour, the local sex industry [in the 1960s and 1970s] was more seedy than sophisticated, laced with the fear of casual violence, an atmosphere expertly evoked by Michael Powell in the 1960 film *Peeping Tom*.[102]

Various forms of commercial sex proliferated in Soho throughout the second half of the twentieth century, most notably strip clubs, sex cinemas,[103] pornography and sex shops.[104] The presence of sex workers has been more than tolerated in Soho throughout its history, with 'men coming in and out with the regularity of a conveyor belt'[105] (which suggests, of course, that those working within them were subject to the same degree of automation). Sex work and workers are widely accepted as an intrinsic part of Soho village life,[106] yet the peep shows, strip clubs and sex shops associated with 'sexpreneurial' figures such as Raymond and Murray Goldstein[107] have been regarded with scepticism if not outright scorn by others who live and work there. As one retired clock-repairer interviewed by Summers put it, 'you accepted the prostitutes as fellow tradespeople', but the sex shops have not (until relatively recently) been accepted as part of Soho's working community.[108] This can be explained in large part because, with the sex industry en masse, came not only rent increases but also a darker, more worrying side to Soho life, in the mid-twentieth century especially: organized crime.[109]

The end of the 1950s marked the beginning of a new phase in the history of Soho and for Britain's sex industry more widely. The Obscene Publications Act (1959) was intended to tighten up on the previously unworkable obscenity laws. With the Street Offences Act (1959), designed to clear prostitutes off the streets, sex workers retreated not only into the 'nether regions of bare, dimly lit staircases'[110] still very apparent in Soho today but also, in doing so, into the 'protection' of pimps and organized criminals, many of whom owned properties used by sex workers to service clients. Until this point, as Barbara Tate (2010) describes it in her autobiographical account of the working lives of 'West End Girls', sex workers routinely solicited outside on the streets and in the many courts and alleyways between the larger buildings. An outcome of the Wolfenden Report (1957), the 1959 Act made soliciting for sexual purposes in public places a criminal offence. On the one hand, this made Soho a (relatively) safer place for sex workers, enabling them to screen potential clients before admitting them onto the premises, including through the use of CCTV and other security devices. If those who had been offended by lines of sex workers on the streets thought that the 1959 Act would result in a 'clean-up', however, they were naively mistaken, at least in Soho's case:

Almost overnight, Soho acquired an uglier face, tacky and sordid. The poorly drafted legislation did not preclude the working girls transferring their trade to clubs, cafes and hostess bars. Within weeks there was an outbreak of outlets devoted to the sale of sex. The gangsters and dodgy entrepreneurs sniffed the chance of making some serious money.[111]

Commercial sex was (and remains) perfectly capable of seeking out and saturating new opportunities to unite supply and demand, and Soho post-1958 epitomizes this. By the early 1960s, Soho's persistent organized crime problem became even more intertwined with its sex industry, as the area established itself as a prime location for protection rackets and pimping. Summers sums up the effect of the Street Offences Act on Soho's sex economy:

Unable to solicit for customers on the streets, prostitutes now had to rely on pimps to tout for them or to meet their clients in special 'hostess' bars, strip clubs, saunas and bogus massage parlors set up expressly to bring prostitute and client together.[112]

The 1958 Act, nicknamed a 'pimps charter' for the reasons Summers suggests, had yet another beneficial effect on the sex industry from a property owner's perspective: 'near beer' bars (immortalized in the Kinks' song 'Lola') sprung up all over Soho serving overpriced non-alcoholic drinks masquerading as expensive cocktails. As Summers puts it, 'the government had virtually presented the vice barons with a license to print money', enabling the owners of properties such as strip clubs and hostess bars to become increasingly powerful and rich. Perhaps the most well known was the aforementioned Paul Raymond, who bought the

Windmill Theatre and many other Soho properties occupied by the sex industry throughout the 1970s.

In yet another irony, while sex work was taking place upstairs, and in the dingy basements of strip clubs and near beer bars, the pornography business, hitherto largely tucked away in the back rooms of a handful of book shops and specialist magazine shops, like the one owned by Verloc in Joseph Conrad's *The Secret Agent*, now came into its own. The Obscene Publications Act of 1959, combined with a relaxation of censorship laws in Denmark and Sweden during the mid- to late 1960s, meant that hard-core pornographic material became widely and openly available in Soho's previously relatively constrained sex shops. In his discussion of the so-called Soho sex barons of the 1960s and 1970s, Martin Tomkinson argues that pornography came to dominate Soho's commercial and cultural landscape at this point, with Soho being one of the few areas where hard-core material was widely available.[113] This was another unforeseen consequence of a legislative change brought about largely by the *Lady Chatterley* trial, introduced ostensibly to enable well-established authors to be able to include more detailed descriptions of sex in their work without running the risk of prosecution.

If the Street Offences Act (1959) was a licence for pimps and property owners in Soho, the 1959 Obscene Publications Act was an open invitation to the area's pornographers, many of whom wasted no time in exploiting it. Many claim that pornographic material overwhelmed Soho by the end of the 1960s, as 'the number of sex establishments mushroomed, and their displays became notably explicit'.[114] Organized crime, police corruption and rent extortion meant that commercial sex rapidly became a multimillion-pound business that seemed to engulf Soho at this point in its history, as the area and the industry became synonymous. As Hutton describes it:

The face of Soho was changing. Small shops were swallowed up by a sea of outlets devoted to the sex industry. Mucky bookshops, strip clubs and clip joints[115] swept all before them . . . as a hardcore pornography boom developed.[116]

It is notable that property owners such as Raymond benefited from the increasing value of Soho property not simply as their strip clubs and pornography businesses flourished but also as landlords. As Soho became more gentrified, thanks to an escalation in land values, rental and property prices generated huge profits.

An enthusiastic supporter of Thatcherism, by 1992 Raymond took the title of the richest man in Britain from the Duke of Westminster, with an estimated personal fortune of £1.5 billion.[117] As Hutton has put it, Raymond became one of Britain's wealthiest men throughout much of his life 'on the back of displays of female flesh',[118] not simply in his own clubs and bars but also through his burgeoning property portfolio. It is perhaps ironic, as Mort notes, that Raymond's business empire benefited so excessively and directly from the Wolfenden Report's recommendations enacted through the Street Offences Act 1959, which 'effectively restructured the sex trade'[119] in Britain. Because of the concentration of commercial sex venues in Soho, the Act's impact was most likely felt more here than anywhere else in the country. As a result, Raymond became the self-styled 'Duke of Soho' and the recognized face of commercial sex in London and well beyond. His expansive business strategy had, and continues to have, major consequences for Soho's development and for the commercial sex industry more generally. As Kirk Truman has recently put it, Raymond's legacy still haunts the streets of Soho today. While the Revuebar closed in 2004, the centre of Raymond's empire of erotic entertainment, sex, publishing and property lives on in the form of The Box, Soho. Billed as London's 'seediest VIP venue', the Box 'remains true to the Raymond Revuebar's legacy, serving up nightly helpings of titillation, nudity and sex'.[120]

Raymond's explicit tactic was to own, rent and control as much of Soho's property as he could in order to promote the area as a sexual marketplace 'organized around his own goods and services'.[121] His wealth and empire spread across Soho as he began to purchase the freeholds of buildings throughout the neighbourhood. He created Soho Estates, amassing around 400 properties in the Soho area. The result, throughout the 1970s and 1980s, was that the sex industry in Soho became something of a 'cluster economy'. But unlike more recent incarnations of this clustering, Soho (as Raymond's commercial manor) became increasingly heteronormative, hypermasculine and seedy: 'the underside of the West End's sexual economy'.[122]

Soho Today

It is against this backdrop, one of growing concern about Soho's future, that in November 1972 a community that had been evolving for over 300 years met to form The Soho Society. Through hard lobbying, members of the Society managed to get Soho declared a conservation area, as evidenced today by the many blue plaques and other artefacts of the area's cultural history that punctuate its urban landscape. Instead of comprehensive redevelopment, the Soho Society championed small-scale renovation based on the preservation of Soho's character as London's oldest urban village. Working with local residents and businesses, ridding the area of its 'plastic vice', as founder member Bryan Barraclough put it, was not a moral crusade for the Society but a matter of community survival.[123] Of primary concern were the rent increases resulting from so many properties being taken over by the sex industry, increasing rents to way above what local residents or businesses not connected with commercial sex could afford. As Theodore et al. (2013) suggest, organized responses such as these to local struggles around affordable housing, living wages and the environment point to progressive alternatives to neoliberal urbanism and to a revivified community solidarity in city centre locales that has the capacity, en masse, to challenge the unfettered 'rule of markets'.[124]

In 1982 and 1986, after heavy community pressure from the Soho Society, Westminster City Council brought in licensing legislation for sex shops and establishments providing sexual entertainment. Under the new legislation, the Council could fix the number (and cost) of licences, so that any business operating without a licence could have its stock seized and be subject to a fine and eventual closure. Glinert describes how, prior to the combined effects of the Soho Society and legislative intervention, Soho had descended into 'a sea of sleaze and sordid sex', having become 'a byword for seediness'. Arnold indicates that in the 1960s there were just under sixty sex shops in Soho[125]. Glinert estimates that at the end of the 1970s there were at least 200; by the end of the following decade, after the introduction of licensing, only thirty-five remained. And the number has decreased considerably since – there were around twenty-four licensed and unlicensed shops when I began researching Soho in 2008, and at the time of writing eleven (all licensed) sex shops are currently trading.

Walkowitz describes how, by the end of the 1980s, Soho seemed to have turned a corner, as the licensing system appeared to have kept the vast expansion of the sex industry in check.[126] The resulting effect is complex. Some argue that Soho has since become overly (and unnecessarily) sanitized and gentrified, citing dramatically increasing rental and property prices in the late 1980s and 1990s, combined with the growing presence of high-street chains and the ongoing closure of local businesses, as evidence of its decline. Erin Sanders-McDonagh et al. argue that Soho has effectively been lost to the sanitizing effects of 'hegemonic gentrification', resulting in the area becoming a playground for the super-rich. Citing the motto of Soho Estates – that the area should be 'edgy but not seedy' – they also draw from the English Collective of Prostitutes. The latter responded to a police raid in 2013 of a number of flats used by sex workers, ostensibly in order to 'rescue' victims of trafficking,[127] by emphasizing how 'if the "girls" go, the whole character of this historic area will be lost forever ... smoothing the path towards gentrification'.[128] But this is not necessarily irreversible, all-encompassing or even new, and Soho remains much more than simply 'another case study in the diverse nature of gentrification'.[129] Throughout its history Soho has been at the mercy of those driven to clean it up, or to clean up on it, and often both; arguably this is when it thrives most (as the formation of the Soho Society in 1972 suggests). Writing in the 1920s, well ahead of what many cultural commentators regard as Soho's bohemian 'heyday', Alec Waugh lamented that Soho was not what it had been, describing the place as 'a dingy and rather pathetic sham' of its former self, over-commercialized and faux-bohemian.[130]

Other commentators have maintained that the introduction of licensing governance in the 1980s, combined with a purge of protection rackets in the area, marked a turning point in Soho's recent history, one that has opened up space for a different kind of sex industry, and sexual ethos, to flourish. Summers closes her historical account of Soho with a note of optimism that reflects this latter view, when she argues that 'Soho has come full circle. No longer the social pariah of London, it is once again the "in" place to be.'[131] Chinatown has grown socially and commercially. With its distinctive pagoda-like entrance, the area is now a major tourist attraction and a culinary and cultural centre. The work of the Soho Society and local business initiatives such as the 'I Love Soho' campaign and social media groups such as Stephen Fry's 'Save Soho' have all combined to breathe new life into the area. And changes in the sex industry have had their own impact as well. As we will discuss in more depth in Chapter 5, although the industry remains heavily male-dominated, important elements have embraced gender fluidity and sexual multiplicity. The sector, and the area's, underlying hegemonic, heteronormative masculinity has been challenged, with a growth of interest in and support for organizations that celebrate LGBTQ lifestyles and provide a focal point for queer communities to flourish.

While to say that Soho constitutes 'the epitome of hard-core hedonism'[132] might be overstating the case, Soho became something of a magnet for gay men in the 1990s, with Old Compton Street rivalling Manchester's 'gay village' as a centre of leisure and consumption as bars and lifestyle stores multiplied, and these continue to have a notable and important presence. Of Old Compton Street, Ed Glinert simply says, '[G]ive thanks.'[133] Again, this reinvention built on Soho's historical associations – Quentin Crisp described how, as 'a reservation for hooligans', he felt safer in Soho than anywhere else, recounting in *The Naked Civil Servant* how the landlord of the Coach and Horses asked anyone who persistently made fun of him to leave.[134] And yet the area's characteristic openness also makes it vulnerable. On 30 April 1999, a neo-Nazi sympathizer, David Copeland, asked the barman of the Admiral Duncan pub on Old Compton Street for directions to the nearest bank, leaving a bag containing a bomb packed with nails in the bar. When the bomb exploded fifteen minutes later, three people were killed and scores of others were badly injured, sending shock waves through the community but also mobilizing its strength and solidarity. The latter was on display once again in June 2016, when a candlelit vigil along Old Compton Street paid tribute to those who lost their lives during a mass shooting at a Latin Pride event at the Pulse nightclub in Orlando, Florida.

But this sense of community is also, at least in part, what makes Soho particularly vulnerable to corporate overdevelopment. Coinciding with its 1990s renaissance was Soho's affirmation as a centre of media and cultural creativity. Soho has a long historical association with theatre and music, and its connection to the film industry was further strengthened by the growth of post-production film studios and distribution companies in the area. Hedge funds and other financial and corporate services businesses have also begun to emerge, trading on Soho's edge and its cachet as a deviation from the norm. The exclusive international chain of members' clubs, Soho House, also cashes in on the area's history and reputation, retaining its name in other cities across the world to signify these associations (whilst remaining entirely separate from the wider community in which it is situated, in the heart of Soho). But again, this apparent 'gentrification' is nothing new: trading on the area's 'exotic' associations began at least with Theresa Cornelys' Society of Soho Square masked balls in the 1700s. Today, as well as clubs such as Soho House and the Groucho, businesses seemingly unconnected to the sex industry, like 'Strip' sportswear and the 'Nudie' jeans repair shop cite Soho's enduring reputation for sex as a semiotic reference point.

Summers signs off with a further note of optimism when she says that 'Soho is no longer synonymous with sleaze but with style'. However, thinking about Soho in terms of a perceptual or aesthetic shift from sleaze to style does not, to my mind at least, quite capture the area's historical complexity, its materiality and meanings, or its contemporary appeal. For many, it *is* Soho's sleaze, even an increasingly sanitized version of it, that characterizes its style and reputation and which explains the place's magnetic capacity. When *Soho: A History of London's Most Colourful Neighbourhood* was published in 1989, Summers noted how in the 1970s there were 186 sex establishments in the seediest parts of Soho. A decade on, as already noted, only thirty-five licensed strip clubs, hostess bars, peep shows and sex cinemas remained, and these were concentrated largely around Brewer Street and Walker's Court. This concentration remains the case today, but the numbers have reduced considerably, and the traditional shops situated in these areas are under increasing commercial pressure. The small area in and around Walker's Court illustrates this. At the time of writing, the area is a building site, with only two sex shops, a tattoo parlour and The Box nightclub remaining open for business. Development plans are in place for a hotel, a revolving theatre and a reconstruction of the Madame Jojo's nightclub that formerly operated on a site in Brewer Street. As a semiotic effort to capitalize on the setting's seedy history, the Raymond Revuebar neon sign advertising 'Erotic Entertainment' is apparently being remade; 'like a Bond villain's lair', the headquarters of Soho Estates will also be re-sited there.[135] An article in the *Evening Standard* that describes the development makes reference to the demolition of 'a couple of old Soho walk-up brothels ... more romantic as an idea than the grubby and sad reality' to make way for a new theatre entrance; new walls will be faced in glazed, handmade bricks to contrast with the plastic-ribboned curtains and blacked-out windows more characteristic of 'old Soho' (and required by licensing conditions introduced in 1982). The whole plan seems to be driven by a mimetic desire to capitalize on Soho's edgy past, but of course this carries with it the risk of crushing its contemporary character in the process, creating the whole area as a clichéd simulacra much like other themed neighbourhoods or living museums.

As already noted, during the years I have been researching this book, the number of premises with sex establishment licences, including sex shops, has reduced dramatically. Yet Soho continues to have a global reputation for sleaze and commercial sex.[136] Undoubtedly there have been huge improvements in Soho, many that have made it a much safer place for those who work and live there. As a working, residential community, Soho is not only stable; it is thriving.[137] Concerns about the effects of licensing, and particularly about the area's gentrification, sanitization and corporate overdevelopment are widespread, however.

These concerns manifest themselves not least in opposition to the effects these combined processes have on rates and rents in the area. Just as the sex industry squeezed out small, family-run business in previous decades, more recently Soho's latest renaissance has resulted in yet another rapid escalation in property prices, so much so that few of the long-standing family businesses remain in an area that seems to be increasingly populated, commercially at least, by refurbished offices, fashionable boutiques and chain restaurants. As a result, an important part of what made Soho distinctive is being irretrievably eroded as the 'casual, haphazard feel of the district is [all but] disappearing'[138]. With all Soho's many gains, there are losses. Despite her optimism, Summers notes that it is the traditional craft industries – so important to Soho's history – that are most at risk.

These combined processes have been led not just by the market but also by government policy and legislation. The Use Classes Order, passed by Westminster City Council in May 1987, abolished the classification of property solely for light industrial use, so that, when leases expire and premises change hands, landlords can turn what might have been a light industrial workshop into office space without obtaining any necessary permission. As office space commands higher rental income than industrial space, this has further perpetuated the erasure of Soho's distinctive character as a working community. As Summers (1989) acknowledges, these changes are by no means unique to Soho. As she also emphasizes, however, and as Stephen Fry has put it more recently, through this process of gentrification 'something extremely valuable is being lost',[139] not least a richness and depth that has taken hundreds of years to, quite literally, 'craft'.

Yet despite, or perhaps even because of, all this, Soho continues to thrive on its atmosphere as an urban village and as a close-knit community. Soho is nothing if not resourceful and resilient. Summers ends by asking whether Soho's vitality and individuality will survive. The Soho Society works continuously to prevent the area from becoming over-sanitized, as do its vociferous supporters within the cultural and creative industries, not to mention Soho's own working population. In the chapters that follow, and in the stories told within them by some of the men and women working in Soho's contemporary sex industry, the aim is to show how, somewhat paradoxically, Soho's simultaneously loved and hated sex industry seems to be playing an important part in ensuring its survival as a thriving, working community of outsiders.

2 Putting Work in Its Place
Space, Place and Setting

Place has often been conceived of in rather unproblematic, commonsensical terms: simply as the setting where social or economic activity occurs. Yet as feminist geographer Linda McDowell noted in her study of the City of London, '*where* things take place' matters.[1] Place matters in a material sense, giving something that is otherwise ideational a substantive form, but it also matters in terms of being 'of importance' to our perception and understanding; place matters insofar as it is of material significance and of significant meaning. Thinking about what place signifies in this way emphasizes that setting is far from a neutral backdrop against which social action occurs; on the contrary, it plays an active role in shaping the nature and lived experience of that action just as the ways in which we make sense of and interact with place impacts upon the setting itself.

Related to, but somewhat distinct from, the more generic notion of 'space', place can be thought of as a series of assemblages and associations – situated configurations of things, people and processes as well as the meanings with which they are imbued that, in combination, constitute particular locations. Like spaces, places are not simply 'doubly constructed'[2] physically and socially, but multiply and perpetually so; they are built in a material, structural sense, but they are also continually 'interpreted, felt and imagined'.

Thinking about place in this way emphasizes that where work takes place plays a performative role in shaping what that work is and how it is organized, perceived and experienced, just as associations with a particular type of work come to shape the situation, setting or location in which it is carried out.[3] In other words, places are performative of particular spatialities and subjectivities – they bring them into being through their associations with particular practices and ways of being. This approach highlights that places are narrated spaces – settings with stories to tell, that are themselves dynamic, complex and fluid. In this sense, places 'trigger and carry sensuous perceptions and embodied memories that influence our ways of being',[4] just as those ways of being in turn influence the stories that particular places tell about themselves and those who inhabit them.

When we think about how different types of work sectors and settings are perceived and experienced in this way, how they are both narrative and performative, we can see the extent to which, as McDowell puts it, 'place matters'. With this in mind, this chapter considers: In what ways are places constitutive of particular kinds of work and work identities? How does place contribute to the ways in which specific jobs and sectors of work are perceived? And in turn, how does an association with particular types of work shape the locations and settings in which work takes place?

Before considering these questions with reference to working in Soho, this chapter will examine the concept of place, thinking in particular about how it relates to work. Contrasting with the more amorphous, open-ended concept of space, 'place' is generally thought, within phenomenological geography especially, to refer to the particular rather than the abstract.[5] For Yi-Fu Tuan, space is connected to movement and place to 'pauses' in the flow of space that we invest with specific and localized meanings; places provide relative stability and attachment, offering shelter and security:

> From the security and stability of place we are aware of the openness, freedom, and threat of space, and vice versa. Furthermore, if we think of space as that which allows movement, then *place is pause*; each pause in movement makes it possible for a location to be transformed into place.[6]

This notion of place as a pause is particularly apt for Soho. With its squares, benches and cafes and its history of migration, Soho has long been thought of as a place where the wider flows of time, capital and people 'pause', whether fleeing from religious or political persecution en masse or simply taking some time out from travelling. One of the risks associated with thinking about place in this rather romantic way, however, is that it seems relatively static and stable, in contrast to the dynamic and constant 'flow' of space. However, as somewhere like Soho, and London more generally, aptly illustrates, the materialities and meanings, assemblages and associations that constitute particular places are constantly changing. Place is more of a process than a fixed point, a change in the pace and tempo of space rather than a distinct pause, or a sensory multiplicity experienced rhythmically, as Simmel describes it.[7] Alec Waugh hints at this in his account of Soho, written in the 1920s, when he notes the place's distinctive transience, 'where life is fleeting and uncertain' and new atmospheres are quickly created and recreated as those who make up Soho's working community are in a 'constant state of becoming'.[8] Waugh's is a migratory point, referring to the constant flow of restaurant cooks and bar and waiting staff, but it could just as easily have been a cultural or ontological one, with Soho's working community, and the place itself, being constituted through a complex process or assemblage of affective entities and associations.

Place might be thought of in this sense as the space we inhabit, as Gaston Bachelard has emphasized in *The Poetics of Space*.[9] This way of thinking about place as spaces of habituation has two important implications: first, as spaces become habituated, they take on particular rhythms that somehow mark them out as distinct through the ways in which they are 'taken up' and made meaningful through social action. Second, they provide a setting in which those who occupy or associate with them can develop something of a distinctive, situated habitus – a way of being (or rather, becoming) in and through the setting. This emphasis on place as coming into being through inhabitation is important to thinking about the social and material production of place as a situated lifeworld, characterized by distinctive experiences, associations and assemblages. In turn, and borrowing from phenomenological writers like Bachelard and others such as de Certeau and Lefebvre, understanding places like this leads us to think about studying them in a sensuous, tactile, immersive and embodied way.[10] Such an approach requires an aesthetic hermeneutic that combines a situated understanding with critical reflection on the broader context in which particular places become what they are. Simmel emphasizes this when he argues that, in order to understand the ways in which urban settings are inhabited, we must appreciate that we do not end with the limits of our physical bodies but occupy the meaningful effects that emanate from our temporal and spatial situatedness. Equally, 'the city' only exists as a meaningful location in the effects that transcend its immediate physical substance.[11]

Arguably, the more mediated and digitized our lives become, including our working lives, the more place 'matters'.[12] This latter point is important to understanding the nature of Soho as a work place – as the specific setting of London's 'centre of depravity'[13] – including the continuing presence of the commercial sex industry there. Much of what is sold in Soho's sex shops is more easily and cheaply (not to mention discreetly) available online, yet the place itself and its commercial sex industry continue to thrive. This supports the argument that 'the geography of sex retailing really *does matter*'.[14] It raises questions: Why do customers shop there rather than online; and why in Soho specifically, rather than in other locations? To turn once again to McDowell, the answer lies partly not just in what Soho has to offer but also in what it *means*. As outlined in Chapter 1, Soho's 'anything goes' ethos has a long history and wide geographical reach; its global reputation as the capital of the United Kingdom's commercial sex industry remains undented by the more diverse range of entertainments on offer there, by licensing regulations or by the increasing digitization of the sex industry. The long-standing association of the place is that Soho sells sex, and sex sells.

But as already noted, places are not simply meaningful points of cultural association: they are the material settings of those meanings and associations; they are 'built or in some way physically carved out'[15]; they are where 'culture *sits*', including consumer culture.[16] In this respect, places constitute an assemblage of meaning and materiality:

> Place is, at once, the buildings, streets, monuments, and open spaces assembled at a certain geographic spot *and* actors' interpretations, representations, and identifications. Both domains (the material and the interpretative, the physical and the semiotic) work autonomously *and* in a mutually dependent way.[17]

A sense of place is not simply, therefore, the ability to locate things cognitively, on a map for instance. It is also the attribution of meaning and emotional, sensual attachment to a particular location – spaces become places when they are physically, materially invested with affective, sensory associations.[18] Places are imbued with associations that are not simply connected to the people or organizations that occupy them; the controlling, compelling or constraining effects of particular places emerge from the location, built environment and symbolic sense we get of specific settings, so that the material and the social are mutually influential.[19] Places are spaces *that mean*; they are the settings that make us feel something in or about them. Again, understanding places in this way helps us to get a sense of why the sex industry, and sex shops in particular, continue to have a commercially viable presence in Soho – people go there not just to buy sex toys and pornographic DVDs; they go there to go there.

Moving away from sex shops for a moment to illustrate what thinking about places as assemblages and associations that 'matter' might mean more widely, Tom Reynolds' book *Blood, Sweat and Tea* is an interesting account of how this sense of place can be experienced in relation to a different type of interactive, but distinctively situated, work. As a London Ambulance Service driver, Reynolds recalls connections between the spaces in which he worked – the homes, hospitals and entrances, as well as the control centre and the streets, the map references and technical layout of the area he and his colleagues covered – and the more subjective meanings he attached to the specific settings in which he treated patients, often in highly pressured and emotionally charged circumstances. Street corners are not simply map references or physical settings to him but memories of impromptu treatment rooms. It is the combination of the materiality and meanings attributed to these interconnected dimensions of his work that gives Reynolds' readers a strong sense of the Newham area of London where he worked not just as a space, setting or location but as his work *place*.[20]

Understanding setting in this way helps us to think about how particular kinds of work or industry 'take place'. *Taking place* refers both to assuming a place (taking 'possession' of it) and in some sense to happening and occurring, to coming to exist in a recognizable form within the context of a particular setting, by assuming a place. To emphasize its performative nature, we may think of this process as one of becoming *emplaced*. 'Placing' is therefore a perpetual process of bringing not just something but some*where* into being, in and through the dynamic relationship between a particular setting or location and the ways in which that setting or location is understood, made sense of and imbued with meaningful associations. Echoing Reynolds' description and resonating with Derrida's notion of 'spacing'[21] as situating space in time, placing involves literally putting something in its place – situating it empirically and epistemologically. Placing, in this sense, is a situated process of social and material enactment that brings meaningful locations into being through the attribution of particular associations. As an area where, historically, 'moral and material blight went hand in hand',[22] Soho epitomizes this way of thinking about how places are enacted through being imbued with distinctive meanings.

To illustrate, like space, place can operate on multiple levels and means different things in different contexts. 'Home', for instance, can refer to a particular address or geographical location (e.g. a village, town, city, region, country and so on) or to a more general, transportable sense of comfort and belonging (as in 'home is where the heart is' or 'feeling at home'). What these different meanings seem to share is an emphasis on the particular, on *place as a situated, specific space* with its associated connotations of attachment and identification.

Linking these conceptual themes to the study of Soho, the socio-materiality of place, and its wider cultural associations are important to our understanding of the lived experiences of the people who work there and in other similar kinds of settings. The sex industry 'takes place' in Soho in the sense that it takes 'possession' of the place or at least has done so historically (see Chapter 1), through a series of associations that continue to have local, regional and global resonance. At the same time, Soho's retail sex industry only exists in the form that it does in that *particular* location – there is something about the sex shops there (as will be discussed here and in subsequent chapters) that is discernibly characteristic of the area. In this sense, the sex industry 'takes place' in and through Soho insofar as it simultaneously happens in and dominates the setting. The materialities that bring it into being include its streets, courts and alleyways[23]; its signage and other urban artefacts such as the many blue plaques that adorn Soho buildings, or its murals and artistic displays; the fronts and entrances of its buildings, including shops, clubs and other venues; the interiors of these settings, including their layout, lighting, 'front-' and 'backstage' areas, their props and product ranges, as well as the physical presence of those who live, work, consume, pass through or settle in the area.

Together, although not necessarily in any harmonious way, these materialities mean that Soho 'takes place' through its physical and embodied substance and the meanings attributed to these – the social, cultural and political associations with the aforementioned substance that brings Soho into being in a very *particular* way. The latter includes the area's accumulated historical and contemporary associations discussed in Chapter 1, what Simmel describes as 'the weight of historical heritage',[24] with bohemianism, artistry and community and with sleaze, exploitation and over-development, as well as sanitization and commercialization. Taken together, these materialities and meanings constitute Soho as a distinctive work place.

Space and Place in Work and Organization Studies

The study of work and organizational life has come a long way since Chris Baldry described space as 'the final frontier', arguing that for too long the built environment had been excluded from the analysis of work organizations.[25] Much of the growing interest in space and place within work and organization studies has taken the phenomenological, social-materialist approach developed in Henri Lefebvre's (1991) *The Social Production of Space* as its conceptual starting point, emphasizing that space is never fixed or stable but exists in a constant state of becoming. What makes Lefebvre particularly interesting is his ontology of space. In characteristically phenomenological fashion, he works beyond a subject–object, social–spatial dualism, insisting that space is '*something more* than ... the disinterested stage or setting of action'.[26] This post-dualist, processual way of thinking about space is central to his understanding of the entwined complexities and contradictions that make up the social-spatial sphere; for Lefebvre, space is both produced and producing, always a becoming of 'something more'.

The Production of Space outlines how space is socially constructed through the dynamic interrelationship between three elements or dimensions. At the risk of oversimplification, these can broadly be summarized as: (i) *perceived space* (the routine, embodied and non-reflexive structuring of everyday reality through spatially situated practices); (ii) *conceived space* (dominant representations of space produced by scientists, planners and technocrats); and (iii) *lived space* (everyday, embodied experiences of space loaded with symbolic images, affective associations and wider connotations). These three dimensions are not separate but are dynamically interrelated in the social production of space, through what Soja refers to as Lefebvre's spatial trialectics.[27]

Thinking about the concept of 'place' through this phenomenological, processual lens highlights how the *conceived* manifests itself in particular settings, the *perceived* is routinely reproduced through dynamic, situated social relations, and the *lived* encapsulates how places are experienced through embodied perceptions and associations. Seen in this way, the dynamic intertwining of these different spatial dimensions is such that places can be understood as being produced and producing of social-spatial meanings and materialities; 'nothing is immobile', as Lefebvre puts it.[28] Developing an embodied perspective on this intertwining is vital to Lefebvre's approach to studying space and by implication, place. As he phrases it, 'this understanding of space . . . must begin with the lived and the body, that is, from a space occupied by an organic, living and thinking being'.[29] This means both understanding others' lived experiences of particular spaces, places and settings and, at the same time, adopting an immersive, reflexive and embodied approach to studying place.

Benjamin's (1928) book *One Way Street* shows how this can be done, by treating place as text. His essay on the cafes and coffee houses of Berlin in particular illustrates how place comes to be 'taken up', as different groups of artists, stock-exchange speculators and theatre directors 'plunge' into the same space, vying to make it their own, with the specific settings along a particular street serving as the organizing devices for his account.[30] In a similar vein, Benjamin's Arcades Project framed the Paris Arcades as a 'dialectical fairyland', 'the hollow mold' out of which consumer culture was cast.[31] What Buck-Morss (1989) describes as the materialist pedagogy of Benjamin's approach developed a stereoscopic way of understanding what the physical aspects of the space come to mean, and vice versa – that is, how layers of historical and cultural association come to take on physical forms in the displays, shops and settings Benjamin scrutinizes.

Of long-standing interest to scholars of social and urban life, Benjamin's attention to the arcades as a place of bedazzlement, spectacle, pleasure and consumption emphasizes how the synesthetic effects of the commodities on display, and the spaces in which they are brought together in an overwhelming mix, diverts expectations from social solidarity towards a 'hollow' preoccupation with individualized consumption. For Benjamin, the Arcades were 'a world in miniature' insofar as they were a constellation of material, cultural and historical referents.[32]

As Featherstone (1998) suggests, were he alive today, Benjamin might study both the substantive and experiential qualities of the settings that interested him, as well as their virtual, digital forms and representations, through films, photographs, music and voice recordings and, we might add, visual and social media.[33] All of this is important, as Featherstone suggests, to being able to develop the kind of immersive account of urban life that Benjamin strove for in his study of the flâneur as someone attuned to both the movement of space and the particularities of place, as well as to the kind of embodied, immersive perspective adopted by Lefebvre. Such an approach might draw from Soja's (1996) concern to move beyond what he called 'first space' – the 'objective' city of architecture, buildings and plans – and to drop down from the 'bird's eye' view of urban life that De Certeau (1984) made the focus of his critique in his advocacy of walking through the alleys, passageways and labyrinths of the city in order to understand it.[34] But it would also problematize this distinction, by showing how moving between immersion and reflection, between the lived and the representational, can maintain the dynamics that are so central to Lefebvre's approach. It would aim to show, for instance, how the physical and virtual materialities of space and place – buildings, streets, shops, websites and so on, are not simply things but 'media of meaning construction'.[35]

Drawing on the ideas considered in this chapter thus far, this is exactly the kind of approach I tried to take to studying sales-service work in Soho's sex shops, deriving additional insights from research within work and organization studies that has also taken phenomenological writing on space and place as its starting point.

Developing the dynamic interplay between the three spatial elements and the processual, performative ontology that is so central to Lefebvre's approach, organizational scholars have drawn on his writing largely to highlight the relationship between space and organizational control. Emphasizing the 'mutual enactment of the social and the material', Dale and Burrell's (2008) analysis of the organization of space takes Lefebvre as its conceptual starting point.[36] Stressing the spatial, embodied and material nature of social relations, their account considers 'representations of space' as 'organized space' – 'spaces deliberately developed for the practices of organization, and the forms of power embedded within them', and 'representational space' – 'the imaginary and lived spaces of organization ... lived through the embodied subject'.[37]

Dale and Burrell argue that, in order to understand the links between these two spatial dimensions, and the connections between space and power, three distinctions can be made between analytically discernible but empirically interrelated processes: *enchantment, emplacement* and *enactment*. Spatial enchantment involves the fusion of the material and the symbolic, 'connecting matter and meaning in such a way as to produce various power effects'. Emplacement refers to the 'construction of certain places for certain activities and certain people'. Whereas emplacement implies 'boundaries and compartments producing effects of fixity', enactment draws attention to how social spaces are 'lived, are processed through, are experienced through mobility and what power effects this brings about'.[38]

Sharing Dale and Burrell's concern with spatial control and power relations, Fleming and Spicer (2004) note that much of the critical analysis of the power-laden nature of organizational spatiality has focused specifically on what goes on *within* workplaces. They maintain that the very boundary separating the inside from the outside of work is an equally important instrument of control, arguing that the spatial regulation of working life involves a 'two way process' in which typically 'private' practices are drawn into working life as a site of production just as organizational norms and imperatives are encouraged outside of the workplace.[39]

The permutation of this spatial boundary has been more widely discussed with reference to the idea that everyday life outside of work is increasingly subject to the discourses and imperatives of managerialist rationalization.[40] O'Neill's (2018) ethnographic study of the 'seduction community' – a commercial, pedagogic network that provides training to men seeking to become more efficient at seducing women – shows how an intensification of the cultural logic of social relations takes the complexity of human relationships and identities and repackages them as a problem to be controlled through an accumulation of the right skills and techniques and by following the correct rules and formula. O'Neill shows how this logic is *spatially* situated in the classrooms, clubs and on the streets where the men being trained in seduction go to practice their 'game', including areas in and around Soho,[41] largely due to the latter's reputation for the consumption of sex.

Combining this critique, one that extends Habermas' writing on the rationalization of the lifeworld[42] with the processual ontology of place discussed thus far in this chapter leads us to consider how a place such as Soho is performative in both an ontological and a productive sense. How does the kind of place Soho is impact upon both the subjectivities of those who work there and the productive processes and pressures to which they are subject? As outlined in the Introduction, these questions are important to understanding the relationship between Soho as a work place setting and sector.

Emerging mainly from the literature on organizational aesthetics and symbolism, growing academic interest in organizational space has tended to focus on space as simultaneously a mechanism of organizational control and as a site on which such control can be challenged and resisted. While the former draws attention to the ways in which the organization of space is linked to identity management as a form of control, the latter emphasizes that the managerial regulation of identity, and of space, is 'a precarious and contested process'.[43] Both approaches draw from Lefebvre's conceptual typology, emphasizing a concern to understand how space is constitutive of social action, and vice versa.

Organizational scholars have argued that the space in and around factories and other settings has been an important mechanism for extending managerial control beyond the immediate sphere of the workplace. Perhaps the most well-known such arrangements revolved around the Fordist assembly line at River Rouge in the United States or Cadbury's planned village at Bourneville, as well as Port Sunlight and New Lanark in the United Kingdom. All of these can be thought of as examples of places that materialize the power relations embedded and enacted within particular organizations. Where Soho differs from these types of spatial arrangements is that the place is organized largely around a particular sector of work rather than a specific employer, although (as discussed in Chapter 1), Paul Raymond's property empire came to dominate the setting and many of the premises it occupied throughout the 1970s. What is also distinctive about these kinds of work places is that they were largely engineered by ostensibly philanthropic mill or factory owners; they were effectively manufactured as work places in order to blur the disciplinary boundaries between work and home to which Fleming and Spicer refer and to extend the supervisory gaze into workers' everyday lives, including (in the case of Ford's Sociology department) their sex lives.

As discussed in Chapter 1, Soho also emerged as a working community housing largely migrant workers employed in the 'backstage' areas that served the frontstage centres of politics, commerce and entertainment by which it is surrounded, as in many ways it continues to do so today. In this sense, whilst not 'constructed' in a way that is comparable to the places noted in the previous paragraph, Soho evolved as a distinctive work place, one charged with particular meanings and associations, where power relations are both reproduced and resisted. This dynamism generates a collective, even creative, energy that characterizes Soho as a working community. As Jason, one of the co-owners of a gay lifestyle store and sex shop on Old Compton Street whom I interviewed, put it:

You see all walks of life in Soho ... Big cities can be soulless and there's no community, but not here ... Soho has a strong community. A lot of people that live and work in Soho have been here for years, but at the same time, because it's such a huge tourist destination and also a migrant community ... you meet as many people from other parts of the world as you do Londoners ... It makes it really exciting. I mean, it's just bustling. Whatever people say about how it's changed, that's what it is – it's always changing. It's not a museum. Do you know what I mean? It's a community – it's a friendly community.

Its proximity to centres of power and its abject nature adds something of a conspiratorial, 'forbidden' element to Soho's working culture, one that its place-related rituals and rites perpetuate, a theme to which we return in Chapter 3 in our discussion of Soho's sex shops and industry. These practices thrive on the blurred boundaries there, resulting in informal working arrangements and conditions that create workplace meanings and experiences that are different from those in other sectors and settings but which are also similar to those in the informal or 'shadow' economies, particularly those in the sex industry.

Organizational scholars such as Felstead et al. (2005) draw distinctions between *work stations* (the immediate location where work takes place); *work places* (the buildings designated for work) and *work scapes* (the network connecting work stations and places, comprising specific sites and the technologies that link them).[44] But work places – as settings like Soho illustrate – are much more than this materialist topology would suggest: they are, as outlined at the outset of this chapter, 'a dynamic nexus of meaning and materiality'[45], a *situated* connection between the spatial and the social. Intertwined with the social production of place in this sense are the specifics of history, location and meaningful association and the social production and perception not simply of space but of *particular* social and economic landscapes. Central to this is what Soja called the 'socio-spatial dialectic'[46]: the mutual constitution and meaning of social and spatial relations. This approach emphasizes that workers are embedded within the distinctive 'fabric' of a particular workplace as different industries, sectors of work and organizations will be experienced in different ways in different locations. In this respect, workers are spatial agents who simultaneously produce their workplaces as they inhabit and embody them. And as Sanders-McDonagh and Peyrefitte (2018) argue, the commercial sex industry has long been part of the fabric of this area of central London.[47]

In their study of the significance of organizational place to work relations and identities, Courpasson et al. (2016) champion what they describe as a 'place-based perspective', arguing for the importance of understanding the relationship between physical location and lived experiences of work. In their study of the meanings attached to places of resistance – settings where mechanisms of corporate control can be challenged – they note that 'the nature and efficacy of resistance can be a direct product of the meaningfulness of a given place for the individuals involved'.[48] Citing Iedema et al.'s (2012) work on hospital corridors as ad hoc places for people to engage in impromptu social exchanges[49] and Casey's (1993) notion of transitory 'dwelling places',[50] they argue that inhabiting specific places permits the development of creative, critical exchanges that facilitate resistance when the place of resistance is particularly meaningful to those involved.

The vibrancy of Soho's cafe culture has been an important contributor to the area's radical politics throughout its history: the York Minster (now French House) on Dean Street is widely cited as the temporary British headquarters of the French resistance movement during World War II; Hungarian restaurant the Gay Hussar was used throughout the 1970s and 1980s as a meeting place for members of the radical left; and, perhaps most famously, the Golden Lion pub on Dean Street was the venue for meetings where early drafts of the Communist Manifesto were presented for discussion by Marx and Engels (the former living in rooms on Dean Street at the time – see Chapter 1).

Taken together, all of these insights and issues point to the importance of 'placing work' in the social, historical and material context within which it is enacted, experienced and made meaningful. Borrowing once more from McDowell, work matters to place just as place matters to work.

Placing Work and the Sex Industry

Social geographers have long since argued that place, as 'a meaningful location',[51] constitutes the material setting for social relations. Places enable us to produce and consume meaning through the emotional and subjective attachments we have to particular locales[52]; this is what Lippard (1997) calls 'the lure of the local'.[53] Place can therefore serve as the focal point for a strong sense of emotional attachment – what geographers call 'topophilia' (love of place). Courpasson et al. (2017) emphasize this in their study of middle managers' resistance to managerial policies and decisions, premised upon the idea that 'place is a centre of security for people'.[54] Yet our sense of place can also be shaped by precisely the opposite – that is, by a sense of revulsion or repulsion, particularly to those spaces deemed contaminated or contaminating (for instance because of their associations with deviant forms of sexuality), so that those who consume or work in such places might themselves become contaminated by association. Places can be tainted and can imbue those associated with them with physical, social or moral taints (see Chapter 4). As a place of 'ill repute', Soho is arguably one of those places.

Just as where work takes place 'matters', so too does the social situation and location of commercial sex, including in the form of sex shops. Relating sexuality to space and setting is by no means new, since this association follows from an ontology of sexuality as a largely situated social practice rather than a 'property' of the self. As cultural geographer Edward Casey has put it, the places we occupy have 'everything to do with what and who we are',[55] and much the same could be said about sexuality, especially when we begin to think about perceptions and experiences of the connections between places and sexualities that we might consider to be 'on the margins', as Casey puts it. Places are embedded within and materialize power relations and vice versa, just as lived experiences of sexuality are intimately entwined with 'where things happen'. To borrow from Shortt's analysis of liminal spaces within hairdressing salons, liminal spaces – in-between spaces on the boundaries or borders of rules, regulations and expectations – can open up within the confines of particular work*places*[56]. As a self-styled 'gay village', Soho is characterized by what Alan Collins describes, in his analysis of sexual dissidence, enterprise and assimilation in Soho's urban regeneration, as a place of 'sexual and legal liminality'.[57]

What Hubbard calls 'the spatiality of sex' is vital to understanding how and why certain spaces come to be designated for commercial sex or become liminal. As noted in our earlier discussion of phenomenological meanings of place, spaces can be homely and defined largely through attachment, as Bachelard (1958) describes, but also the inverse – certain spaces, places and settings come to be associated with exploitation, violence and degradation.

Legislation and regulation govern sexuality and gender in the ways in which they situate and perpetuate established power relations. Urban geographers have developed a range of perspectives on the strategic containment of behaviours deemed undesirable and on tactical responses to urban regulation. In his discussion of the neo-liberal city, urban geographer Phil Hubbard has shown how new modes of urban governance increasingly exclude minority groups from city-centre spaces, emphasizing the gendered, sexual and class-based dimensions of this. His analysis highlights how neo-liberal policy serves to 're-centre masculinity in the cityscape at the same time that it encourages capital accumulation'.[58] Focusing on the regulation of female sex workers in particular, he argues that such policies 'serve both capital and the phallus'.

One of the forms this takes is through direct subsidy or flexible application of planning regulations for developers prepared to invest in inner-city districts. Hubbard emphasizes how this underpins 'the reinvention of city centres as corporate landscapes of leisure, with the re-aestheticization of the city centre accompanied by the development of consumerist "plays-capes" catering to the affluent'.[59] With reference to the displacement of sex workers, Hubbard emphasizes how urban governors have sought to revitalize city centres largely through the adoption of 'place marketing' or 'urban branding' designed to improve the prospects of attracting inward corporate investment and to reframe designated areas through a reorientation of their consumer landscape.[60]

The Disneyfication of New York's hitherto notorious Times Square is a notable example of this process. In her study underlying the emergence of what Neil Smith has characterized as the revanchist city,[61] a concept on which Hubbard also draws, Marilyn Papayanis shows how 'quality of life' discourses continue to stand euphemistically for the domestication and sanitization of central New York's urban landscape. The latter's perceived unruliness, she argues, was emblematized not only by the presence of large numbers of homeless people but also by concentrations of 'sexually explicit imagery associated with XXX-rated businesses' until the mid-1990s. By focusing on the discursive strategies that sought to identify sex shops with so-called secondary impacts such as increased crime and decreasing property values, her analysis emphasizes, in a similar way to Hubbard, the social biases and political-economic motivations that continue to work to reshape the urban landscape in particular settings such as Times Square.[62]

To clarify, zoning ordinances introduced in New York in 1995 made it illegal for any commercial sex establishment (including clubs, bookstores selling explicit material, adult video and DVD outlets, and hostess bars) to operate within 500 feet of residential areas, schools, places of worship or each other (a practice known as 'dispersal')[63]. Of the 177 businesses affected at the time, only twenty-eight were allowed to remain in their established premises. The other 149 were forced either to cease trading or to relocate to an approved zoning area – an industrial/manufacturing district near the waterfront.[64] Given the lack of police resources in this area and its established reputation for danger, this relocation posed a significant increase in the threat of violence and the risks attached to engaging in commercial sex for LGBTQ consumers and workers.[65]

However, the Meatpacking District to which adult stores were relocated was already central to New York's sex industry, with many sex workers and clubs operating there in the 1970s and 1980s. This policy was effectively framed as a regulatory 'win-win' for legislators and city planners, with the area formerly occupied (Times Square) becoming heavily sanitized and the place to which sex businesses were re-located becoming (perhaps not surprisingly) increasingly gentrified.[66]

This is but one example of the ways in which, as commentators such as Hubbard and Papayanis argue, neo-liberalism thrives on the rhetoric of 'urban renaissance' as it allows the state to maintain a laissez-faire aura, enabling the private sector to orchestrate urban redevelopment ostensibly unfettered by governmental interference, *at the same time* as moulding particular locales in its own image. Neo-liberalism is thus entwined with gentrification and sexual regulation, as Hubbard emphasizes, so that for gentrification to succeed it must not only maintain the illusion that excessive regulation stifles urban creativity; it must also remove, through 'strategies of containment', 'Other' groups from re-valued spaces.[67]

Like zoning in the United States, licensing practices in the Britain have encouraged, Hubbard argues, the 'upscaling' of sex-related businesses while reducing their overall number and visibility, so that licensing provides a flexible mechanism through which the state is able to reconcile the demand for commercial sex with concerns about community life, urban aesthetics, public safety and property prices. In this sense, he says, licensing operates as a 'field of governance' in the Foucauldian sense, one orientated towards capital accumulation and gentrification.[68] As he puts it, 'licensing constitutes a site of struggle in which different constituencies fight to have their understanding of what is appropriate land-use legitimated'.[69] But licensing is arguably about much more than land use and struggles over public order and morality; it is a complex site on which the assemblages and associations that *constitute* places of work and consumption are played out.

For places like Soho to thrive, even against the regulatory backdrop of corporate development and neo-liberal governance, they must maintain the 'edge' that makes them distinctive both from other similar settings and from the wider urban spaces and entertainment economies within which they are situated. Struggles revolving around the management and marketing of this 'edge' have created something of a turf war in the regulation of space and sexuality in places like Soho.[70] Those who work in Soho's remaining sex shops are acutely aware of this. Phoebe, who worked in a specialist lingerie shop (now closed) on Old Compton Street when I interviewed her in 2009, said, 'I worry that it's all being cleaned up ... because they want to make Soho into a very unified area full of generic, blueprint coffee shops, so there's not much space for anything that is perceived as an eyesore.' Andy, who worked in a traditional sex shop in Walker's Court, said similarly:

It's all getting a bit quieter because they're trying to tidy Soho up. So they're trying to get rid of the [sex] market. There used to be brothels and about fifteen illegal shops where those luxury flats are now that they're building. They've knocked them all down. I mean, the worry is that once all the sort of edgy bit of Soho disappears, then bars and nightclubs will be next, and there'll just be offices and Costa coffee shops and that kind of thing ... It's just going to end up looking like anywhere else in London.

Yet as critics such as Houlbrook put it, what defines Soho as a distinctive space and place is a heterotopic sense that conventions constraining 'respectable urbanity' can (should?) be discarded there.[71] As Mark, who works in a 'traditional' sex shop on Brewer Street, put it, however, the view that Soho 'is not as edgy as it used to be' is fairly widespread among its working community. Houlbrook's view builds on Mort's earlier emphasis on Soho as a place in which differentiated histories have intersected 'to produce the area as a hybrid or heterotopic site of city life'[72] and, specifically, of sexuality. In effect, this means that Soho has become a de facto tolerance zone[73], which in itself raises the question: tolerant of what, and on what basis? Mort and others have written about Soho's story by exploring the associations between space and distinctive styles of consumption within a specific setting.

While emphasizing the importance of context, what is missing from these accounts is a consideration of Soho as a work place within this nexus of space, consumption and setting and a consideration of how this relationship is regulated through licensing policies, practices, and the imperatives and assumptions by which they are underpinned. Crucially, what struggles over licensing illustrate, and situate, is the extent to which sexuality constitutes a medium through which the dynamics of control and resistance are played out within particular workspaces and settings, with licensing assuming an important regulatory role in shaping the ways in which this dynamic is perceived and experienced. Fleming (2007) describes this dynamic in his account of a high-commitment work environment, in which sexuality is simultaneously a site of managerial intervention and control *and* a source of empowerment and resistance.[74] His analysis draws on Burrell's (1984) earlier work on life-affirming assertions of eroticism in intensive settings such as naval ships, prisons and concentration camps, places that might be regarded as sexually heterotopic in Foucault's terms. Both Fleming and Burrell draw on Foucault to emphasize how sexuality is socially and culturally situated and character-ized by 'fluidity, interpenetration ... ambiguity and flux'.[75]

Burrell's desexualization thesis also extends Weber's classic argument that the formation of modern bureaucracy is dependent upon the elim-ination of 'love, hatred and all purely personal, irrational and emotional elements' from organizational life.[76] Burrell extends Weber's critique of the dehumanizing effects of this, arguing that human feelings 'including sexuality have gradually been repulsed from bureaucratic structures and have been relocated in the non-organizational sphere – the world of civil society'.[77] As a result, expressions of sexuality – what Burrell advocates as a re-eroticization of work – 'may be expressive of a demand not to be controlled'.[78] In an over-rationalized world, expressions of erotic desire, although vulnerable to exploitation and appropriation, may be inter-preted as resistance to social and managerial control, not as some inevi-table outburst of a biological need but as a tactical form of erotic political engagement.

What this might mean for those who work in 'the business of sex' is important to consider. As Brewis' writing on sexuality in organizational life emphasizes, we need to think about how work in the commercial sex industry is constructed and perceived, lived and experienced.[79] And to this we might add *situated* within the context of particular spaces, places and settings through the combined effect of a 'discursive and material placing'.[80] Turning to ethnographic work potentially delivers, as Mort has put it, insights into the relationship between intimacy, identity and place that cannot be gleaned from formal maps of the city, providing an opportunity to understand how specific settings produce distinctive ways of being or 'stories of the self' and vice versa[81] that convey some-thing of the complex dynamics to which Fleming, Burrell and Brewis refer.

What does 'placing sex' mean? In part it means understanding that, although sex is ostensibly 'private', it is also commercially ubiquitous. It also means setting sexuality within its social – and organizational – context in order to understand how sexuality is perceived, lived and experienced within particular assemblages and associations. This, combined with insights on the meaning and organization of space and place, leads us to questions such as: How is commercial sex materialized in Soho's built environment, its geographical location and its cultural materiality? How is Soho perceived and associated with commercial sex? How do these materialities and meaningful associations intertwine in shaping the experiences of those who live, work and consume there?

Soho as a Work Place

Understanding place as a dynamic nexus of meaning and materiality provides an important starting point for thinking about how Soho's status as a 'commodified centre of cultural and sexual tourism'[82] impacts upon the work experiences of those employed in its sex shops. As Hubbard et al. have put it, perhaps more so than any other British city or distinctive place in the United Kingdom, the West End of London 'projects an ambience of hedonistic leisure in which pleasure, excess, and gratification are intertwined'.[83] What does this mean for those who work there, in its many sex and related businesses?

As suggested thus far, place is not 'something that is done to workers',[84] but, at the same time, places compel and constrain the ways in which particular forms of work are experienced and enacted. This applies perhaps especially to those places, sectors and settings that bear a heavy weight of social and commercial expectation, such as the sex industry in Soho. To borrow from Lefebvre's reference to the production of space, place is the outcome of past actions, but it is also 'what permits fresh actions to occur, while suggesting others and prohibiting yet others'.[85] Places constitute the material setting for social relations, including those in workplace settings, 'enabling humans to produce and consume meaning through the emotional and subjective attachment people have to a particular locale'.[86] What does the commercial sex industry, and Soho's many sex shops in particular, call on the place and its workforce to become? What kind of Soho do they construct, compel, and constrain into being, and, in turn, what kind of work place identities and experiences emerge there?

Even though his writing (in the 1960s) predated the virtualization of social life and the digital mediation of sexuality,[87] Foucault's point that our lives are governed by a distinction between public and private life shored up, rather than challenged, by our institutions and practices continues to have resonance when thinking about these kinds of questions. For Foucault, heterotopic spaces – 'different spaces . . . other places' – are those that blur this distinction.[88] Although they vary in form, heterotopias, he argues, are a constant feature of all human societies and groups. Linked by a rupture or pause in time, echoing Tuan's notion of place as a 'pause' in the flow of space, they can be shaped by a quasi-eternity, like a museum or a cemetery, or be hyper-temporary, as in the case of a festival, fairground or circus. Heterotopias are capable of juxtaposing several spaces in a single place, including 'several sites that are in themselves incompatible'. They presuppose a system 'of opening and closing that both isolates them and makes them penetrable'; heterotopias cannot be freely entered but are either controlled, as in the case of a prison, or a ticketed event for instance, or must be entered through ritual or purification, such as a sauna or a temple. This means that to get in 'one must have a certain permission and make certain gestures'.[89]

Promoted as somehow 'authentically Other', the place marketing that surrounds sexualized spaces such as Soho – not just now but throughout the last century at least (see the discussion of the promotion of Soho's culinary and cultural eclecticism in Chapter 1) emphasizes that they can only 'truly be understood by the cognoscenti, or initiated'.[90] At the same time, however, what makes places like Soho distinct is perpetually vulnerable to co-optation by market forces through a 'fetishization of difference'[91] akin to heterotopic branding or simply to a commercial exploitation of Soho's past or present associations with particular communities.

As Frank Mort has summarized it in *Capital Affairs*, Soho's location is fundamental to understanding its significance as 'London's exotic foreign quarter and long-standing centre of the capital's sexual economy'[92] and to making sense of its simultaneous vivacity and vulnerability. If contemporary patterns and experiences of consumption are shaped by specific spatial arrangements whereby commodities are invested with densely localized as well as global meanings, then Soho is an illustrative example of how these local and global associations interconnect; that is, 'of the ways in which large-scale movements of capital and culture are played out in intensely local settings'.[93] In this sense, places like Soho materialize capitalism's capacity both to create and destroy. It is a 'transnational/trans-local space' – a social-spatial materialization of a global sex economy in which particular cultural imaginings are embedded.[94]

As Saskia Sassen has emphasized in her discussion of the 'borderlands' of culture and economy in global cities, recovering 'place' in this way in the analysis of economic activity 'allows us to see the *multiplicity of economies and work cultures in which the global information economy is embedded. It also allows us to recover the concrete, localized processes through which globalization exists.*'[95]

As outlined in Chapter 1, Soho's provenance as the centre of London's cosmopolitan pleasures and dangers dates back at least to the early eighteenth century. The area's proximity to political and legal power bases, and to the retail and entertainment heart of the capital, created an exceptional atmosphere that brought migrants, tourists and visitors in from across the world. This has defined Soho throughout its history and continues to do so today. This history intersects not only with the area's location but also with Soho's distinctive geography and the materiality of its built environment, and these patterns of social and physical space shape the contemporary sex industry there and the meanings attached to Soho as a very particular work *place*.[96] Soho's symbolic and social geography, its location and its accumulated history have all played significant roles in imbuing its streets and shops with a distinctive atmosphere constituted through the ways in which the area's social materiality is enchanted, emplaced and enacted, to borrow from Dale and Burrell (2008). This helps us to understand both how and why the sex industry has flourished there in such a concentrated, clustered form.[97]

As Mort notes, Soho's 'assorted codes of urban spectatorship have been skillfully marketed', not just recently but throughout its history, by those who have wished to promote the area's uniqueness[98] in order to preserve it but also so as to capitalize on it. This has been achieved principally 'by astute marketing of its spatial and cultural distinctiveness and its historical accretions of bohemianism'.[99]

As discussed in Chapter 1, in the 1950s local alliances gave up on trying to contain Soho's edgy reputation and instead embraced it, reconstructing Soho as dangerously compelling for an increasingly permissive, affluent generation of post-war consumers. In doing so, they echoed earlier efforts to market Soho's long-standing associations with cultural hybridity and culinary eclecticism. From the mid-twentieth century, live sexual entertainment became hugely profitable, as eroticized displays of female nudity at venues such as the internationally famous Windmill Theatre and the Raymond Revuebar took centre stage. As noted in Chapter 1, Paul Raymond, the self-proclaimed 'King of Porn', became the richest man in Britain on the back of his growing property portfolio, much of it used to house his share of the commercial sex industry that dominated Soho through the last three decades of the twentieth century. This dramatic and dynamic coalescence of sex and setting is, as we shall consider in the next chapter, what made Soho distinctive as a place to shop and work, then and now.

Soho's day- and night-time economies blend into each other, both contributing in important ways to what makes Soho the *place* it is; in the daytime, the cafes, restaurants and local businesses shape the area's distinctive sights, sounds and smells; at night, the bars, clubs, theatres and entertainment venues come into their own. Although Soho's neon lighting is rapidly becoming a thing of the past, this too makes its own contribution. Connecting Soho's temporal economies and their spatial location, and generating its own series of contested associations, is the way in which Soho's sex industry is encoded into the area's cultural landscape. Signs for 'models', 'girls', 'masseurs' and 'sex shops' signify this connection and the extent to which it is embedded in the place and the sector, enacted by those who work and consume there.

The twenty-four-hour city has been put forward as an urbane solution to many of the problems associated with central city life in areas such as Soho in which the commercial pursuit of pleasure continues long into the night. The expansion of Soho's night-time economy has not surprisingly been a contentious issue for its residential and working communities, with concerns about the impact of increasing levels of noise, waste and anti-social behaviour being raised by residents, and issues associated with personal safety and security being of concern to those who travel to and from Soho in order to work there (an issue returned to in Chapter 5).

With growing trends towards gentrification, mainstreaming, feminization and online shopping, the residual character of the retail sex industry in Soho has also raised concerns. In their discussion of erotic retailing in the United Kingdom, Kent and Brown argue that place is an important part of the 'marketing mix'[100], with the location where the product or service is available to the customer being a significant factor influencing consumer choice and experience in the sex industry. For some, the sex shops that are characteristic of Soho are regarded as the 'dregs' of the industry, anachronistic overhangs from the sector and the area's seedy past that have long since outstayed their welcome. For others, however, the place itself is what appeals to those who seek out Soho's 'seediness' as a setting in which to live, work and shop (a theme we return to in our discussion of Soho as an abject place in Chapter 4).

Manchester (1986) describes the antecedents of Soho's sex shops as the pornographic bookshops and retailers of poor-quality imported films in the 1950s[101] (although Conrad's *The Secret Agent* suggests that Soho's early forms of sex shop date back much earlier, to at least the late nineteenth century). From about five shops in the 1950s, store numbers grew in the 1960s due to changing social attitudes and legislation, starting in 1959 with the Obscene Publications Act (see Chapter 1). The product ranges changed in the 1960s after the prohibition of pornography was abolished in Denmark, followed by Sweden in the 1970s. Importing pornographic films from both countries resulted in an increase in the number of shops throughout the 1970s, as well as their redefinition, from adult bookstores to sex shops, to reflect their broadening product ranges. Amongst these was a branch of Ann Summers, on Wardour Street, selling what were referred to at the time as 'marital aids' – sex toys, erotic lingerie and so on. Customers were mostly male, enticed by the private viewing booths that also became a feature of Soho's sex shops throughout the 1970s and 1980s (a contentious issue returned to in Chapter 4).

Jacqueline Gold, who is the daughter of one of the owners of Ann Summers and who later became its chief executive (but has since retired), said that she found these shops 'very seedy', explaining that her reaction was largely to the setting and environment of these more traditional shops rather than to their products.[102] In 1982, the licensing of sex shops drew a clear distinction between shops selling sex toys and 'soft-core' pornography and those selling 'hard-core' material, rated as R-18 by the British Board of Film Classification (see Chapters 1 and 3). Many of the shops in Soho sell both, differentiating one area from another through the use of spatial layout, curtains and in-store signage. Admittance to licensed shops, or sections within shops, is limited to those aged eighteen and over, as indicated by Figures 2 and 3.

These kinds of 'traditional', male-orientated sex shops continue to have a strong presence in Soho, in a more distilled form than perhaps anywhere else in Britain. As Kent and Brown have put it, there is

no other concentration of specialist erotic retailing comparable to London's Soho, which remains a uniquely-themed neighborhood, despite efforts to re-brand it, and periodical attempts by local government to clean it up.[103]

The place itself – the physical environment and its cultural associations – is an integral part of the experience of working and consuming in a sex

Figure 2 Sex shop signage indicating licensed areas, Brewer Street

Figure 3 Sex shop signage indicating licensed areas, Brewer Street

shop in Soho. This is evident in the continued existence of the area's more traditional shops, as well as the growing presence of more gentrified, feminized and themed lifestyle stores. This diversification reflects changes in the industry more widely, with the growing presence of sex shops orientated towards a female customer base, as well as the LGBTQ market.

A notable example of the former is London's Sh! – a shop which markets itself as a play space in which women can explore their sexual desires in a gynocentric environment. In parallel with this feminization of the sector has been a notable mainstreaming, with Ann Summers and other brands featuring as concessions in department stores or being sold on the shelves by high-street retailers.

A third, related trend is that of gentrification, with retailers such as Coco de Mer and Myla featuring design-led products sold in relatively luxuriously appointed stores charging considerably higher prices than others for stylized products on the premise that the high price tag 'wipes away the sleeze'.[104] The latter creates a distinctive environment in which to work and shop through an elevated combination of the style and location of the shop itself, as well as through the design and quality of its product range.

It is largely an aesthetic, class-based distinction that differentiates the 'traditional' sex shops associated with Soho from more feminized, mainstream and gentrified shops. As Crewe and Martin have argued, this distinction materializes a range of ironies and contradictions, not least that the encroachment of feminized stores and gentrified 'erotic boutiques' onto the high street means that, whilst traditional sex shops remain subject to licensing and zoning regulations, 'geographically marginalized and hidden because of concerns that they can pollute and contaminate their surrounding areas',[105] upscale boutiques and those marketed primarily at women carry no such restrictions and can thus locate themselves in design- and market-led settings, including adjacent to family stores and leisure outlets. This highlights that 'it is not the presence of sex in public space', or even its blatant commercialization, that ignites or fuels anxiety but its gendered and classed connotations.[106]

Working in Sex Shops in Soho

The Local Government (Miscellaneous Provisions) Act (1982) makes provision for the licensing of sex shops in the United Kingdom; the Cinematographic Acts (1982, 1985) control sex cinemas; and, in Westminster, the area in which Soho is situated, the City of Westminster Act (1996) allows licensing inspectors and enforcement officers to serve an immediate closure notice on any sex shop operating without a licence; it also fixes the maximum number of licences that will be granted in the area at any one time. Following Hubbard, licensing policies and practices can be understood as underpinned by the combined imperatives of gentrification, corporatization and control, to which we might add feminization, all driven by the pursuit of capital accumulation. Similar processes have been identified in relation to Manchester's gay village. Drawing on Žižek, Binnie and Skeggs examine how the capitalist drive to open up new markets of leisure consumption intertwines with a political desire to secure a distinctive space on the part of LGBTQ groups, leading to the formation of a discernibly gay space 'marketed as a cosmopolitan spectacle'.[107] This resonates but also contrasts with Soho.

In Soho, these largely commercial imperatives combine to produce what some have argued is a sanitizing effect which, coupled with the prohibitively expensive cost of a licence, produce an 'upscaling' of sex businesses, with independent operators being squeezed out in favour of corporate chains. Licences are clearly an important source of revenue for Westminster City Council, but, more significantly, licensing constitutes a form of governance that enables the Council to harness the area's inherent malleability in its own neo-liberal image. As Hubbard has put it, 'the system does so by reaffirming "community" as the seat of moral order, banishing potential contradictions through a logic of prevention that views certain venues as antithetical to the cultivation of "family values"'.[108] But as Chapter 1 emphasized, this is nothing new – since its very inception as a distinctive place, Soho has always been a playground (or, perhaps more precisely, a hunting ground), materializing a distinctive set of meanings and associations with commercial sex in all its forms, to which we turn in more detail in the next chapter.

3　Shopping for Sex
Situating Work in Soho's Sex Shops

Michael, one of the many participants in the study on which this book is based, described how, on a rainy Monday morning, he had spent time explaining the relative merits of a small selection of soft-porn DVDs to a recently widowed elderly man who had never been in a sex shop before but who was in need of some 'company'; he had been asked to model a pair of leather chaps for a gay couple looking for party wear (finding out only some way into his modelling session that the party they had planned was for three, if Michael was interested?); and he had been invited to try on the newly delivered store-branded T-shirts designed to convey the sexual eclecticism and corporate identity of the store in which he worked on Soho's Old Compton Street, known as the United Kingdom's 'gay capital'.[1] And a 'local' (the term used to describe regular customers rather than people who necessarily live or work in Soho) had asked Michael if he would let him have the socks he was wearing, as the customer said he wanted to smell them while he masturbated. For reasons unknown to me at the time, and seemingly to Michael, this was not an uncommon request.

In a little under an hour, Michael had performed many elements of what sociologists call emotional, aesthetic and sexualized labour. He was probably also performing some other types of labour, and engaging in interactions with products and customers, as well as providing services, that these terms don't quite capture.

Following Hochschild (1983), emotional labour involves the commodification of emotion within the labour process,[2] while the term aesthetic labour describes those workplace activities that, broadly speaking, 'generate an atmosphere'.[3] The latter, Gernot Böhme explains in his critique of what, borrowing from Horkheimer and Adorno,[4] he calls the aesthetic economy, 'embraces all human activities that lend to things, people and ensembles that *more* which goes beyond their handiness and objective presence, their materiality and practicality' to endow them with an aura.[5] At its heart, he argues, is the performance of aesthetic labour as a means of *staging* the sphere of exchange. This exchange does not take place in a vacuum but within the context of specific locations and settings that, in the case of Soho's sex industry, integrate the commercialization of emotion, aesthetics and sexuality. How these different elements of sales-service work interact and the various roles that shop workers such as Michael move between in a setting such as Soho are the focus of this chapter.

While there have been several ethnographic studies of sex shops, these have focused largely on customer behaviour, drawing attention particularly to the management of stigma[6] or to the negotiation of gender performance on the part of customers.[7] Yet as Malina and Schmidt (1997) have noted in one of the few published academic studies of working in a sex shop:

> Sex shops are an example of service where *all aspects of the service encounter are arguably heightened* because of the still fairly sensitive nature of the encounter. Potential customers in particular are *sensitized to their surroundings* and to the actions of staff and other customers in ways which may not be observed in more mundane settings.[8]

Although, as discussed in Chapter 1, much has been written about Soho itself, relatively little is known about the work experiences of those employed in its many sex shops. How does Soho's global association with commercial sex impact upon the work experiences of those employed there? What are the emotional, aesthetic and sexual demands of the role, and how are these demands shaped by the place itself? The place, the sector and the shops there, while continuing to exert a strong influence on the area's distinctive associations and assemblages, are changing rapidly. For now, as a recent (and rare) article on sex shops in the *Journal of Management History* put it, there is 'no other concentration of specialist erotic retailing comparable to London's Soho, which remains a uniquely themed neighbourhood'.[9]

For how much longer this will be the case remains to be seen, but in the ten years or so that it has taken to research and write *Soho at Work*, it seems fair to say that it's genre has shifted somewhat, from a 'sociology of work' book to something more akin to a social history, as many of the shops have closed down or been taken over by high-street chains. When the study began in 2008, there were twenty-four sex shops in Soho; at the time of writing there are eleven. This compares to Thompson's (1994) account of fifty-four sex shops, thirty-nine sex cinemas and clubs, and twelve licensed massage parlours in 1982.[10]

None of the shops in which I undertook interviews or observations fit into a neat categorization: some are 'traditional', seemingly male-orientated shops; some fall into the classification of erotic boutiques;

others are feminized high-street chains; others are LGBTQ lifestyle stores, orientated largely (but not exclusively) towards a gay male clientele. Ownership of the shops in Soho broadly falls into three categories: most are owned by (absent) holding companies and operated by managers, some are owned by national or international chains and (at the time of writing) only one is run by co-owner/occupiers, who have invested their life savings and more in the design and development of the business.

On the basis of a series of interviews with men and women working in Soho's sex shops spanning a ten-year period, between 2008 and 2018, this chapter will concentrate on providing a detailed, ethnographic account of lived experiences of working in the area's remaining sex shops at this particular point in time. Drawing on relevant sociological literature on emotional, aesthetic and sexualized labour as well as the stories told by the men and women who work in Soho, the discussion will explore the ways in which sex shop work is *embedded* in Soho itself; it will consider how retail sex work is *enacted embodied* by those who perform it; and it will also examine some of the ways in which interactive work in sex shops is *encoded* into Soho's cultural and semiotic landscape.

Before we begin, it is important to try to get some clarity on what actually constitutes a 'sex shop', although it should be noted that the legal definition in the United Kingdom and elsewhere remains somewhat ambiguous.[11] Because of this, it is difficult to give an exact figure on the number of sex shops in the Britain, or even in London, as classification varies depending on exactly what products are sold. But while legal definitions might lack precision, perceptual ways of knowing what a sex shop is are arguably much clearer, with their discernible aesthetic marking them out in the places in which they are situated or, as in Soho, are particularly concentrated. Sex shops are a common sight in red-light districts across the world, but their distinctive blacked-out windows and neon triple-X signage have been a ubiquitous feature of Soho's semiotic landscape for decades, signifying their distilled presence as a characteristic and enduring feature of the area's visual culture.

Sex Shop Legislation and Licensing

The applicable legislation in the United Kingdom – the Local Government (Miscellaneous Provisions) Act (1982) – leaves much of the licensing and regulation of sex shops to the relevant local authority; in the case of Soho, this is Westminster City Council. As Coulmont and Hubbard (2010) note, licensing legislation was largely the result of Westminster City Council petitioning central government for powers to exercise control over sex-related businesses given growing concerns among Soho residents and the Soho Society in particular about the character of the area in the late 1970s and early 1980s (see Chapter 1).[12] Premises licensing had been used as a mechanism for controlling contentious land uses since at least the nineteenth century, and so, following MPs raising the possibility that licensing might be extended to cover sex shops during the second reading of the Bill in the House of Commons, a system of sex shop licensing was introduced through Schedules 2 and 3 of the (1982) Act. Section 3, 4(b)(ii) allowed any local authority in England and Wales[13] to issue a licence for:

Any premises, vehicle, vessel or stall used for a business that consists *to a significant degree* of selling, hiring, exchanging, lending, displaying or demonstrating sex articles or other things intended for the purpose of stimulating or encouraging sexual activity or acts of force or restraint which are associated with sexual activity.

Though the 1982 Act allowed limited discretion over what was sold in licensed shops (unless stock was deemed to 'corrupt or deprave', in which case it would be covered by relevant obscenity legislation), local authorities were permitted to impose conditions in three key areas: shop window displays; admittance or employment of under-18s, and opening hours. Refusal of a licence on the basis of the applicant's character or the unsuitability of the location[14] was also permitted by the Act, which was backed up by the imposition of fines or imprisonment for those failing to comply with these licensing terms and the powers to serve enforced closure notices on unlicensed premises. The 1982 Act thus gave unprecedented discretion to local authorities in the control of sex shops; it also allowed them to generate considerable revenue through licence fees, which the Act permitted being set by the relevant authority.

Section 4(b)(ii) of the Act covers any recording or display of vision or sound which is 'concerned primarily with the portrayal of, or primarily deals with, or relates to, genital organs, or urinary or excretory functions'.[15] In June 1999, the Westminster Planning and Transportation Committee (under Schedule 3 of the 1982 Act) decided that the maximum number of Sex Establishments within the locality of Soho should be sixteen.

In administering the relevant legislation, the Council takes account of the views of local residents and community groups, including the Soho Society. The Westminster City Council Sexual Entertainment Venues statement of Licensing Policy (2012) states that its aims are to: (a) prevent crime and disorder, (b) secure public safety, (c) prevent public nuisance, (d) protect children from harm and (e) improve the character and function of the city, or areas of it.[16] Explicit reference is made to other statutory regulation that pertains to Sex Establishments, including sex shops, such as fire safety, planning, building control, public health, food hygiene, and trading standards,[17] but no specific mention is made of the working conditions of those employed in sex shops or other establishments (with the exception of a passing reference to the provision of suitable changing spaces for performers). Westminster's (2012) Licensing Policy effectively makes the 'business case' for Soho's sleaze in an allusive reference to its commercial value as a place to visit and consume when it states that:

the mixed character of the CAZ (commercial activity zone) is central to its economic vibrancy and crucial to attracting visitors and businesses. It also makes a significant contribution to the unique character of Westminster.[18]

In what might be read, following Hubbard, as a charter for gentrification, the Policy also makes explicit that 'the layout, character or condition of the venue' is an important factor that the Council takes into account when considering licence applications or renewals, the aims being to 'reduce existing concentrations of licensed premises, particularly in Soho'.[19]

During the period in which I have been studying Soho, all of the unlicensed shops have either closed down or applied for licences.[20] One example is Adult World, located in the notorious Walker's Court, which applied for a licence in 2014 after previously operating as an unlicensed store, selling mainly pornographic DVDs and sex toys. The written application states that the anticipated annual turnover for the business was approximately £300,000 and that 'the sale, hire, exchange, loan, display or demonstration of sex articles' accounts for 100 per cent of this amount, specifically the sale of 'R-18 films, sex publications and sex toys'. The application received four objections: two were from the Council's Environmental Health Service and District Surveyor, and two were anonymous. The Environmental Health Service objected on the grounds that the basement toilet needed refurbishing, as did emergency lighting and escape signage. Also recommended was the installation of CCTV equipment, 'due to the *location of the premises* and the nature of the proposed retail goods'[21]; the District Surveyor objected to the licence being granted until these refurbishment works were completed. Of the two anonymous objections, one was from a local resident who wrote that s/he has lived and worked in Soho for over thirty-five years and has 'seen the area change many times'. This resident was particularly concerned that the area around Walker's Court had become a 'haven for drug dealers and thieves', to the extent that 'I and many others are afraid to be in the area and this is not just at night'. The letter sent to the Council from this particular resident ends: 'I have no problem with the sex industry as such but think that premises such as the one in question are to the detriment of the area. The sooner the lower end of this trade is removed the better.'[22] The second anonymous objection was also raised by a local resident, on the basis that '*there is a saturation of sex shops in the area, which leads to a general atmosphere of sleaze.* I thought that we were trying to improve the area not bring it down. We should be closing these places down not legitimizing them.' Reference is made to local schools and places of worship, as well as to the irony of Westminster City Council pursuing a policy of closing down unlicensed stores by licensing those that have been operating illegally for some years[23].

In Foucauldian terms, Coulmont and Hubbard argue that the 1982 Act constituted a new regime of sexual governmentality, designed to address precisely these kinds of social and moral concerns by protecting communities or populations deemed to be vulnerable and regulating sexualities regarded as deviant or potentially corrupting. They cite the local media portrayal of Trafford Council's decision in 2005 to refuse a licence for a sex shop as a victory for a local schoolgirl who, with other objectors, had written a letter to the relevant Licensing Committee, expressing her view that: 'this shop will attract paedophiles, perverts and rapists ... [W]e will be letting children in the community get contaminated.'[24] Views such as this, and by implication licensing and legislative responses to them, arguably discursively position those who work in sex shops 'as professional perverts'[25] intent upon facilitating predatory and contaminating behaviour through their work and workplaces, a theme returned to in Chapter 4.

Since 2001, the need for a licence in the United Kingdom has been largely determined by the sale of R-18 films (those that graphically depict sex acts). Local authorities retain the discretion to set their own fees and to refuse any license, with license renewal being required every twelve months or less. Legislation in Westminster precludes the admission of anyone aged under eighteen into licensed stores and the display of sexually explicit material in the windows, with fines beings imposed for any violations. Encoded as heavily male spaces, their physical location and aesthetics have created an understanding of Soho's sex shops as 'sleazy and inadequate spaces, requiring legal regulation to protect the general public from their obscenities'.[26]

To my mind, one of the most useful descriptions of what constitutes a sex shop is based on a study conducted in the United States, where sex shops have been regulated not through licensing but zoning. Michelle Edwards' research on the social organization of commercial sex in New York focuses (not surprisingly) on the Times Square area of the city. She explains that, in 1976, the Supreme Court introduced a legal definition of adult or sexually orientated businesses as those that display 'material distinguished or characterized by an emphasis on matter depict-ing, describing or relating to 'Specified Sexual Activities' or 'Specified Anatomical Areas'. The specified list includes: adult bookstores, adult entertainment clubs, adult sexuality boutiques, massage parlours, cabaret clubs, adult theatres, escort agencies, and nude modelling studios. Edwards notes that 'the divisions between these categories are, to a certain degree, subjective, with some of these labels overlapping'.[27] To give an indication of the distilled concentration of commercial sex even in contemporary Soho, following years of licensing and 'clean-up' campaigns by regulatory bodies, it is worth noting that *all* of the examples of 'adult or sexually orientated businesses' in Edwards' list can still be found in the square mile of space that the area occupies.

Situating Sex Shops Historically and Geographically

Perhaps one of the first recorded descriptions of a London sex shop can be found in Georges-Louis Lesage's account of his visit to London in 1713, in which he recalls women in St James's Park carrying baskets full of dolls, which seemed to be in great demand. These 'dolls' had cylinder-shaped bodies instead of legs and were approximately six inches long and one inch wide. According to Lesage, one young woman complained that her doll was too big and asked to exchange it for one with a smaller body; but the vendor refused, explaining that it would be impossible to resell it to another customer[28]. Since then, the sex industry has flourished in London, with Soho being its commercial and cultural centre.

As Frank Mort describes it, and as discussed in Chapters 1 and 2, the cultural and geographical contrast between shops in Soho and its surrounding streets is quite dramatic. Soho possesses few of the distin-guishing features of shops on Oxford or Regent Street. With its narrow streets, squares, courts and alleyways, much of Soho is still largely pedes-trianized or inaccessible to flowing traffic. Unlike Oxford Street's linearity or Regent Street's sweeping grandeur, the layout of Soho's smaller streets and lanes remain remarkably similar to those mapped out in Cardwell's *Two Centuries*, and earlier (see Chapter 1), reflecting patterns of aristo-cratic land ownership and the hunting grounds on which Soho was built and from which the area takes its name.

Most of Soho's retail history is one of small, family-owned or -run businesses that contrast markedly to the large department stores and retail chains that line the neighbouring retail thoroughfares of Oxford and Regent Streets. With the notable exception of the Soho Bazaar, a social enterprise that epitomized the philanthropic orientation of Soho's more wealthy business owners in the nineteenth century (see Chapter 1), shops in Soho have always been small scale and specialist. Until recently, very few names that would be recognized beyond Soho operated there. This is in part due to Soho's reputation, but it can also be explained with reference to its geography: though accessible by taxi, car and van, Soho has never been crossed by any bus routes, nor has it been as easily accessible from an Underground station as other shopping areas, except at its outer edges. As Mort has summed it up, 'this sense of Soho as culturally amenable to the pedestrian rhetorics of strolling, spectating and loitering [has been] … a significant asset for widely different groups of users'[29] throughout much of its history, particularly those looking to consume what Conrad described as the area's 'shady wares'. It is Soho's combined history, geography, culture and economy that constitute what Peter Speiser refers to as its 'urban fabric' and which, in my view, accounts for the emergence and endurance of the area's sex economy.[30]

All of Soho's major boundaries signal the resumption of 'normal' forms of metropolitan life: mass leisure, shopping, transport, tourism and commerce that are generally not found en masse in the district. Indeed these kinds of activities are either relatively 'marginalized in Soho or differently inflected within its extremely localized spaces',[31] and its sexual economy and culture are no exception.

As the product of ongoing redevelopment, as Mort notes, Soho's surrounding streets epitomize many of the hallmarks of urban modernity described by Georg Simmel in his essay on the social impact of metropolitan life: speed of movement, massive capitalization of the commercial and technological infrastructure, and the 'chaotic excitement' of the city's anonymous, sensory multiplicity.[32] Soho's relative physical and social separation from these processes shored up its status as a world somehow 'set apart' from – yet intimately intertwined with – mainstream commerce; as a result, the area's cultural economy is characterized by 'notoriety as a site of urban danger, sexual transgression and exotic cultural fantasy'.[33]

It is the latter in particular that helps us to understand how and why its sex shop business continues to exist in the face of the combined forces of technological, social, commercial and legislative changes. Much of what is sold in a licensed sex shop can now be purchased online,[34] either on that same shop's own website or from other retailers, or (in the case of pornography) accessed free or via subscription websites.[35] Further, changing social attitudes to sex means that consuming in a high-street sex shop or concession is increasingly easy and socially acceptable, particularly in those stores that are more gentrified or feminized and which deliberately provide an alternative to the concentration of more 'traditional' retail outlets in places like Soho. Added to this, legislative changes mean that a significant proportion of what traditional sex shops sold until relatively recently – namely amyl nitrate or (original formula) 'poppers' – is no longer available (or, like porn and other products on sale, can be bought online). The cost and complexity associated with obtaining a licence constitute a further challenge to the continued existence and commercial viability of the retail sex industry in Soho. And yet, although declining in number and changing in nature, over the course of the ten years or so that I have been researching sex shops there, a remarkable number have survived. Some of these appear to be thriving, particularly those that have positioned themselves as branded lifestyle stores or which are situated along Soho's main thoroughfares, particularly along Brewer Street, Wardour Street and Old Compton Street, in the 'heart' of Soho's consumer economy. Against this backdrop, the decline of the sector is perhaps less sociologically interesting than its continued survival, even revivification.

As well as the place and the sector's enduring reputation, the continued presence and commercial viability of sex shops in Soho can also be explained, at least in part, with reference to the market characteristics of the area itself. In his discussion of the evolution of paid sex markets, Samuel Cameron outlines how the emergence of commercial sex 'is a product of various locational economies', including *laddering* – an escalation of involvement in the range of activities and opportunities that constitute a paid sex market.[36] Laddering, he argues, is one of the reasons why sex markets might emerge and flourish in a particular location, producing 'spillovers in network demands due to the presence of other sex market products'.[37] City-centre settings may also produce a 'herd effect', increasing demand due to passing trade on the basis of spur-of-the-moment decisions including occasions where immediate gratification may be desired. The latter produce what Cameron calls 'atmosphere benefits' whereby, although some may frown on the ambience associated with a particular area, others are attracted to 'the frisson of excitement and danger that is perceived to reside there'.[38] Here Cameron emphasizes the extent to which the pursuit of sexual gratification within specific settings can be linked to other consumption elements.

In Soho this is particularly apparent in the sense that visiting a sex shop not only provides a source of social interaction and advice, including product recommendations; the shops are also sites of sexual pleasure in and of themselves, as is Soho more generally. Julie explained this to me when she described sex workers bringing clients in to the store as part of both the 'experience' and the transactional relationship:

We get some punters who come in with people they are paying to go on a date with and to have sex with them. They will come in here and look at things together. Often she will talk about the things and say what she likes. It's all part of the experience. More often than not, we know them, but even if we don't you can spot them. But we pretty much always know them, so we say we can give them a good price, but we always give them discounts. She might buy what she needs for the session or, more likely, will take him for what she needs and get him to pay.

Connecting otherwise disparate sex-related businesses in a market cluster, Cameron argues, are specialized buyer–seller relationships such as these. Given the relationship Julie describes, we might add that Soho's clustered sex market also involves specific relationships between different types of sales-service encounters, workers and environments. These capitalize on the area's accumulated atmosphere, reputation and history. Comparing sex work, erotic dancing and retail work in a sex shop, Cameron notes that 'one skill that is common to these employments is putting new and apprehensive, or morally inhibited customers, at ease'.[39] Soho, he argues, is a classic example of how this clustering works, as is Amsterdam. In both places, demand complementarity creates and sustains an incentive for sex-related businesses to remain in close proximity. Although zoning restrictions have prevented the emergence of full-scale laddering and clustering in the United States, this is not the case in Soho, in which a clustered market has been sustained for decades if not longer.

Daniel, who had worked in Soho for about a year when I met him in the sex shop in which he worked on Wardour Street, explained some of the characteristics of the area's clustered market economy to me. As he put it,

The shops are a real community – not really competing because everyone specializes in different things. The Oxford Street branch [of the feminized chain of sex shops he works for] is more 'vanilla'. It sells more lingerie, whereas our branch is more focused on toys but still vanilla, not like the more specialist stores for people who are really into this as a lifestyle. Some of their toys are more extreme – some are really out there.

[‘Why is Soho different to Oxford Street?’] There's more of a vibe here. More of an expectation that the shops will be more specialist. And the customers are different. It's mainly just shoppers on Oxford Street, but here you get people who have come to go to Soho, you know? They come here knowing what kind of things the shops will be selling, and that's what they want. They're more prepared for it, and they have an expectation. The toys in some of these shops are eye watering, including the costs. You can see that you really have to invest in some of these, so it must be a big part of people's lives.

Borrowing from Alan Collins' account of the evolution of urban gay villages in UK towns and cities, it is possible to discern four key stages in the development of the retail sex industry in Soho as a 'clustered' sex economy in Cameron's terms and in the way that Julie and Daniel describe it. These are: (i) *pre-conditions* (an urban area in decay or decline, combined with the specific location and history of sexually and legally liminal activities in the area); (ii) *emergence* (a clustering of social and recreational opportunities, including conversion of established businesses, with an increasingly specialist focus, creating a 'distilled' market); (iii) *expansion and diversification* (widening the service base, through increasing numbers of premises and related businesses making a contribution to revenue streams, and raising 'increasing physical visibility and public awareness'); (iv) *integration* (assimilation into a 'fashionable mainstream' through growing presence and association, and regeneration of customer bases, as well as an increasingly significant and sustained contribution to enterprise revenue streams within the community).[40] With regard to the latter, Brents and Sanders show how commercial sex has undergone a gradual process of mainstreaming in recent years. As they put it, 'cultural changes and neo-liberal policies and attitudes have enabled economic mainstreaming, whilst social ambivalence continues to provide the backdrop to a prolific and profitable global industry'.[41] As already suggested, this integration of sexual services into the mainstream economy has both reaffirmed and challenged Soho's reputation as the heart of the United Kingdom's commercial sex industry, both intensifying and undermining its specifically local character and the situated nature of its clustered sex market.

Key to understanding Soho's sex shops is that, as a place to visit, Soho's reputation, combined with its pedestrian orientation, paucity of civic grandeur and official landmarks, means that those who go there tend to do so quite purposefully, including specifically to engage in the area's sex economy. Many of those who visit the area's sex shops, clubs and other establishments such as massage parlours tend to be people who consciously and deliberately seek them out. And they do so within the context of a very particular set of cultural and sexual associations, as sex has played 'a major role in the development of Soho's consumer economy almost from the area's inception'.[42]

If prior to and during World War II Soho's sex industry was dominated largely by street-based sex workers and the erotic tableaux on offer at places like the Windmill Theatre (see Chapter 1), by the 1950s it was the strip clubs that began to hold sway and, by the 1960s, the pornography industry.[43] By the 1980s, so-called near-beer bars, peep shows and clip joints, 'the glummest alternative of all',[44] shaped the commercial sex landscape, combined with the large number of sex shops with which the area had come to be associated. For clarification, clip joints are places of sexual entertainment that became notorious for overcharging or cheating customers by enticing them into paying an excessive amount for non-alcoholic or watered-down 'cocktails' through the underlying suggestion of freely available sex with hostesses. Customers are ejected as soon as they become unable or unwilling to pay. Clip joints trade on the assumption that, due to the combined effects of the illicit nature of the services on offer and the shame of having been duped, customers are unlikely to contact the police or take any recourse through official or legal channels. In theory, they are all but extinct in contemporary Soho, but their permanent closure is difficult to maintain, and their legacy lingers on in Soho's residual reputation as a place of extortion and exploitation. Maxine White, who worked in a Soho clip joint in the 1980s, describes how clip joints work:

A typical scam is when a customer is shown in and offered a drink or the company of a hostess at their table. Acceptance means they will be presented with an outrageously inflated bill, sometimes for several hundred pounds, for the drink, service charges, or hostess's company. Immediate payment is demanded on pain of criminal charges or the threat of physical violence. Clip joints exist on the fringes of legality, as there is no law against overcharging and the onus is on any customer to discover what, and how much, they are paying in advance of any purchase they may make.[45]

Recent years have seen a combined task force consisting of the police, fire brigade, council inspectors, immigration officers and an investigative unit of the Inland Revenue, known as the Joint Shadow Economy Team, making a concerted effort to close Soho's clip joints once and for all. In 2004, the Illusions clip joint on Great Windmill Street was closed after the fire brigade discovered that (sadly, not surprisingly) it had no emergency exits, thereby putting its customers and particularly staff at considerable risk. While closures are hailed as a success, other clubs quickly spring up in their place.[46]

Clips joints are but one manifestation of the reality and reputation of Soho's sex economy, which has historically thrived on exploiting customers' naivety and shame and, at the same time, as the case of Illusions illustrates, often trades on working conditions for staff that are on the fringes of the law, at best.

Hutton lays out what he describes as 'the bare facts' of the historical origins of contemporary manifestations of commercial sex in Soho. As he puts it, while post-war Britain may have been outwardly prudish and sanctimonious, it was also largely hypocritical. Sexually repressed Victorian society had helped to create an army of sex workers (many of them children) in the West End of London, and this largely unrecognized army continues to support the city's contemporary sex economy. Dickens sought to raise awareness of the exploitative nature of London's sex industry through characters such as Nancy in *Oliver Twist*, as did other social reformers such as Thomas De Quincy, whose heart-wrenching account in *Confessions of an Opium Eater* describes the help given to him by child prostitute, Anne. Cardwell's *Two Centuries in Soho* also alludes to the situation (see Chapter 1), as do Hogarth's engravings. Well into the twentieth century, Hutton notes, British consumers of commercial sex sought to condemn those who made their living in the industry, at the same time as they 'indulged their excesses guiltily and hopefully out of the public's gaze'.[47]

Perhaps because of this, a sense of community thrives beneath and behind the commercial exploitation of those working in the area's sex industry, affirming a sense of connection in what can be particularly negating circumstances. Echoing Cameron's account of market laddering and clustering, Hutton describes how, in the 1950s, most of the women who worked in the increasingly popular strip clubs saw themselves as colleagues of the sex workers who lined the streets around the clubs. He notes that this connection was not merely a platonic one but a transactional one as well: many of the strip club audiences would become customers of the sex workers, 'having had their appetites whetted'.[48] By the end of the 1950s, following the introduction of the Street Offences Act (1959), the sex workers who had been moved off the streets started to advertise as masseurs or models and so relied on this interrelationship – as well as on remaining on good terms with local bars, restaurants and shops (above which many of them operated) – to sustain their business. Many Soho sex workers continue to advertise as 'models', working in flats above sex shops (see Figure 4), with signage in stairwells by shop entrances.

Few accounts of Soho as a working community consider the significance of its sex shops to the area's evolving and enduring character, and most that do are particularly scathing. A notable example is Daniel Farson's (1987) *Soho in the Fifties*. In his Introduction to the book, the jazz and blues musician George Melly argues that 'the suppression of most of the squalid sex shops' following the combined influence of the Soho Society and Westminster City Council was 'an event to be praised on aesthetic rather than moral grounds'.[49] For Farson, what he describes as 'the cynical seventies' came close to destroying Soho. For him, the proliferation of the area's sex shops in the post-war era was underpinned by a growing permissiveness that

Figure 4 Signs advertising 'models' in upstairs flats next to a sex shop, Peter Street

had little to do with sexual freedom and everything to do with commercial exploitation:

The worst consequence was the sprouting of sex shops selling identical goods to the same nondescript and rather gloomy men. Instead of being erotic, the effect of these places was deeply depressing with the realization that even the permissive society desperately needed further arousal. Evidently, the carbon-copy shops met a genuine demand and the owners made a fortune in the process, sometimes an alleged £10,000 a week, and the temptation to make such money must have been irresistible when the law allowed you to get away with it and no one particularly cared.[50]

Whereas Melly's main objection was a largely aesthetic one (concerned with the impact of the sex shops on the look and feel of Soho), Farson's focused more on the effect of the shops on Soho's working community, 'ousting many of the old-established stores which gave Soho its character', cautioning that, once gone, Soho's traditional stores would not return, along with its residents, the latter being pushed out by rising rents in the area.[51]

Towards the end of *Soho in the Fifties*, Farson concludes that the dramatic reduction in the number of sex shops in Soho since the introduction of licensing regulations in 1982 meant that Soho was beginning to enjoy 'a new prosperity' that celebrated, rather than cynically capitalized on, its past. Taking a sideswipe at one of Soho's nearest neighbours, he concludes:

Sex has always been an essential part of Soho life and it would be a pity if the atmosphere became hygienic. Better a seedy Soho than a tarted-up tourist attraction like Covent Garden.[52]

The type of shops that proliferated in the 1970s (prior to the introduction of licensing regulations) – 'traditional' sex shops selling sex toys, pornographic magazines and R-18-rated films – came to characterize Soho's retail environment, so much so that Soho and the commercial sex industry almost became synonymous during this period, a reputation that persists. Maxine White's memoir of working in a clip joint in the 1980s recalls around sixty or so shops operating at that time, many of which, she suggests, offered 'under the counter or backroom services' or sold illegal pornography (e.g. material involving children or animals).

Echoing Cameron's discussion of laddering and clustering, White outlines how the clubs, clip joints and shops were often integrated, being either run or owned by the same operators, with staff frequently switching between the different businesses as required. This degree of integration meant that, if a shop were raided, it would affect the hostess bar in the same building. White describes the raids as something of a game and highlights how the shops worked together to provide an early warning system:

The police were always plainclothes officers and usually the same ones would carry out every raid. We got to know some of them and would have a laugh when they asked if we had hidden the videos in the toilets or elsewhere. It was a game of cat and mouse. The lads upstairs always left a couple of videos for them to find but the rest were taken away just before the raid, unless ours was the first club on the list. *As soon as one club in Soho was raided a quick call or dash through the tunnels to the other shops warned them they could be next.*[53]

Recalling her time working in Soho in the 1980s with a tinge of nostalgia, White describes how Soho's vibrant night-time economy, combined with this strong sense of community within the setting and sector, meant that, for many of those working in the clubs and shops, leaving work late at night was relatively safe. As she recounts: 'The strange thing about Soho was that I could walk around it any time of the night or day without fear. In most cities you would think twice about doing the same thing. *We all looked out for each other and it really was an extended family.*'[54]

When I first met him, Michael (who worked in a traditional sex shop on Brewer Street) similarly emphasized to me how safe he felt in Soho when leaving work late at night, often after a thirteen-hour day, 'because Soho's such an all-nighter. It's such an all–night-time place. There are always people around. It never feels deserted.' As well as security and connection, the network to which White and Michael both refer also provides a mechanism for transferring knowledge and expertise for those working in sex shops. As White put it in her account, 'the longer I worked in and around the sex industry the more I learned. I learned something new every day.'[55] It also illustrates how central this sense of being part of a working community is to Soho's laddered market. As White also recalls:

> We had become friends with the model who worked above Green Court and we used to send her quite a bit of business from punters who thought they would get a bit of something in the club. We charged them a small amount, maybe fifty pounds and then took them up to the model. The model would then charge them again for whatever they were after.[56]

Stacey Denekamp begins her account of working in a sex shop in the United States, *Sex Shop Education,* with a disclaimer that resonates with White's recollections and with the experiences of many of the people I got to know; namely, of being thought of as personifying this clustered market and therefore of embodying all its various specialisms: 'I am not a sex therapist, a doctor or any kind, stripper, or prostitute, nor have I had any formal training … Yet according to my customers, … [I am] all of the above.'[57] Denekamp evokes the informality of employment practices that are also characteristic of the sector and setting, describing walking into a shop to inquire if they were hiring and being asked 'Are you comfortable talking about sex?' Replying in the affirmative, she was then asked only when she could start. The men and women I spoke to referred to similar processes in my conversations with them about how they came to be working in a Soho sex shop. As Michael put it:

> Literally I saw an advert, saw the address, 'Ring this number for a retail position.' I rang it up … It didn't say what it was or anything. No idea … They said what day to come down and I basically went … in for the interview and I'm pretty much like, "Oh right, this is interesting," and straight away I'm into advising on what to do with which products, advising on really intimate things. It was a steep learning curve!

Toby, at eighteen the youngest of the participants in my study, also explained how he had somewhat fallen into the job, having had no intention of applying to work specifically in a sex shop:

> It was a mistake! I was handing out CVs on Tottenham Court Road/Oxford Circus and my friend went into the shop. So I handed my CV in and then four

days later I was working there. It was literally ... Well, the day I handed my CV in then [someone] left, and it was just like, "Do you want to work?" and I said, "Yeah, yeah," and here I am. No interview, no training, nothing.

While Toby describes the process as a 'mistake', he elaborated by emphasizing his attraction to the setting: 'I mean I've always loved Soho and I just like ... I don't know. You come to a cafe and you can go to, I don't know, a restaurant or you can go to a bar or a club and you're literally walking everywhere. You know, you're smack bang in the middle of everything.'

This combined informality and intimacy, and the attraction of Soho as a work place, means that workers in sex shops there don't seem to experience the clear awareness of being 'on' and 'off' stage or of having a clear 'backstage' area to use as a space for respite and to resolve tensions that other sociologists have described in studies of interactive service work, with clear 'transition rituals' and 'boundary markers' between their working selves and everyday lives.[58] One notable exception to this applies to the ways in which they manage the stigma that is widely perceived to be associated with the sector and, in particular, their place of work – a theme returned to in Chapter 4.

Broadly speaking, sociological analysis of the different forms of labour underpinning interactive service work has tended to coalesce around three concepts, each emphasizing different aspects of the commodification process involved. Following the publication of Hochschild's (1983) groundbreaking account of 'the commercialization of human feeling', much of the field has been shaped by a primary concern with the performance of emotional labour – that is, the commodification of emotion within the labour process and exchange relationship. Taking its analytical cue largely from Hochschild's hints at the ways in which emotional labour is embodied, attention has also been drawn to the performance of aesthetic labour, involving the incorporation of workers' embodied capacities and attributes into the labour process, but this research has largely focused on the aesthetic aspects of workers' looks. Alongside this literature on emotion and aesthetics has been a growing interest in the commodification of sexuality within sales-service environments through the performance of so-called sexualized labour. The work undertaken in sex shops considered here highlights how these different dimensions of the commodification process might be analytically distinct but are empirically, experientially intertwined and *situated* within the specific associations and expectations that characterize distinctive places of work and consumption. And the performance of emotional, aesthetic and sexualized labour in sex shops moves well beyond a commodification of how workers look or even interact with customers, into a relationship that capitalizes on Soho itself as a working community and setting. This came across in the stories that people had to tell, in their variation but also in the patterns that began to emerge in the accounts of their work and work place that were shared with me.

Encoding Sex Shop Work: 'Not in This Place, and Not in This Industry'

Broadly speaking, encoding involves imbuing material artefacts with specific cultural associations or meanings – literally converting a particular message into a sensory code.[59] In contrast to previous research on the aesthetic sexualization of primarily female service providers, the people I interviewed who had managerial responsibility for shop-floor staff all explained how, in order to discourage predatory behaviour from customers, the only rule that was relatively non-negotiable related to the maintenance of a neutral, de-sexualized appearance at work. This contrasts markedly with the requirements of other forms of sexualized labour, particularly those associated with the expectation that women will embody the seductive qualities of the products or services on offer. It reflects the precarious position of sexualized workers and the ambiguous nature of their work, as described by Diane Kirkby in her study of Australian barmaids, which emphasizes how the sexualization of women working in bars

has been part of that culture of enjoyment that has mystified and obscured the skills demanded of workers while simultaneously rendering their workplace a space for sexualized encounters they have had both to repel and attract.[60]

In many sectors of work involving intimate forms of labour, women's bodies especially are called upon to mediate between the organization, the products or services provided, and customers or clients; in such instances, bodies are hailed (to borrow Althusser's term[61]) into acting as 'both a receptor of discursive practices and a purveyor of social meaning'.[62] Sociologists of work have long since recognized that 'interactive jobs make use of workers' looks, personalities and emotions, as well as their physical and intellectual capacities', and many studies have developed what McDowell and Court call a 'materialist semiotics' to study the ways in which workers' bodies are required to signify a particular ethos.[63] This research highlights how the mediating role that workers' bodies play, and the ethos they are required to embody in particular settings, connects to localized experiences, assemblages and associations.

In Soho's sex shops, workers are required to embody discursive ideals of professionalism in a similar way to those working in say, the City, as described by Waring and Waring.[64] In both cases, this connection could be based on a desire to 'clean up' the perceived taints routinely associated with both types of work and workplaces. But in the case of sex shops, workers' need to embody an ethos of neutrality was also a moral projection, designed to emphasize an attitude of openness towards customers and co-workers, an ethos that is located in commercial pressures but also in an understanding of the wider social context, including HIV/AIDS awareness and queer politics. This echoes Goffman's (1969) classic work by highlighting the communicative significance of the working body and its potential to symbolize occupational status and legitimacy and a wider contextual ethos.[65]

Evoking three important themes in his reflections on the dress code within the store for which he had overall responsibility as an area manager, Nathan explained the significance of maintaining a relatively neutral, 'presentable' appearance that was explicitly de-sexualized, with reference to the effects of Soho on customer expectations, as a place of work and consumption with a global reputation for commercial sex:

All I ever want is for people just to be smart and presentable really ... You really, really don't want people turning up for work looking sort of tarted up, *not in this place and not in this industry* [emphasis added].

Echoing Nathan's concern that staff should look 'presentable', Toby reflected on the importance of looking 'approachable' on the shop floor in the store where he worked:

I just try and look as normal as possible, because, I mean, it doesn't matter what I wear ... [B]ut then you just kind of think *you've got to look approachable*, you've got to look nice and well, not smart ... *You've got to look approachable, neutral I guess* [emphasis added].

But Toby also emphasized the importance of maintaining a look that is appropriate to the sector and setting. He felt that – at the same time as appearing to be approachable – in order to signify a non-judgemental ethos and neutralize any potentially negative associations he also needed to embody Soho's 'edge':

I think I just try and look as normal as possible because ... you've got to look approachable, you've got to look nice and ... well, not so much smart because people don't care about smart when they're buying dildos. People want something a bit edgy, a bit exciting ... When customers come into the shop, they want

Figure 5 Store manager Shirley's 'neutral' but 'edgy' style of dress

something a bit . . . Do you know what I mean? *When you come into a sex shop you're not expecting a cardigan* [emphasis added].

Echoing this concern to embody the ethos of the place and setting, Shirley, who was the manager of the shop where she worked, explained her preference for staff to 'look smart casual': '[Staff appearance has] got to have quite a casual, relaxed feel about it, because if I was walking around in a suit it's a bit of a barrier for customers.' Shirley explained how her own fairly typical style of dress was designed to signal this preference to other staff in the shop she managed, as well as to customers. As shown in Figure 5, her clothes were relatively neutral, but – dressed in figure-hugging black and accessorized with a hip slung 'dollar sign' belt – Shirley also embodied the 'edge' to which Toby and others referred.

Julie, who worked in a notably feminized sex shop in the heart of Soho, also emphasized the importance of looking 'just professional really, neutral', both to discourage predatory behaviour on the part of

customers, as Nathan describes it, and to embody an ethos of professionalism to neutralize any associated stigma. This concern to embody neutrality was articulated not only with reference to clothing but also to the
embodied labour involved in maintaining particular facial expressions.
When describing dealing with customers, as Michael put it, 'you have to
sort of *remind yourself* to keep your face fairly blank and neutral' (emphasis
added).

Yet at the same time as a de-sexualized aesthetic is being actively
pursued, sex shops in Soho are, not surprisingly, replete with highly
sexualized iconography, manifest in a range of ways such as the names
of the shops themselves, their colour schemes, their window displays,
their product range, their merchandising and point of sale material, and,
of course, their ubiquitous display of hard-core pornography.

In practice, this means that, while explicitly de-sexualized in their own
presentation of self, those who work in Soho's sex shops perform sexualized labour against a semiotic landscape, or 'servicescape'[66], that
frames the encounter as highly sexualized. This, coupled with Soho's
long-standing global reputation for commercial sex in all its many
forms, plays a significant role in shaping staff and customer expectations
of the sales-service exchange involved. In other words, the way in which
their work is encoded into the setting, both now and historically, means
that staff have to continually negotiate customers' expectations of the
place itself as a sexualized setting and of the shops in particular as places
associated with – sometimes direct and immediate – sexual gratification.
As Toby puts it, again evoking the setting:

You get people coming on to you all the time . . . You know, everyone gets that.
I mean you have to deal with it . . . It's the wrong job and the wrong area to work in
if you don't like that sort of attention . . . [*I*]*t's just part of the job, and the place*
[emphasis added].

Toby returned to the same issue in a later interview, indicating his
strength of feelings about this and his perception of the pervasive nature
of the problem:

The more you learn how to deal with people, you can tell when they walk in the
shop after about ten seconds, are they a thief, crack head . . . and you can always
tell the ones who are going to start coming onto you because they always [say the
same thing] . . . You literally say . . . Because of where we work, it's less formal, and
you can just say, 'Get the fuck away from me!' and, like, 'If you take one step
closer to me I'm going to ring the police', or 'I'm going to hold you down on the
floor'.

As Toby emphasizes here, the sexualized nature of their work role,
place and identities therefore means that, because of the ways in which

sexuality is encoded into the sector and setting in which they work, sales-service staff in Soho have to continually mediate between, on the one hand, a formally de-sexualized aesthetic in their employment relationship combined with the evocation of an aesthetic of neutrality and a 'normalized' ethos of professionalism and, on the other, a hyper-sexualized semiotic landscape shaping customer expectations of the sales-service encounter and of the place and spaces within the shops themselves. Further, they have to do so largely beyond the confines of a stringent corporate aesthetic or set of formal guidelines but within the more amorphous context of an aesthetic shaped by, and shaping, social perceptions and historical accumulations particular to, and situated within, the sector and setting. This means that their day-to-day experiences of work are effectively framed by the materiality of their work place, as well as the meanings with which it is widely associated, by customers, managers and by themselves; as Toby put it, 'It's the wrong job and the wrong area to work in if you don't like that sort of attention.' What Toby suggests, however, is that, while he didn't really like this situation, he did expect it, and he perceived and experienced it as the norm in this particular work place.

Enacting Sexualized Labour: 'It Gives You Such a Buzz'

As a consequence of the meanings attached to the setting and the sector, and to the landscaping of the spaces within and around Soho's sex shops, a high level of presumed intimacy shapes the sales-service encounter. As noted, those who work in the shops normalize this, and rarely feel embarrassed or awkward about the discursively intimate nature of day-to-day interactions with customers and co-workers. As Stephen put it, 'I never get embarrassed. *Never. It's my job* ... You have to know everything about every product and to keep up with the current trends' (emphasis added). Soho's status and reputation as an LGBTQ community is important in this respect, as shop workers frequently give advice on how to access social and support groups as well as HIV and other testing services and treatment centres in the area. They also advise on safe sex practices – many shops provide 'safe sex tours' of product ranges to anyone who asks, and staff will often offer these to any customers who they think might welcome them. Stewart described his experience of giving this kind of advice:

We always try and answer the best we can, but that's just the way it is and that's the lie of the land.

['In what sense?'] *It's just where we are, you know.* I mean we get so many different types of people in ... I mean today we had somebody in asking if there was any other form of protection apart from condoms as I said, 'Well, between men and men, no, as far as I'm concerned' . . . You know, you try and be as honest as you can. *I mean, we are used as advice in a sense . . . Some is sexual and some isn't at all.* It's a bit like a general . . . I mean [I think we're viewed] as a general sort of information centre [emphasis added].

While most workers refrain from offering specific medical advice, mindful of the risks attached to this given their lack of formal medical training or qualifications, they are very aware of the potential significance of their guidance, particularly in relation to safe sex. As Michael put it, for instance, when a customer comes in to buy an oil-based lubricant with condoms, staff will always make it clear that the two should not be used together, potentially saving someone from the risk of injury or infection.

Nathan articulated his more general experience of giving advice and reassurance when he recounted the extent to which many customers are relatively nervous and require sensitivity or discretion. Nathan also described, however, how customers who are more confident can be much more forthright in articulating their needs and that staff have to be able to deal with these kinds of regular customers as well:

I always say [to the staff he manages] . . . 'Be polite and offer people your services because a lot of people come in and they are nervous' . . . But then you get other people come in and some people just don't care. They'll come in and talk to us like they'd talk to their doctor and say, 'Well, I've got this problem' . . . Some people do ask you some of the strangest things, like you're a sex therapist or their doctor even. *They come out with such personal stuff* [emphasis added].

The well-established historical association of sexuality with shame and embarrassment,[67] coupled with the gender politics of consuming commercial sex (with its associated connotations of 'spoiled masculinity'[68]), means that the dominant customer-service discourse of consumer sovereignty is arguably temporarily reversed in a sex shop. Evoking the significance of the locale twice in his reflections on this, Michael echoed Nathan's description when he referred to the presumed intimacy of some customers who talk to staff as if they were sex therapists, explaining how such customers are often self-consciously 'not sure of themselves' and seem to display signs of their awareness of the stigma attached to the sector and setting, even those who otherwise appear to be confident:

Some of the locals [regular customers], they come in and speak to me as a local sex therapist! They say, 'Oh, I'm having a bit of trouble with this,' and they really look to you for help. They really need you to listen and give them advice, and they're not sure, really, not sure of themselves shall we say? They feel self-consciousness. The burliest men can be quite shy and just, well, not sure of themselves.

This emphasizes the extent to which much of the work that sales staff undertake involves offering advice and putting people at ease, at the same time as drawing on their own sexual expertise and experience. Shirley emphasized this in her account of what she sees as a central aspect of the job, namely reassuring people that they are not 'different' and that she has 'heard most things before':

> You get people coming up to you and it's like, 'Erm . . . I've got to ask you a really sort of peculiar question,' and, you know, you have to put them at their ease, and you laugh and you sort of say, 'Look, in this business nothing is peculiar. You know, you're not going to tell me anything I haven't heard before' . . . Most things I've heard of and problems that people have I've heard about, and *it's just a case of making people feel comfortable and not feel inadequate or that they're different.* So even if you told me you've got a problem and I've never heard of that one before, I would go, 'Oh, don't worry. You're not the only one,' because actually you won't be . . . *So it's putting them at ease, and drawing on your own specialist knowledge of the products and of things that people do* [emphasis added].

Here Shirley also emphasizes how this performance requires her to draw on her own 'specialist knowledge' of sexual products and practices – 'of the things that people do', a recurring theme that highlights important ways in which much of the work that is undertaken in sex shops involves investing in and drawing on reserves of sexual capital. Shirley highlighted the satisfaction she derived from helping people rather than simply pursuing a sales imperative in this respect:

> There's times when you know you've really helped somebody out, and it's just that little bit of satisfaction rather than just going, '£10 please, £20 please, £20 please'. There's no interest in my day for something like that. It's actually engaging with people and having a conversation, and when you can help somebody, yeah, it gives you a buzz . . . Somebody will come back and go, 'You know, that really did a treat,' or something, and that actually makes my day worthwhile.

Sociologists of work have long since recognized that 'organizations deploy the sexual skills of their employees to flatter, to soothe, to satisfy, and to ensnare customers',[69] and sex shops are no exception, with workers being required to draw on their own sexual experiences and 'know-how' in order to embody the skills they have to deploy in interacting with the wide range of customers they encounter, especially in a place like Soho.

Embodying Sex Shop Work: 'You Learn from Your Own Experience'

In a way that goes beyond simply an aestheticization of the body's appearance, staff often have to draw on considerable reserves of embodied sexual capital during their interactions with customers in order to cope with the presumed intimacy of the exchange and to be able to offer the necessary advice and guidance that many customers seek, as noted earlier. Michael summed this up when he referred to the high level of specialist knowledge the role demands: 'If you asked the average person on the street how you'd use a [particular kind of sex toy] or something, I don't think they'd know. You do have to have a lot of specialist knowledge and to be able to draw on your own reserves.' Most of the people I interviewed emphasized how much of their product knowledge is acquired from customers: 'You're learning something new all the time. I've been here eight years and some twenty-one-year-old kid will come in and go 'blah, blah, blah'. Well, I never knew that! You do hear things all the time. You learn stuff from customers. Most of the stuff we know … [is] because the customer's telling you,' said Nathan. Throughout the fieldwork period, I often observed customers asking for advice and found that staff frequently drew on their own sexual experiences when they advised customers about particular products and their potential uses. As Toby put it in this respect,

I use the toys and I know people who use the toys. Like I work with a couple of girls and they use all the vibrators and we use lots of the other stuff … [S]o you learn from customers, you learn from the people you work with, from what people say, and you learn from your own experience.

Seemingly making the 'business case' for sexual diversity in the store where he worked, Mark also explained how the shop employed staff with a range of sexual interests and expertise – something he felt was useful when advising customers with different interests:

There are guys here that are into fisting and there are guys here that are quite vanilla, so there's a wide variety and broad spectrum, so we all have, you know, different knowledge of products and of how they might be used, depending on what your interests are.

As well as non-professional customers, the job frequently involves learning from the many regular customers ('locals') who are professional sex workers in the area. As Jason explained,

We get a lot of people in here who work in the sex industry, be it escorts or hookers, so they're obviously a big part of our trade and obviously a lot of those workers use our products in their trade, so we learn a lot from them about what works and what doesn't work so well and about what people are asking for.

Working in a sex shop in Soho thus involves investing in and drawing on reserves of sexual capital, incorporating knowledge acquired from workers' own sexual experiences, relationships and identities, as well as those of co-workers, (non-professional) customers and customers who are professional sex workers, each of whom constitute the wider community within which those employed in the sex shops in Soho work. This incorporation of sexual capital into the work involved means that it is not simply workers' looks that are sexualized but rather their embodied, sexual know-how and understanding of the intimate nature of what is at stake. Sexualized, aesthetic and emotional forms of labour become fully integrated. As Toby put it,

You've got to remember that, first of all, sex toys aren't cheap, and you've got to think people don't have the money to go shelling out hundreds for stuff, and you do actually think, 'Do you know what? If you're going to spend that money, they're going to have something good,' and especially with the recession and stuff. But you've got to give people what they want because it's kind of nice. You know, you're buying that because you want an orgasm or you want to feel this or you want to achieve something or whatever you're into . . . People have got a lot invested in it, and a lot of people aren't very comfortable coming in, so to get out of them what they want is hard. It's an important part of what we do because you've got to understand what they want. You've got to be able to read them.

Dealing with the more explicit side of the job comes easier to some than others. To assess this at the recruitment stage, Nathan described how he lays sex toys out on the desk when he interviews potential employees, asking applicants to handle and talk about them, to 'test' how embarrassed someone is likely to be with a customer.

On one of the occasions when I chatted to him whilst undertaking observational research in the Wardour Street shop where he worked, store manager Daniel mentioned to me that he was advertising for two new staff – both to do sixteen hours per week and to work flexibly. One was needed for two eight-hour shifts during the week, the other for eight hours on a Saturday and Sunday. Taking the time to elaborate while we unpacked stock together, Daniel referred to many of the issues raised by others about being able to the 'handle' the sector and the place, as well as the relative informality of the recruitment and training process and the nature of Soho as a work environment. I asked him if he was looking for someone with previous retail experience, and he explained why that wasn't the case:

No, we can train for that. It's the personality I look for. Can you deal with people? We don't have an application form, just ask people to send in a CV. But I can tell from talking to someone, even on the phone, whether they're cut out for it.

['Cut out for it how?'] Friendly, outgoing. Not having a problem working here. With where we are.

['Meaning?'] People come here because of where we are. And because of where we are they are more confident. And we get all sorts in here, so you've got to be able to deal with that, handle it, be okay with the people we get in.

['Such as?'] Well, drunk people, smack heads, and some of the nicest people we get – the sex workers, the girls from the massage places. They are lovely, but not everyone could work in this sort of place, you know.

['How could you tell if someone could?'] You can just tell. I prefer to interview in the store. I do it for this one and Oxford Street. I can tell if someone is okay in here. If they are okay with what we sell, but mostly with where we are. It's not for everyone. I assume that if someone comes in then they are okay with it, but that's not always the case, especially when it comes to dealing with customers. We can train for pretty much anything – using the till, stock-taking, layout etc. We have plans for stock layout that I draw up, so they just have to be followed, but not for that.

['For what?'] Being able to handle the place and the people who come in here. Just that, really, that's the most important thing.

Mark, who worked in a specialist lifestyle store on Old Compton Street, explained how his accumulated experience of working in Soho and his sense of humour had helped him to overcome an initial sense of discomfort and his own concerns about whether or not he could 'handle' working in a sex shop:

You have to deflect that seriousness and ... just make it as light-hearted as you can, you know. I mean, it is embarrassing to talk about, you know, bottoms, and things you might want to shove up bottoms.

['Do you still feel that?'] Yeah. I mean, I'm not that sexual as a person. Sometimes people find talking about [sex], you know, really easy, but others don't and I myself don't, but you've just got to get over it, and, you know, the longer I've been here, the easier it gets.

As these accounts highlight, in this particular sector and setting, the shared understandings and expectations involved are shaped, in part at least, by the ways in which they are embedded within the place and space of Soho itself.

Embedding Sex Shop Work: 'It's Because of What and Where We Are'

As an entwined social and material process, 'embedding' refers to the mechanisms of organization whereby a particular entity becomes an integral part of a broader whole and must be understood as such in order to make sense of the dynamic relationship between the parts and the social and material context within they are situated, and placed, geographically and historically. In the case of emotional, aesthetic and sexualized labour, to argue that work in a Soho sex shop is embedded is to emphasize that it is enacted and experienced within the context of the specific sector, setting and place within which it is performed and perceived, and must therefore be understood as such. The sexually explicit expectations and behaviour of customers, the presumed intimacy that characterizes the service exchange and the embodied commodification of sexual capital involved result from Soho's long-standing association with commercial sex and with the ethos of sexual openness and experimentation that characterizes this specific setting. In practice, this means that customers come to Soho with a particular expectation of their experience as a consumer in mind, and this has important implications for those who work in its sex shops. Andy summed this up when he said, '*They come to Soho* ... there's probably two or three licences in every town in Britain, so they don't need to come to London to get an R-18 [a 'restricted' film that can only be purchased, by those aged eighteen or above from a licensed sex shop, or shown in a licensed cinema] ... *They come to the place*' (emphasis added).

This means that much of the demand for sexualized labour originates from the commercial associations of the place itself and from the 'anything goes' ethos for which Soho has a long-standing, global reputation. This ethos can be identified in the industry more widely, but in Soho it takes on a particular character. Echoing Shirley's phrasing above, Stacey Denekamp describes the terms of the 'non-judgmental' ethos that shaped her experience of working in a sex shop in the United States:

We are not judgmental. That is so important. We never judge. As long as there are no kids or animals and no one is being hurt who doesn't want to be hurt, I really don't care what anyone is into. I have seen and heard it all before. Nothing fazes me in the least. Anything between consenting adults is fine by me.

She goes on:

Any reputable sex shop is a 'no judgment' zone. It's a place where you are free to be yourself. *A place where anything is normal, whatever your normal is.*[70]

In Soho, as Nathan explained, this ethos means that customers presume an immediate level of intimacy in their encounters with sales staff that he admits to sometimes being surprised by, even after working in the sector and in Soho specifically for over two decades:

I mean I get stunned sometimes by the honesty when people ask, because they're just perfect strangers and they just ask us anything ... Yeah, you do get asked weird and wonderful things every week. It makes you laugh, afterwards, but obviously not when you're with a customer.

Yet Soho's 'anything goes' ethos and liminal reputation mean that customers coming in to request 'under the counter' illegal pornography (i.e. featuring children or animals) is a daily occurrence for those who work in the shops. Nathan explained what seemed to be a fairly universal view of such customers, connecting their behaviour specifically to the place itself:

Everyone is different, but to me, even to come in and ask me for that [child or animal porn], that insults me. It insults all of us, doesn't it? Because they do think ... *because we're a sex shop, and because of where we are, that they can ask for whatever they want, which they do* [emphasis added].

Nathan went on to emphasize the regularity with which requests for 'under the counter' material are made, reiterating his feelings about such requests and those who make them as violating Soho's ethical code:

You've got to be eighteen to come in the shop. We don't sell anything that I would class as offensive. Obviously no under-age ... We get asked all the time. 'Do you have films with under-age children? Do you have films with animals in?' and you just go, 'No, it's highly illegal. Get out of the shop,' but you still ... It's a weekly – no, I would say daily thing we get asked.

For some, this is the worst aspect of the job: 'People asking for kiddie stuff or animals, which you get asked a lot ... That's the downside, definitely,' as Graham put it. Toby said that the regularity with which customers ask for this kind of material, coupled with his awareness that some shops do stock it, is the only aspect of the job that he really dislikes:

The only thing that ever gets to me is the child porn because it really disturbs me. Like I don't understand ... at the end of the day it's wrong. It's non-consenting and it's children ... That's – it's just so wrong. That's the only thing that really bothers me here and in this job.

At the risk of over-simplification, the ethos that characterizes Soho as a working community and which Toby and others (including Denekamp) allude to can be summed up as 'anything goes' as long as it is between consenting adults: anything deemed to deviate from this is not tolerated by those who work in (or regulate) the sex shops operating there. Shops believed to sell pornography that violates this code (e.g. involving children or animals) are clearly outside of the community to which Julie and others refer, and are positioned as Other to its constitutive ethos.

To contextualize this, Soho is a compact working environment, in both a geographical and a social sense. Shops operating there, and with which the area is largely associated, can be distinguished from more gentrified boutiques or feminized stores that occupy high-street settings in other locations. Despite this, the sex industry there is in so sense homogenous. As Nathan put it, 'every company is different ... even within a small place like Soho. They're all the same business, but they're all completely different.' Some shops are more 'traditional' than others in their design and product range and in their location – skulking in courts and alleyways, in contrast to the louder, brighter more mainstream or specialist (e.g. LGBTQ lifestyle) stores in the main shopping streets, particularly Old

Figure 6 Sex shop signs and entrances in and around Walker's Court

Compton Street, Wardour Street and Brewer Street. It is the latter that
seem to be thriving, but it is the former that Soho continues to be largely
associated with in terms of the persistence of its reputation for 'seedy'
shops and clubs.

Noting this in one of my field notes from March 2016, what seems
particularly marked in Soho is a distinction between the extent to which
more 'traditional' shops continue to categorize their product ranges and
customers, whereas more contemporary stores are more fluid in their
orientation to gender and sexuality, a theme returned to in more depth
in Chapter 5. In my notes and photographs, I recorded:

All shops in and around Walker's Court feel anachronistic – like they haven't changed
in their decor or style, or indeed product ranges, since the 1970s. Compared to the
main streets (Brewer, Old Compton, Wardour) they seem very quiet, separated off
somehow not just from the outside street area but also from the world and time
around them by their strip curtain entrances. Their entrances all have a 'dated' feel
[see Figures 6, 7, 8 and 9], signified by advertisements for dolls and clear categories of

Figure 7 Sex shop signs and entrances in and around Walker's Court

taste and identification (e.g. signs for different sections in the shops pointing to porn magazines and films for 'hetero', 'gay', 'les', and a few 'trans') which more contemporary stores don't have. The latter still tend to divide up by practices and tastes but not to 'categorize' products and people in this way.

Despite these important aesthetic, commercial and locational differences, certain features and experiences shared amongst those who work in the shops are relatively common. For instance, in all of the shops I studied, customers would often act as what Dana Berkowitz, in her research on an adult store in the United States,[71] calls 'video voyeurs'. This is a term she uses to describe the solo men who enter the store specifically in order to browse at pornographic DVDs either on the shelves or playing on screens that are fairly ubiquitous in traditional sex shops. In Soho, some of these men take DVDs to the counter to ask about their content. Female staff especially understood this to be because the men wanted to get them

Figure 8 Sex shop signs and entrances in and around Walker's Court

to 'talk dirty' and to use certain words or phrases while describing the films. Julie explained this to me:

Some people want to get us to say or touch things and talk about them. Sometimes they phone and get us to talk. Mostly they just want to hear us use certain words. I am pretty much used to it by now, but they are the only ones that make me feel really uncomfortable.

Other (male) customers come into the stores to masturbate whilst browsing or watching hard-core films. Referring to the first time he encountered a man pulling his trousers down and masturbating in the store during his first week of working there, Toby described his attempt to deal with this kind of situation humorously:

You know, you've got to take it for what it is and it's funny. And that's how you see it. You laugh it off. It's entertainment. Like, really all of us are so used to it, I don't think we're really bothered by it at all.

Figure 9 Sex shop signs and entrances in and around Walker's Court

Workers and managers alike related this kind of customer behaviour and staff views on it to the sector and setting: as Shirley put it, referring to customers who she thinks overstep the mark and become aggressive towards staff, 'you will get customers that think that because you work in a sex shop, here, they have a right to abuse my staff, and I'm on that straight away. I've never tolerated anybody swearing at me in whatever store I'm in.' Soho's global reputation for commercial sex and its attraction as a tourist destination were cited as important factors shaping customers' expectations in this respect. As Michael put it, alluding to a trope that would be familiar to anyone who has undertaken research on sex tourism, 'If you're a Soho tourist, you're a different character ... You're going to be different. It's almost like you can be a different person and there's less of being embarrassed about things because the chances are you're not going to come back again anyway.'

As well as the video voyeurs, a regular encounter for those who work in Soho's sex shops is with customers who are widely referred to as the 'fitting

room fiddlers'. The latter are also thought to have become more ubiquitous and 'blasé', as Shirley put it, since the closure of the sex cinemas, but
they are generally seen as less predatory and seem to be more widely
tolerated (perhaps because the fitting room accords at least a degree of
privacy) compared to those who masturbate on the shop floor. Nathan
described how these customers are often just left to 'get on with it':

We do get some people who look, yeah. As I said, you get used to it and you end
up ... You get a feel and you just ignore them. You ask if you can help [with
a purchase], 'No' and just let them get on with it.

Toby's view is that customers using the shops for sexual purposes is
a widespread issue that is tolerated but not exactly appreciated by staff:

I mean [we get] people touching themselves, people coming on to us like I said,
people trying to go into the stock room and people trying to use the toys on the
shop floor, you know, and people reading the back of the DVD and thing and you
can see one hand down their trousers . . . It's the same people. The ones that come
in that we know why they're here . . . you see them and you get to know them after
a while . . . They used to go in the cinemas and . . . they were happy with that, but
now they haven't got that. So they come in here. They come in here.

Almost everyone I spoke to had stories to tell about the voyeurs and
'fiddlers', articulated through a shared lexicon and set of understandings.
Mark referred, on the one hand, to them not being tolerated, but, on the
other, to his sense that such customers are 'just a bit misguided' and are
generally dealt with in a fairly informal way:

We have our share of what we call the fiddlers in the fitting room. We had a guy in
here a couple of weeks ago. You know, 'Please can I try on a pair of [crotchless
leather trousers]?' And you think they're serious to start with, but you wise up
pretty quick smart as to what is actually going on, and, like I said, we don't tolerate
that sort of behaviour, so they're just asked to leave the shop. But this one chap in
question was trying on things with nothing else on apart from these trousers and
he decided to have a little play with himself and try and have a little play with
myself and also another member of staff – he came back later whilst I was out at
lunch. He was pretty harmless, really, just a bit misguided.

As Mark intimates, humour and a fairly relaxed attitude is deemed to
be an important coping mechanism for those who work in Soho's sex
shops and who regularly encounter this kind of behaviour and have to take
it in their stride. Stewart emphasized the importance of having a strong
sense of humour and of sharing jokes with co-workers and customers to
diffuse any awkwardness or embarrassment. Julie also emphasized the
significance of shared humour to the sense of community experienced by
those working in the shops: 'You can normally have a laugh with other
people and ... sort of laugh it off and say, "Oh my God, we had this

person or that person in. They wanted this or that," and they know what to look for in case they go to them! [laughs]'. Michael also emphasized this in reference to his tactic for dealing with any potentially tense encounters with or between customers:

I do worry [about potentially aggressive or violent customers] . . . One of the weapons we've got is a double-ended dildo. You know, it's a solid sort of penis and double-ended, so if they come back I'd [holds the item in question up and over his shoulder, like a baseball bat ready to be swung, and laughs] . . . Yeah, because they're just going to laugh, aren't they? You'd actually get a laugh. 'What, are you going to hit me with that?' You know, it almost diffuses the situation instantaneously. . . . You know, I can square up to them, but you'd maybe use humour to diffuse it better.

Many participants spoke of their discomfort with the men who come into the shops specifically to look at the screens. This was widely seen as a growing problem created largely by the closure of the sex cinemas in the area where previously these men would have gone. As they saw it, the closures meant that more explicitly sexual behaviour – hitherto contained in designated spaces – was now 'spilling over' into the shops and onto the streets. To deal with this, it is common for staff to regularly pause the DVDs in the shops so that the screens freeze, as a way of ejecting or deterring in-store voyeurism relatively easily and discretely. Nathan explained what happens:

We've got screens above us [points to screens playing hard-core porn above the sales counter][72] . . . We get people come in and we know them now. There's certain faces that come in, and as soon as they come we just put them on pause and then they walk straight out again. We used to have cinemas, but they've nearly all been closed by this Council . . . I mean just smutty, grotty places, but they've mainly all been shut now. So it's changing a lot in Soho. Mind you, they all come in here now!

While the location is significant to the prevalence of voyeurs and fiddlers in Soho's sex shops, the place itself is also an important resource for workers to draw upon in order to cope with their regular interactions with these kinds of customers. Michael emphasized how staff from the shops and sex workers constitute a mutually supportive working community, a theme that recurred in the observational research I undertook during which I frequently observed the kind of interaction he describes:

When I first came here, the first week, every night I had two or three [sex workers] always approach me, but now I know them all it's like, 'Hello, how are you? Alright? Are you alright tonight? Are you being careful?' 'Yeah.' You know, things like that.

Similarly, Julie explained the sense of community that characterizes the sector and the setting, describing how those working in the stores and on the streets support each other: 'everybody, especially the businesses, everybody practically knows each other and everyone looks after each other's back, so it is a little community' – a theme to which we return in Chapter 4.

Toby echoed Julie's feelings when he reflected on how 'at home' he feels in Soho as a place of work, because of the intimacy and sense of community associated with the sector: 'I feel more at home here than I do where I live. Because it's so intimate. It's quite a small area. Because all the shops know each other, we all look after each other.' What these references suggest is that place is central to understanding both the nature of the work undertaken in the sex shops *and* the coping strategies and techniques deployed by those who perform it. In other words, to make sense of lived experiences of working in Soho's sex shops, we need to take account of the interconnected ways in which the work involved is encoded, enacted, embodied and embedded within the material and meaningful environment in which it is situated.

In the performance of sales-service work in Soho's sex shops, emotion, aesthetics and sexuality are all brought into play, as workers are often required to perform emotion work on themselves and their co-workers, and their job routinely calls for the performance of a sexualized form of emotional labour in their interactions with customers. The aesthetics of sales-service work in a sex shop are also important to understand, as the aesthetic management of the space – both within the stores and in the place itself, provides an important contextual setting for staff–customer interactions: the sex shop as a work setting does not constitute a neutral backdrop but a carefully managed, encoded and meaningful materiality shaping and shaped by the social relations of production and consumption that take place within it. In this respect, experiences and perceptions of the work involved cannot be separated from precisely where the work is placed, in a complex relationship that constitutes the social materiality of the exchange, one that is constantly evolving through processes such as gentrification and feminization.

Feminization: Gynocentric Playspaces or Novelty Shops?

As Crewe and Martin (2017) note, while sex shops have traditionally been perceived as masculine spaces of consumption, 'frequented at the margins of both the city and the clock',[73] the retail sex landscape has shifted considerably in recent decades, with marketing sex products to women becoming a 'huge growth area' since the 1970s.[74] The Ann Summers chain has been a key player in the mainstreaming of female adult retailing or the 'feminization' of sex shops: a cultural and commercial trend towards 'representing women's sexual pleasure as fashionable, safe, aesthetically pleasing and feminine',[75] not to mention commercially lucrative for the retail sex industry.

Inspired by the commercial success of the Beate Uhse chain of sex shops in Germany, entrepreneur Kim Caborn-Waterfield (known as 'Dandy Kim') launched the first Ann Summers store in the United Kingdom, hoping to cash in on the increasingly liberal moral climate of the late 1960s. The name 'Ann' was apparently a sign of affection for his secretary, Annice, who had taken on her stepfather's surname of Summers. He is alleged to have liked the name because it conjured up an image of an English rose, 'which was just the thing for what he hoped would become the acceptable face of the British sex industry'.[76]

The first Ann Summers shop opened at Marble Arch in September 1970, fronted by Annice, who 'became a sort of agony aunt to dozens of customers who came into her shop seeking advice on how to spice up their sex lives'[77], an expectation that is now (as discussed already in this chapter) fairly widespread in the sector. Jacqueline Gold describes Ann Summers, in her autobiographical account of the company, as a retail environment that is intended to provide some 'balance' in the industry, aiming to create 'something for women, run by women and with women's needs and desires in mind'.[78] This commercially driven gynocentrism has clearly been a very successful (i.e. profitable) formula, with its distinctive focus on 'shocking and titillating fun' that materializes the de-sexualized, infantilization of sex. Gold's own description of the Ann Summers ethos emphasizes this when she states: 'Ann Summers is a unique operation: it offers housewives and mothers, often tied to the home, a chance to escape', going on to note that, in such a male-dominated business as the sex industry, Ann Summers offers a 'softer, more feminine approach'.[79]

Echoing similar themes and imperatives, Williams (cited in Edwards, 2010) describes her female-orientated business as different from traditional adult stores insofar as it is 'safe', 'comfortable', 'female-centred', and committed to promoting women's 'sexual health, independence and self-growth'.[80] Evoking similar aesthetic reference points, Loe's study of a feminist, collectively owned sex shop in the United States cites customers' descriptions of the shop as a 'well lit, respectable enterprise', 'non-threatening' and explicitly 'not penetration-centred'.[81] Edwards (2010) describes how the targeting of female customers in the US sex shop business requires spaces that are 'open, as opposed to secretive'[82] and situated in locations where women would not feel threatened or uncomfortable.

In her discussion of the ways in which 'feminized' high-street sex shops engage with feminism and questions of identity and taste, Clarissa Smith argues that the emergence of specialist erotic retail for women indicates a shift in perceptions of women's sexuality and 'the construction of a particular form of hedonistic femininity'.[83] Indicative of this, she argues, is the discursive production of the sex toy as a stylized accessory or fashionable domestic appliance, based on the premise that 'every household needs a vibrator and every woman deserves a stylish one'. Attwood notes the importance of sex shop websites to the feminization process, describing their signification of 'a safe, accessible, mainstream address to women' that articulates sexuality through a discourse of safe play.[84]

Masquerading as feminist empowerment, this largely market-driven feminization and differentiation of the retail sex market is an important part of the industry's (and in the case of Soho, the area's) 'clean up' and its inclusion into the consumer mainstream. For a place like Soho, this is a process that has been as important, if not more so, than licensing or zoning, for it has 'tamed' the industry from within, complementing the more external, legislative measures. Intersections of class, gender and geography have been central to this. Against the backdrop of these combined processes, Soho's traditional shops – stoically persistent and stubbornly resistant to being domesticated – remain something of an oasis of ugliness, a 'no-go area' for women[85] characterized by an objectifying culture of patriarchy that positions several of the remaining shops there as the contemporary industry's anachronistic Other.

In Attwood (2005) and Storr's (2003) accounts of Ann Summers, feminized high-street stores are contrasted with 'real' sex shops, such as those with which Soho continues to be associated, on the grounds that they are 'bright and lit … no different than walking into Top Shop'[86]. Encoding 'cleanliness' and accessibility into the format is an important part of the feminization process, as Attwood notes:

It is striking that in this repackaging of sex across the range of brands, there is a very clear perception that sex must be made over as nice, bright, and accessible. This is achieved by clearly signifying sexual representations, products and practices as stylish, classy and fashionable.[87]

'Re-packaging sex as pleasure for women'[88] might seem like a generous, politically engaged feminist gesture; however, in practice it also often enables sex businesses to work around licensing regulations, by selling primarily lingerie, toys and accessories rather than sexually explicit pornographic material.

Perhaps for this reason, or possibly because of good old-fashioned misogyny and a dose of commercial resentment, this feminization of the retail sex industry was subject to a stream of disparaging comments by many of the more 'hard-core' sex shop workers in Soho, who saw shops such as Ann Summers (those that managed to evade licensing requirements by selling what were often described as 'novelty' items) as 'vanilla' – 'they're basically novelty shops. That's all,' as Andy put it. These were contrasted with the more 'traditional' shops selling pornographic DVDs, magazines and books, sex toys and so on, catering mainly to a male clientele, and with the more specialist 'lifestyle' stores marketed largely at LGBTQ (but in practice, gay male) customers. Few shops in Soho cater specifically for female customers (with the exception of Ann Summers and Agent Provocateur). Some sex boutiques in London (Sh! for instance) are owned by women and emphasize women's sexual health and pleasure, orientating themselves largely towards female customers. Their openness arguably provides 'an antidote to the embarrassments of licensed premises'.[89] However, shops geared towards a heteronormative male clientele continue to dominate Soho, with a few catering primarily to gay men but with an open remit that reflects the ethos of the place itself. Jason, one of the proprietors of a gay lifestyle store on Old Compton Street, described how his store materializes this:

I think you should be proud of who you are ... so when people look at our store, I want them to see a nice, contemporary environment. You know, it's welcome to everybody, gay, straight, whatever ... We're focusing on gay men because we're in a gay area, and we're gay, and that's where we want to focus on, because those are the people that we want to be our customers. However, we don't want to alienate or discriminate against anybody else.

In terms of merchandise, there is some overlap between the products sold in all types of Soho stores, but the more upmarket boutique-style shops sell primarily lingerie and 'designer' sex toys, while some sell fetish accessories, others novelty items intended for hen nights and so on. It is the latter that are particularly disparaged by those in the more specialist or traditional (largely male-orientated) shops in Soho. Whether this is a comment on the shops themselves, or on a perceived inequity in the application of licensing regulations, or whether this reflects a particular view of women's sexuality it is hard to say. Several participants shed some light on this, though, with older men in particular referring to the more traditional, heteronormatively male-orientated shops as 'real' sex shops and the others as novelty or lifestyle stores, as noted above.

Gentrification: Location, Location, Location

Another important trend in sex retailing that has also contributed to the regulatory effects of licensing and feminization is gentrification. Clarissa Smith refers to the emergence of so-called designer sex shops as indicative of a 'poshing up' of commercial sex[90] aimed at refashioning outdated boundaries between eroticism and pornography for a culturally knowing consumer base. The latter are frequently represented in mainstream and social media through references to their knowledge, taste, culture and experience, articulated through what Williams (1977) described as 'structures of feeling'.[91]

In a (largely class-based) distinction mirroring one that is often made between lap or pole dancing and the cultural sophistication attributed, knowingly and ironically, to burlesque, Crewe and Martin (2017) describe upscale erotic boutiques such as Agent Provocateur, Coco de Mer and Myla as presenting themselves as bespoke spaces catering to a more sexually 'self-aware' clientele. Such stores often use black and red colour schemes to differentiate themselves from the more 'tacky' aesthetic associated with high-street feminized stores such as Ann Summers. They also signify their difference from the more traditional sex shops that continue to be associated with places like Soho through their location and carefully crafted aesthetic. As Crewe and Martin describe it, the stores themselves evoke 'a sense of grandiose, decadent luxury' through their designs that give 'an air of wealth, luxury and seductiveness'.[92] Their study highlights the significance of the sensory environment or 'atmosphere' of a sex shop to its market positioning, hinting that locale is an important part of the affective branding and commodification of sexuality on offer. Smith adds to this by noting how the '"nicer" environments of these shops, which are often situated in more up-market shopping areas, offer "semiotic" benefits over traditional "dirty" sex shops'.[93] The products they sell, she argues, are not just sex toys but a 'reworking of symbolic capital, offering distinction and status to their purchasers'.[94] In a culture in which sex is increasingly part of the public mainstream, exuding sexual style and sophistication can be an important basis for class and gender distinction, demarcating particular instances of sexual consumption as 'liberated' and liberating and others as not.[95] Falling into the latter category are Soho's traditional shops that carry a product range dominated by hard-core pornography, the design aesthetic of which, such as it is, appears to have remained unchanged for several decades. In contrast to erotic boutiques such as Myla and Agent Provocateur, Soho's backstreet shops continue to feature plastic curtains, functional metal shelving, square carpet tiles and fluorescent strip lighting.

A parallel trend, although less well developed in the industry, is the growing popularity of 'fair trade' and ethically sourced products.[96] Examples of the latter include, for instance, vegan, cruelty-free bondage equipment and products made from recycled plastics or from natural, sustainable materials. However, increasing customer demand in this field appears not to have extended, at least yet, to a concern for the working conditions of those involved in the retail sex industry or in the production of products on sale, with the notable and long overdue concern to, as Brooks-Gordon sums it up, 'take the sexism out of the sex trade'.[97]

Erotic boutiques and those that identify themselves as in tune with a feminist sexual and ethical politics – such as the afore-mentioned Sh! in London or Maison Mika in Singapore[98] – tend to position themselves discursively and aesthetically as more 'authentically' sexual than more traditional sex shops such as those associated with Soho. Thus, 'the dichotomies of high and low culture are employed as organizational structures of distinction'[99] that are *situated* within the settings in which these are perceived and experienced.

As well as intersections of control and containment, what these combined processes of gentrification and feminization emphasize is the significance of retailing styles and practices to the conditions in which the experiential dimensions of sexual consumption are felt and can be understood, highlighting the importance of *where* this consumption takes place to how it is perceived. This provides an important counter to the growing virtualization of the sex industry, although it is uncertain how long this will be sustained as online sales in retail sex markets continue to increase.

Virtualization

The emergence of new visual and communications technologies has transformed the meaning and experience of commercial sex. In her discussion of female sex workers and their male clients, for instance, Elizabeth Bernstein argues that the virtual nature of commercial sex has the capacity to imbue transactional encounters with a 'new respectability' for those who participate[100] against the wider backdrop of an 'increasingly unbridled ethic of sexual consumption', as evidenced by soaring demand for pornography, strip clubs, lap dancing, escort services, telephone sex and 'sex tours'.[101] As many of the participants in my study emphasized, much of what is sold in sex shops can be purchased more easily, not to mention discretely, online.

Between 2013 and 2018, the number of licensed Sex Establishments (lap-dancing clubs, sex cinemas and shops) fell by a third in England and

Wales, from 386 in 2013 to 256 in 2018, when the number returned to its 2011 level after peaking in 2013.[102] By far the biggest decline was in London, and in the Westminster area in particular, where 65 per cent of licensed sex establishments have closed since 2013. The number of active licenses for Sex Establishment Venues (SEVs) has fallen by over two-thirds in Westminster since 2013,[103] although the area still has the highest concentration of licensed premises in the United Kingdom.[104] As suggested, this has had the effect of bifurcating the remaining shops into those that occupy positions along the main thoroughfares – and which appear to materialize a gentrified, feminized or specialist (e.g. LGBTQ, bondage) aesthetic and range of products and services – and the more traditional shops. The latter seem stoically to resist any of the above processes, signifying this in their distinctive aesthetic, as well as somehow being able to (appear to, at least) ride out the full commercial effects of virtualization. Yet – even in Soho – these shops feel increasingly anachronistic: most are tucked away in courts and alleyways, separated off geographically and aesthetically from the main flows of people and capital and from the changing semiotic landscape that characterizes the commercial centre of contemporary Soho.

Across all of these different types of shops, the combined effects of regulation and virtualization have impacted on the sales techniques and experiences of those who work in the sex shops. 'Trading up' is widely used to boost sales, and those who have worked in Soho long enough to compare the shops now to the 1980s and early 1990s when they were less tightly regulated commented on how trading up is still ubiquitous but is more difficult to 'get away with'. Nathan and others attributed this, in part, to changes in legislation and tighter regulation by licensing enforcement officers and trading standards. But it is also attributed to a perceived 'mainstreaming' process and to a gradual reduction in the stigma associated with shopping in an adult store:

It's different now. Before it was … I mean, we're the largest in the country of licensed shops and we always have been. We've got 106 shops. It sounds blasé, but we could literally do and say whatever we wanted to. It was a very harsh environment … Before, as I said, you could talk to and treat people however you wanted and it was easy to take £100, £200 off people eight or ten years ago. I mean easy … It's a different profession now, and as we take people on now we do train them completely differently.

['In what ways is it different?'] Well, just the way … Anyone who comes in, as with any sales, the aim is to get more money off them. If they want to spend £20, get them to spend £40. If they want to spend £100, get them to spend £200. We call it trading up. We train them to get away with whatever they think they can get away with.

In the past, Nathan recalled, it was easier to trade up, because the stores were less tightly regulated and the stigma attached to consuming in a sex shop, particularly for men, made it easier to exploit a customer's combined sense of shame and bewilderment:

You'll have blokes that come in and they'll come and stand at the counter . . . 'I don't know where to start.' 'Start at the beginning. Start at the beginning.' And they go, 'Right, my wife's moaning because I can't get a hard-on,' and they're blurting it out, and you go, 'No problem . . . ' 'Well, which one do you recommend?' You just tell them what you think and then you leave the choice down to them. I won't ever push anything . . . I would love to go, 'Here, have this and have this.' We used to be able to do that. You used to be able to get a carrier bag, grab a bloke round the shoulder and walk around the shop, going, 'Here, have one of these and one of these. I'll do you a deal. How much do you want to spend? £100? £200?' and they'd go, 'Well . . . ' and you just literally used to walk around the shop – 'There you go, look, £150' – take their money, and people'd sort of walk out the door thinking, 'I didn't want all this.' You used to be able to work like that.

Times have changed, and there is a strong sense that customers now expect a more honest approach, particularly as they tend to be more open about their needs and desires, ironically perhaps as a result of the mainstreaming effects of virtualization on the sex industry. As Martin, who worked in a traditional sex shop on Brewer Street, explained to me, referring to some sex toys being sold at a reduced price that he had just recommended to a customer: 'I don't know why these are reduced. I would put them at full price myself. I have two and they're great. Much better quality than these [he shows me a similar product marked at ten times the price of the item he has just sold] for a fraction of the price.'

Shop workers assume that customers come to Soho, at least in part, for this level of interaction, rather than buying sex toys and DVDs online. As Toby put it,

What customers are expecting most is honesty, you know, and that they're confident you know what you're talking about because you are selling things that people . . . in the end they're sticking them inside themselves. So you need to give advice. It's not like you're selling them, I don't know, a T-shirt. You're selling them something they're going to put inside. We get asked advice everyday. *It's part of the job* [emphasis added].

Unaware of how things 'used' to be, younger workers such as Toby and Michael highlighted the level of informality they associated with the sector and setting as a particularly enjoyable aspect of the job:

The shop and the trade are so fun because you can give discounts left, right and centre and there wouldn't be a care in the world. You know, someone'll come up with £100 worth of gear and you'll say, 'I'll tell you what, you can either have another two toys for free or I'll give you £20 off that,' and they'll be, 'Oh, thank you!' and it's like, 'You're thanking me and I've done nothing' ... and I'm getting thanks for it. It's brilliant. That's nice. That's a really nice thing about working here, in the trade. It's that level of informality to be able to give discounts like that.

Mark, who worked in a busy lifestyle store on Old Compton Street, showed similar enthusiasm for the relaxed nature of the work environment and in particular the collegiality he experienced working in Soho:

We have a great bunch of staff here who are lovely and the manager's great. It's great people and it's just really quite relaxed and a fun environment to work in. You know, it's not serious. They're not hard on us, as far as sales go, so it's just very relaxed and good fun.

In contrast to Michael and Mark's shared enthusiasm, Andy, who worked in one of the more traditional shops near Walker's Court, was much more pessimistic about the combined effects of the internet and economic recession. He expressed concern not just about the commercial implications for the sex shop he worked in but also for the sense of community and the 'banter' that he enjoyed with regular customers as opposed to 'passing trade':

It used to be good. Maybe until two or three years ago, but not anymore ... It's changing because there's no money in it, really, because the internet's just giving it away for free. The things we sell you can get for free. We don't have as many regular customers as we used to ... There's so much change – there's not the money, we don't have as many regulars, there's no banter. It's just passing trade now.

From Andy's point of view, regulation has also had a negative impact on the sector and the setting: 'When it was illegal it was good fun, but now it's just boring.'

The accessibility of online pornography, which is widely and often freely available, is clearly a significant and ongoing threat to the commercial viability of Soho's retail sex industry; pornography dominates the product range in many of the remaining shops. A little like the sex workers in Bernstein's study, the men and women working in Soho's sex shops are keen, as a result of this perceived threat, to emphasize the 'authenticity' of the experience on offer in their shops as opposed to buying products online. The customer's experience is premised on the fantasy that what is being purchased is somehow more 'genuine'. Soho itself plays a significant role in nurturing this fantasy, based on the premise that being in/of Soho provides an important locus for authenticity and mutual understanding.

Bernstein outlines, in her discussion of the meaning of the 'purchase' in transactional sex encounters, that the pursuit of bounded authenticity that is encapsulated in the demand for sexual commerce has been augmented by several interconnected social phenomena: the shift from a relational to a recreational model of sexual intimacy; the symbiotic relationship between virtual technologies and commercial sexual consumption; a global economic reliance on working patterns that facilitate the temporary insertion of (predominantly) men into commercial sexual marketplaces and settings; and, more generally, 'the myriad mergings and inversions of public and private life that are characteristic of our era'.[105] Taken together, these factors help us to understand the continued presence of Soho's sex economy and the importance of its sex shops to that economy.

Those who are the agents of this 'authenticity', whose emotional, aesthetic and sexualized labour is encoded, enacted, embodied and embedded within this very particular setting, are drawn to working there – much like their customers are attracted to consuming there – by the 'edge' that Soho maintains. It sustains this edge in the face of the combined sectoral processes considered here – licensing regulation, feminization, gentrification, virtualization and ongoing attempts to 'clean up' Soho as a working community. Yet at the same time, as outlined so far, there are many aspects of working in a sex shop, in Soho, that those who are employed there find particularly difficult, demanding the constant, integrated performance of emotional, sexual and aesthetic forms of labour. Understanding how they perceive and experience this simultaneous sense of attraction and repulsion, to their work and place of work, is explored in the next chapter.

4   It's a Dirty Job ...
Performing Abject Labour in Soho

As a consequence of the meanings attached to the setting and sector, and to thelandscaping of the spaces within and around Soho's sex shops, a high level of discretion as well as presumed intimacy characterizes the sales-service relationship. As discussed in Chapter 3, encounters with customers are neither a direct sexual exchange nor a simple sexual aestheticization of the service interaction. Sitting somewhere between the two extremes of sex work and sexualized labour, retail sales work in a Soho sex shop is a kind of abject labour, in an abject work place. As will be discussed here, it is experienced and perceived as both compelling and unsettling by those who perform it.

Drawing on the concept of abjection, this chapter considers this sense of simultaneous attraction and repulsion to the work, and to their place of work, that Soho's sex shop workers describe. As Davina, who worked in a (now closed) specialist lingerie shop on Old Compton Street, put it, '[I]t's seedy and it has an edge, but that's what makes it exciting.' For the many sex shop workers I interviewed, the very attraction of the place and the job was its 'dirt' – physically, socially and morally.[1] Soho is both a source of taint and a resource for deflecting the potentially stigmatizing effects of that taint.

In his discussion of communities of coping, sociologist Marek Korczynski (2003) argues that collective emotional labour is an important mechanism for coping with the demoralizing effects of dealing with irate or abusive customers in sales-service work. For him, it is the structure of workers' social situation that means they are likely to turn to each other to form what he calls 'communities of coping'. These communities are primarily social processes, cultures and associations, as part of 'the social relations of the service workplace' rather than lived materialities experienced within the context of specific settings and locations.[2] In Soho, the actual setting, the place itself – its assemblages and associations – is both a source of the various taints that workers in sex shops experience and an important part of the communal reference points for coping with these taints. In a slightly different way to the call-centre workers in Korczynski's research, and more like the sex workers in Sanders' studies, sex shop workers in Soho form a community in a very material (although not necessarily homogenous) sense, seeing and experiencing themselves as working together in and through an albeit competitive work environment. The specialist nature of the stores and the clustered market mechanisms discussed in Chapter 3 through which the sex industry in settings like Soho tends to operate, however, mean that this competition is often more complementary than divisive. Andy explained how this tends to work:

> This is like a marketplace here … You know, there's people who come in because they want a certain thing and the dealer says, 'I haven't got that, but I know someone who has,' and then, you know, another week, they'll send someone to them … There's no point going all the way up to London when you can get an R-18[3] in your local town.
>
> ['Is that why people come, for the R-18s?'] No, no! They come to Soho … there's probably two or three [shops with] licences in every town in Britain now, so they don't need to come to London to get an R-18 … *They come to the place* [emphasis added].

'Good' customers (those who spend money and/or don't cause any trouble) routinely get referred from one store to another. At the same time, virtual networks, using direct or group messaging, for instance, are frequently used to warn colleagues in rival stores about difficult or potentially dangerous customers (e.g. those deemed to be drug users and/or possibly violent or predatory). During observational sessions in shops, and whilst undertaking interviews in situ, I often noted messages being sent around warning others about voyeurs or fiddlers such as those discussed in the previous chapter.

As this indicates, as a work place, Soho continues to have a strong sense of community – as Julie put it, 'We've all got each others' backs.' At the risk of over-homogenizing or romanticizing, the shared feeling of belonging and working together in a sector and setting that others often perceive as tainted or 'dirty' provides an important sense of camaraderie and connection for Soho's workers. It also provides an important mechanism for being able to cope with the more disconcerting or abject aspects of the job and the setting.

But unlike many of the dirty workers described in other sociological studies of work that carries physical, social or moral taints,[4] the sex shop workers I interviewed did not simply want to 'clean up' their work: they were generally dismayed by governmental or commercial attempts to sanitize Soho and its retail sex industry, preferring instead to revel in its 'filth', metaphorically at least. Hence their work is discussed here as not simply 'dirty' in a sociological sense but as abject. An association with contamination and contagion is one of the many points of identification for those who work in Soho's sex shops, themselves ostensibly 'matter out of place' in anthropological terms.[5] Making sense of how this process of abjection is perceived and experienced means *situating* it within the wider context within which it takes place, including processes of gentrification and sanitization, introduced in earlier chapters.

Situating Abjection

In his discussion of the neo-liberal regulation of urban 'play spaces' as settings orientated towards capital accumulation and a reiteration of virile masculinity, urban geographer Philip Hubbard (2004a) high-lights the purification strategies that gentrification depends upon. For gentrification to succeed, he argues, it is necessary for the state to remove 'Other' elements that may threaten or destabilize its efforts to pull off a convincing act. Attempts to regulate the visibility of dis-orderly bodies in city centres make perfect sense, he emphasizes, in the context of policies designed to re-orientate commercial and con-sumer investment. As he puts it, 'it is those who are Other to real estate developers and their target markets who are subject to such exclusionary urges, depicted as perpetrators of "quality of life" crimes that threaten "urban renaissance"'.[6] For Hubbard, this kind of 'fron-tier policing' amounts to a successful and distinctly neo-liberal recipe for capital accumulation that effectively depends upon the displace-ment of anything and anyone associated with 'filth', reinventing the city centre as a 'purified arena'.

Much of this resonates with Soho, as does Marilyn Papayanis' (2000) account of governmental attempts to clean up New York City, which highlights the ways in which zero-tolerance policing displaced expressions of desire deemed Other in the Disneyfication of the city's Times Square area, cultivating an aesthetic atmosphere and semiotic landscape geared towards family-orientated consumption that represented a distinct break from its seedy history, particularly the area's association with the porn industry.[7]

Hubbard shows how Westminster City Council's attempts to clean up Soho's sex industry through the regulation of window displays, the intro-duction of high-level taxes on films rated R-18 and reductions in the number of licensed sex shops and clubs permitted to trade in the area (see Chapter 3) have all combined to create a 'happy family atmosphere'.[8] Many cafes and bars (although not sex shops, which are not permitted, under Westminster City Council's licensing terms, to admit anyone under the age of eighteen) now display signs welcoming children and families.

Hubbard cites the Criminal Justice and Police Act (2001) that made it an offence to place an advertisement for sex work in a public telephone kiosk as 'a classic piece of "moral panic" legislation' intended to continue the process of cleansing commercial sex from the streets that began with the Street Offences Act (1959). What drove the 2001 Act, he argues, was a concern with policing the boundary between public and private space and with the maintenance of social order through the containment of sexuality to the private, non-commercial sphere.[9]

And yet, in the face of these regulatory mechanisms, as well as place marketing and corporate redevelopment, Soho maintains something of its abject character despite ongoing attempts to purify it beyond recognition.

Abjection – A 'Tempting' and 'Condemned' Elsewhere

The concept of abjection draws on the work of feminist writer Julia Kristeva, who emphasizes that abject phenomena are simultaneously repulsive and fascinating. 'There looms within abjection', as she puts it, '*an elsewhere as tempting as it is condemned*'.[10] This concept is relevant both to Soho itself and to the (increasingly residual) retail sex industry there, with workers describing their place and sector of work as both compelling and repulsive. As Davina, the former lingerie shop worker referred to near the start of this chapter, put it: '[Soho] is a similar universe to me. It's an inspirational place to work in ... It's what makes it what it is.'

In understanding how Davina and sex shop workers like her experience the 'edge' with which their work and work place are associated, this chapter draws on the 'dirty work' typology, developed in the 1950s by sociologist Everett Hughes,[11] and on the concept of abjection, articulated most clearly by Kristeva. While the few studies of work that engage with abjection tend to adopt a psychological or psychodynamic perspective, my aim here is to take a more sociological approach to *situating* abjection within the social and cultural geography of Soho as a work place.[12] Maintaining the focus on 'putting work in its place', the aim is to reflect on the role of place in shaping the construction, perception and lived experience of work that carries negative physical, social or moral associations, considering the different ways in which work in sex shops carries multiple taints, reflecting on how these are lived and experienced. Various techniques used by workers to manage the taints with which their work, and indeed their place of work, is associated will also be considered, highlighting the ways in which the place itself is significant in this respect. Here Ashforth and Kreiner's (1999) linking of the recasting of dirty work to strong organizational and occupational cultures is extended by drawing attention to the role of place and locale in shaping the meanings attached to dirty work[13] and to abjection as a workplace phenomenon.

The final part of the chapter argues that, as well as these coping techniques, lived experiences of working in Soho's sex shops emphasize the need to appreciate what, borrowing from Kristeva (1982), we might describe as the 'power of horror' in the performance of dirty work. For many of those who work in Soho, the very attraction of the place, the sector and the job is precisely its 'dirt' – physically, socially or morally; 'that's what makes it exciting', as Davina put it. With this in mind, the chapter concludes by arguing that working in a sex shop, in Soho, is a form of 'abject labour' – that is, work that is simultaneously attractive and repellent, 'as tempting as it is condemned', for those who perform it. It emphasizes the role of place in shaping this simultaneous sense of attraction and repulsion and the significance of the place itself as an abject work setting to workers' perceptions and experiences of it.

Although there is no direct exchange of sexual interaction (as in the case of sex work) or obvious aesthetic sexualization of the service encounter (as has been argued to be the case in the performance of sexualized labour – see Warhurst and Nickson, 2009),[14] important emotional and aesthetic aspects of the service interaction are heightened in sex shops because of the intimate nature of the exchange. The encounter is arguably relatively intense because the performance and consumption of commercial sex raises physical, social and moral issues arising from the transgression of perceived boundaries generally considered necessary to the maintenance of the social and moral order, the latter involving the containment of sex to the private sphere (and space) of intimate relations rather than to its enactment within a commercial transaction between relative strangers and, in the case of a sex shop, in a relatively open, public environment. Michael hinted at this when alluding to the 'dirty' nature of a commercial exchange, as opposed to the relative 'purity' and special nature of sexual intimacy, when trying to explain how he negotiated this boundary during his first few days of working in a sex shop. Speaking with reference to the materiality of the products, he said:

At first it was kind of embarrassing because I was ever so timid and gentle with it [a sex toy] because I didn't want to touch the actual vibrator. It felt wrong, intrusive somehow, and basically . . . I was worried because I didn't want to get it dirty or anything. I didn't feel like I should be touching it.

A number of studies have drawn attention to the ways in which customers negotiate sex shop encounters,[15] focusing on themes such as shame, stigma and embarrassment.[16] Geographers have emphasized how the spatial organization of sex reflects and reproduces wider normative notions of morality; Hubbard in particular highlights the contested nature of this process, arguing that moral spaces are 'always fought over and in a state of becoming'.[17] Urban settings such as Soho that are associated with a concentration of commercial sex come to be perceived as 'immoral landscapes' – spaces of desire and disgust that bring together particular sexual, spatial and temporal contexts.

How does Soho's reputation as a place 'abandoned to sleaze and inadequacy'[18] impact upon the work experiences of those employed in its sex shops? Are those who work there 'dirty workers' because of the shops and the sector they work in, and the jobs they do, or particularly because of where these shops are located? How are these associations with abandonment, 'sleaze and inadequacy' perceived and experienced? When work is tainted, in what ways does place contribute to that taint – does it accentuate or alleviate it?

Thinking through these kinds of questions with reference to place is important, because while on the one hand the taints with which particular types of work are associated may in part relate precisely to where they are carried out, it may also be the case that the settings in which dirty work is performed help workers to cope with the stigmatizing effects of their work. Hughes et al. (2017) in particular demonstrate the significance of considering what they describe as 'the co-constitution of the material and symbolic dynamics of dirt' in understanding how workplace taints are embodied, experienced, and, crucially, *embedded* within the material settings in which dirty work is carried out.[19] Similarly, Ashforth and Kreiner (2014) note how, although the taints with which certain occupations are associated are widely recognized as being social constructions, relatively limited attention has been paid to 'how … context shapes those constructions'.[20]

Insights like these lead us to even more questions such as: How do those employed in sex shops experience the stigma attached to their work and to their place of work? How does their place of work shape not only the various taints with which working in a sex shop is associated but also the coping techniques they deploy? How do they negotiate their own perceptions of their work, and their place of work, as well as those of others? What attracts sex shop workers to the work they do and to their place of work? What role does their place of work play in shaping employer, customer and their own expectations of what the job involves?

Hughes (1952) argued that dirty work might be dirty in several conceptually distinct but empirically interrelated ways that are important to how we respond to these kinds of questions. He defined dirty work as work that carries a physical, social or moral taint; dirty work 'may be simply physically disgusting. It may be a symbol of degradation, something that wounds one's dignity. Finally, it may be dirty work in that it in some way goes counter to the more heroic of our moral conceptions.'[21] As Ashforth and Kreiner (1999) outline in their development of Hughes' typology, physical taint occurs when an occupation is thought to be dirty or disgusting in a material sense or when it is performed under particularly 'dirty' conditions. Social taint occurs when a job involves sustained contact with people who are stigmatized or where the worker has a particularly servile relationship to others. Finally, moral taint is attached to work that is regarded as sinful or of dubious virtue or where the workers employ methods (e.g. being deceptive, intrusive or confrontational) thought to be immoral.[22]

In his original typology, Hughes (1952) emphasizes that what constitutes 'dirt' is very much a social construction, the common denominator being not the attributes of the jobs themselves or the assumed characters of the people who perform them but rather the reactions they provoke. The boundaries between the three forms of taint are relatively blurred, and many occupations of course carry multiple taints – retail sales work in a sex shop being a case in point. Hughes is also at pains to point out that 'dirt' is not restricted only to certain occupations: it is hard to imagine, he argues, that at some point we don't all find ourselves 'having to do something that is *infra dignitate*'.[23] Yet some occupations not only carry multiple taints but are also perceived to be more consistently and substantively 'dirty' than others, particularly, Hughes emphasizes, those that are 'on the margins' of mainstream economies. Again, working in a sex shop in Soho is a notable example.

Sex Shop Work as Physically Tainted

In contrast to the manual labour performed by street cleaners and refuse collectors in Hughes et al.'s (2017) study, retail sex work is primarily dirty in a symbolic rather than a physical sense (although, as with any retail work, aspects of the job such as unpacking and stacking or shelving stock, merchandising, and cleaning the store involve the performance of manual labour). Aside from what might on occasion be relatively physically dirty manual work, there are other important physical elements to the 'dirt' involved, however. The physically intimate nature of the products on offer means that the job often involves handling 'dirt', including bodily matter. Shirley described her own reluctance to touch products that have been used by customers precisely because of this, an issue rarely encountered in such an extreme way in other forms of retail sales work:

You have people trying to return products that have been used in personal areas because they don't think they do what it says on the packet, and they're trying to give me something that's been inside certain parts of their anatomy and wonder why it's like, 'Whoa!', you know? A gentleman bought [a particular product] three months ago and he over-used it. The instructions say twenty minutes a day for four days; leave it for a week and do it again. He decided to do an hour a day every day of the week, and he wondered why he got swollen and ... in fact he needed to go to a doctor – and then thought I was going to give him a refund! I was like, 'No, I'm not going to touch it, thank you very much.'

This 'dirt' relates not just to the products, however, but also to workers' perceptions of customers (or at least some customers) and their behaviour on the shop floor. Many staff reported their difficulty in coping with what they perceived to be a rather abject, boundary-threatening physical transgression. Stewart described how he found it difficult to deal with the idea that customers would masturbate in private viewing booths[24] and then, as he put it, 'walk out ... as if everything's normal'. For Stewart, echoing the views of many others, this was a physical, symbolic dilemma rather than a moral one: 'I mean, I haven't got anything against it, but I just think with the set-up in here [in a shop], *it's odd really, just a bit dirty*' (emphasis added).

The demand for viewing booths and the ubiquity of 'video voyeurs' (see Chapter 3) was widely thought to have worsened since the closure of Soho's sex cinemas as part of Westminster City Council's concerted attempts to clean the area up and rid it of its residual associations with sleaze. When I first began researching Soho, several sex cinemas remained (see Figures 10, 11 and 12), but their subsequent closure meant that, for the men and women I interviewed, the 'dirt' with which they had been associated had not been swept away but now spilled over into the shops in which they worked, increasing the presence of 'fiddlers' and voyeurs and the demand for 'preview booths', which several of the stores have (see Figures 13 and 14).

As Michael put it,

A lot of people come into these types of shops expecting private booths. Yeah, because all the cinemas have been shut down now ... Which is something this company's pretty into which I'm not really liking ... They're not prepared to pay what it would cost to have to maintain them ... you know, clean them up and ... you can guess who would end up having to do it.

The physical taint with which retail work in Soho's sex shops is associated relates not simply to the physicality of the products on sale or to the nature of staff-customer interactions, as Shirley, Stewart and Michael explained, but also to the broader social materiality of the work, and to its spatial context, and particularly to the meanings associated with the

Figure 10 Adult cinemas, Soho

place where it is carried out. As Shirley put it when she explained to me why she had chosen not to tell her eighty-year-old father where she worked: 'He lives up in Scotland and he hasn't been in this neck of the woods for thirty-odd years. He would still remember Soho as cheap and dirty, and he would be worried – not because of what I'm selling; more worried about me being in Soho.'

The location of shops in courts, alleyways and basements often with no natural ventilation or daylight accentuates perceptions of the shops as dark and dirty. Mark, who worked in the licensed sex shop in the

Figure 11 Adult cinemas, Soho

basement of a gay lifestyle store on Old Compton Street, described how the materiality of the setting impacts on the work experiences of staff: 'We all, you know, take turns coming down here ... It's like a cave down here. There's no light, so it's just nice to rotate the staff so you're not stuck down in this hole all day long.' He went on to elaborate on the interrelationship between the materiality of the shop layouts and the social stigma attached to consuming in a sex shop, emphasizing the importance of a sense of informality to managing this relationship:

Figure 12 Adult cinemas, Soho

Approaching customers upstairs [in the gay lifestyle store selling mainly clothing] is so much easier even if it's just a "hello" when they come through the door, but down here [in the licensed sex shop in the basement] some people don't even want to be, you know, greeted because, you know, they're here for personal reasons and some of them have embarrassing . . . well, not embarrassing, but are embarrassed about buying products or whatever. So we tend to keep it less formal down here as opposed to upstairs.

['How do you do this?'] Well, you just try to put them at ease and make them as comfortable as possible. You kind of crack a joke or talk about the weather. You know, you kind of deflect from the main issue as to why they're down here.

Stewart also made explicit reference to the aesthetic experience of working in basement settings with no air flow when asked about the aspects of the job that he particularly dislikes: 'The downside is the smell . . . the fact that the drains make the shops downstairs smell so bad sometimes, especially when it's been raining a lot'.

Daniel, a manager in a feminized chain store on Wardour Street, who had worked there for a year when I met him in 2016, after working at a branch of the company in a suburban shopping centre, told me that the

Figure 13 Neon sign advertising 'preview booths', Brewer Street

shop was only just being refurbished after being open for 'thirty-odd years'. He said that the floor constantly lifts because it is damp and uneven and that 'the basement smells because of the drainage system'. He also said that 'the office is down there, so thankfully customers don't have to smell it, just staff, because it's a bit off-putting'. Daniel went on to explain that the basement of the building next door, which is a club, is constantly flooding. And as the shop and club are located between two pubs, people who are drunk regularly come into the store late into the evening, 'often lying on the floor'. 'It's a nuisance,' he said, 'but you get used to it.'

What these points highlight is that, while the work is physically tainted, the nature of this taint extends beyond that which is 'simply physically disgusting' in Hughes' terms,[25] encompassing a broader social materiality of taint relating to the physical nature, setting and location of the work, one that is intimately bound up with the social stigma with which the sector and setting are also associated. Mark hints at this in his comments about the challenge of putting customers at ease in what can be quite an off-putting space, one that, as descriptions of the smell and lack of natural air and light suggest, can often be quite a noxious environment.

Figure 14 Private viewing booth inside a basement sex shop, Brewer Street

Sex Shop Work as Socially Tainted

Those who provide and consume the goods and services on sale in Soho's sex shops, particularly because of enduring perceptions of the place as 'cheap and dirty', as Shirley suggests, are also socially tainted. Reflecting on how even long-standing customers seemed conscious of the social taint attached to frequenting a sex shop, and particularly one located in Soho, Nathan described how 'even regulars who've been coming in the shop for years ... will never, ever pay on credit card even now ... *It's*

stigma stuff because of what and where we are, a sex shop … in Soho'
(emphasis added).

Reflecting on the social taints associated with working and consuming in a Soho sex shop, Michael described the importance he attached to not transferring any sense of stigma or shame onto customers when describing how he tries to take most aspects of the job and the place in his stride, including some of the more intimate or unusual requests from customers:

> Well, if you get fazed by things like that [a customer asking him for advice on how to use a particular anal toy] … it'll show to the customer, so it kind of works against you and it might make them think, 'Well, why are you doing that? Is there something wrong with me?' No, it doesn't faze me at all.

Toby summed up his awareness of a mutual understanding of the importance of a non-judgemental relationship between customers and staff: 'I can't figure out the people who are [awkward] because it's like, if you're embarrassed to be in here, what does it make me to work here? Do you know what I mean? You feel they're judging you by being embarrassed.'

In addition to their awareness of customers' experiences of a consumption stigma, sex shop workers also described their own sense of performing stigmatized work, reflecting on the impact of the social taint with which working in a sex shop is associated on their relationships with others, including casual acquaintances, and friends and family. Michael, for instance, described how a woman came into the shop where he works with a friend and started chatting to him, but when he asked her if she might like to meet for lunch one day, he recalls how 'she wouldn't do it, and she was really honest. She was like, "I'm a bit put off by where you work." You just have to accept it I suppose, but it was a shame'. Nathan similarly explained that when friends and acquaintances ask what he does for a living 'they turn their noses up':

> If some people say, 'What do you do?' I just say 'sales' and I don't really go into it. If some people ask, 'What type of sales?' I go, 'Oh, retail.' 'Well, what type of retail?' 'Oh, a private shop.' Some people haven't got a clue – 'private shop?' – and other people, their eyebrows go up … Some people sort of turn their nose up when I've explained 'It's licensed.' They really do … It's still that image of 'Oh, my god, it's sex'. It's still taboo.

Many of the people I got to know connected the relatively transient nature of the place and of their work to the social taints associated with the combined effects of the setting and the sector. In this sense, their accounts echoed Soho's long history as a place of fluidity and flux. Stewart summed up what seemed to be a fairly widespread view – namely, that the social taints associated with working in a sex shop meant that few people saw it as anything other than a temporary arrangement:

You get a lot of people coming and going and . . . obviously a lot of people come in who just want it to be a temporary thing . . . I mean I think a lot of [workers] . . . sort of want to see themselves in a respectable job . . . I suppose you don't imagine many kids going to the . . . school careers advisor and saying, 'I really want to work in a sex shop.'

Echoing themes discussed in Chapter 3, Nathan explained how he used the recruitment process to test out how affected potential employees were by perceived social taints, seeking to appoint only those he thought could 'handle' the place and its products:

We've got a few set questions that we ask people that all the supervisors ask. But mostly we show them a few bits of literature [porn]. I've had people in before and they've answered questions quite well and then I've said, 'Right, this is a magazine we sell. This is [name of explicit magazine]' . . . and some blokes'll go, 'Oh, I'm not looking at that,' and you go, 'What do you mean, "I'm not looking at that"? Well, this is what we sell,' and you're sort of pushing it around. 'If you can't even look at that, then . . . ' Some people are literally like, 'Oh no, I'm not sure,' and you go, 'Well, sorry for wasting your time.' So you just know if that's going to put them off, *they're just not going to be able to do the job or the place for that matter* [emphasis added].

What struck me as being particularly interesting about what Nathan says here is his phrasing: the concern he expresses is that people might not be able to 'do' the job or the place, by implication framing the latter as something that workers *enact* through the work they do. And he seems as aware of the social stigma attached to this 'doing' of the work and the work place as he is of the requirement to be able to 'handle' this as an important part of the job.

Largely as a reflection of the social taints with which commercial sex is associated – and in a similar vein to the sex workers described by Sanders (2005) in her study of sex work[26] or by Grandy (2008) in her research on exotic dancers[27] – many of those who work in Soho's sex shops described themselves as leading 'double lives'. Some were explicit that they would lie about where they worked or would be vague about the precise details of the location and nature of the job. When asked about his job, Andy said: 'I'd just lie – I'd just say I sell DVDs. If I know them well enough I'd just say I sell adult DVDs.' Stephen similarly explained how he deflected questions from family and friends about the specifics of his job:

I tend to lie, you know! I say publishing or media or something . . . I don't know. What's the best way to describe it? My friends know and they think it's funny, but I have a master's degree [in Fine Art], and I'm very conscious of the fact that it's all gone a bit tits up really [*laughter*] . . . Actually, my family don't know. They'd be a little disappointed I think . . . I tell them I work in a bookshop [*chuckles*]. I'm so bad!

Julie evoked an intertwining of sex and gender as shaping her perception of the stigma attached to where she works: 'I'm proud to work at this store. The only place I wouldn't really advertise it so much because I'm a mum of two is at school because *it's still very taboo*. So, *there's some sort of boundary there that I wouldn't want to cross.*' While Shirley suggests a protective paternalism at stake in her decision not to tell her father that she works in Soho, as she felt he would worry about her safety and security, perceiving Soho to be 'cheap and dirty', Julie had decided to conceal the place and nature of her work because of its assumed transgression of gender roles and expectations. For those who took part in the research, a sense of working across boundaries, including moral boundaries, was a common experience.

Sex Shop Work as Morally Tainted

The very nature and location of retail sex work in Soho means that it also carries an implicit moral taint, largely because of its association with relatively stigmatized people engaging in what are generally perceived to be immoral, possibly illegal activities or simply with the transgression of boundaries, evoked by Julie and others. For the people working in the sex shops, most customers are regarded as perfectly 'normal' and 'ordinary': 'We get everything in here from eighteen year olds to eighty year olds and everything, and I do mean everything, in between', as Nathan put it. Customers that are generally perceived to be outside of this 'norm', and who are deemed to be predatory or perverse, and who violate the strong moral code that characterizes the place and sector are a regular and potentially increasing feature, however. Stephen explained the effects of the moral taint associated with these types of customers on his experience of the job, and on his sense of self, as someone employed within the industry:

You just get certain types. You get the browsers. You get the people that are wanting to buy stuff. You get collectors … and then you get the occasional perv, which isn't pleasant. That's really not pleasant … Sometimes they touch themselves, or … but you're kind of immune to it. I can put on my very polite face and smile and do whatever because I work on commission. It's when you get the perverts, the ones that ask for really nasty stuff … mainly kiddie stuff, and animals.

['What do you do? How do you cope?'] 'Sorry, out.' Done … *I just feel a little bit degraded by stuff like that* [emphasis added].

Michael explained how customers regularly behave in ways that violate wider social boundaries that they assume to be suspended in places like

Soho because of the nature of the sector and setting. As noted earlier, he recalled that, during his first week at work, 'a man walk[ed] over with his penis out in the shop. You do get that ... That was one of my first breaking moments ... When I say 'breaking moment', [I mean] as in 'If I can handle this I'll stay.' This blurring of boundaries often became more predatory, however, in a way that made workers feel uncomfortable and exposed to perceived taints associated with the place. As Toby recalled,

I've been [smelt] before. That made me feel sick. I had a good two-hour shower after that. *It just made me feel so dirty.* Just like the idea of someone smelling you ... Fair enough if you put your hand on my shoulder and I can push your hand off, but the idea of someone ... *That's really intimate. Oh, it was horrible* [emphasis added].[28]

Taken together, these accounts suggest that working in a sex shop carries physical, social and moral taints owing largely to the long-standing associations of the sector and the setting with a particular type of work and consumption that transgresses boundaries deemed necessary to the social and moral order. In other words, the 'dirt' with which retail sex work in Soho is associated constitutes 'matter out of place' (Douglas, 1966) that occupies an abject, 'boundary-threatening' status, to borrow from Kristeva,[29] ambiguous in its status and 'in-between' what are otherwise perceived as socially and sexually distinct spheres. What the participants' accounts also suggest, however, is that Soho – the place itself and the cultural meanings attached to it – constitutes both the source of these multiple taints, as well as an important coping mechanism that workers draw on as they perform a type of work, in a place of work that, as Stephen describes it, makes him feel 'just a little bit degraded'.

Place, Space and Community: Coping with the Business of Taint

In order to cope with some of the negating effects of their work, dirty workers, Ashforth and Kreiner (1999)[30] argue, develop 'strong occupational or workgroup cultures'. At the risk of oversimplifying their classification, the coping techniques they describe include *reframing*, *recalibrating* and *refocusing* the ways in which dirty work is perceived. Reframing involves transforming the negative meanings attached to dirty work, either through imbuing it with positive value – what they call infusing – or through neutralizing the negative value of the stigma. Many of the people I interviewed 'normalized' the work they do, neutralizing the taints with which it is associated. Nathan, for instance, described how working in a sex shop is 'no different to normal sales. It's just sales ...

[You] just take people's money and put it in a till. As simple as that.'
Davina similarly described how 'basically it's like working in any other
place. It's like it's a normal shop.' This neutralization process was also
extended to the shops themselves, and to Soho as a place of work, and to
the way in which the sector is framed as serving a basic consumer need. As
Shirley put it, evoking a 'naturalistic' discourse:

People don't seem to realize the way Soho's developed and *this is just normal* …
We may have a recession going on, but everyone still eats and still has sex. They're
like the two things that we're not going to stop doing, so business is there … and
you have to run it professionally *like any other normal retail store*. I apply basic retail
principles – *keep it clean, neat and tidy* [emphasis added].

Shirley went on to connect this normalization process to the regulation of
Soho's sex shops and to concerted attempts to clean up the area and the
industry:

It's all about image. No longer is Soho a dark and seedy place … Everybody has to
have a license now. We're regulated … and we have Trading Standards in on
a regular basis – probably more so than any other retail outlet. So yeah, *it's just
business* and we just happen to sell different products [emphasis added].

The relative informality of the sector, and the ethos by which it is
underpinned, also assists in this normalization process. Describing his
decision not to sack a member of staff who was caught masturbating
behind the counter, Nathan reflected, 'I don't really care. As long as
they're in every day and they're good at their job, we let a lot of things
go by, really.'

As Shirley suggests with her 'basic retail principles' of 'clean, neat and
tidy', this normalization process was also an aesthetic one that involved
making the shops 'light and bright' as a way of cleaning up sleazy associations with Soho's past, connecting its sex shops to the design imperative of
more gentrified and feminized sectors of the industry discussed in
Chapter 3. This was also partly in an effort to tackle some of the off-
putting implications of the materiality and location of many of Soho's sex
shops (e.g. in basements, below street level), particularly drainage smells,
already noted in relation to the more physical aspects of these taints. As
well as dealing with the olfactory issues, the use of colour to make the
shops, and their product ranges, seem brighter and more accessible was
also cited as an important aesthetic management technique, one that was
widely used in the more contemporary-style stores. Toby, for instance,
described the store where he worked, on Brewer Street, as pursuing this
kind of approach, comparing his shop to more traditional stores that are
(by implication) positioned as dirty and dark:

Ours has a nice, clean, bright feel compared to some of them ... We do it on purpose. We try and make it less intimidating. And we order colourful toys ... because [we] know how awkward people are and how intimidated people can be.

Mark placed a similar emphasis on physical cleanliness as a mechanism for reframing 'dirty' associations, including perceived physical taints:

Everything's got to be very clean and neat and give that impression ... We've got alcohol wipes which obviously we use for things ... that aren't packaged, but *we try and keep it as clean as possible* ... and that's all we can do, is just try and keep it as clean as we can [emphasis added].

Echoing her comparisons with other retail settings, Shirley similarly emphasized the importance of physical cleanliness as a way of challenging the dirty and dark connotations of the place and the sector. Echoing Mark's references to the persistent problem of bad smells, she affirms the importance of freshening the air as a technique for reframing associations of sex with 'dirt', linking the latter specifically to the setting:

There's an image with sex *here* that it has to be seedy and dirty, so therefore you have to be exceptionally clean and we've probably [got] a higher standard of cleanliness than clothes shops, shoe shops ... We have an air freshener system going on which keeps the air constantly fresh ... It's important to us that the whole place smells clean, fresh [emphasis added].

Referring to the gay lifestyle store he designed and co-owned, Jason went into some detail about importance of the store's aesthetic to reframing established perceptions of the industry and area, an imperative that he linked to challenging the social stigma associated with commercial sex as 'sleazy' and to his desire to make the sector and setting more 'respectable':

When I designed the shop there's a few factors that I took into consideration. Number one is that I don't think the sex industry necessarily needs to be sleazy. You know, it was more about being sexy rather than sleazy, so for me it was about bringing the whole place and the market into a contemporary image. You know, if you go around and look at retail in general, in London particularly, and ... you look at the style of the shops, a lot of them are very nicely designed with very interesting interiors, and I don't really see why that couldn't transcend into a sex shop environment here.

It is interesting that Jason implicitly links this aesthetic pursuit to an ethical, political one in his reference to 'opening things up' and also to 'transcendence', the latter suggesting something of an elevation of the sex industry and, by implication, of Soho itself:

You get a lot of people who before now have been quite shy and ... snuck into sex shops secretly and have come in here and sort of said, 'I really like this store because it sort of makes it not sleazy.' They feel like they're coming into something that's respectable ... *The whole feel of our shop is opening things up* ... I mean, that's what we're trying to do. We're trying to change, in a small way, people's perceptions of sex shops and the sex industry, I think, you know, in a way that's ... *aiming to be sexy, not sleazy* [emphasis added].

Recalibrating dirty work involves adjusting the perceptual and evaluative standards involved in order to 'make an undesired and ostensibly large aspect seem smaller and less significant and a desired but small aspect seem larger and more significant'.[31] To illustrate, the fire fighters in Tracy and Scott's study of sexuality, masculinity and taint management engaged in a recalibration of their work, emphasizing the excitement and danger associated with dealing with fires in order to maintain 'an esteem-enhancing identity' that detracted from the more mundane or physically dirty and degrading aspects of their work such as dealing with clients they referred to as 'shitbums' – among them, homeless people with drug problems:

They call 911 and [know] we'll have to take them to the emergency room, where they'll be cleaned up and referred to some homeless shelter or some other place that'll give them a handout.[32]

In a similar vein to the slaughterhouse workers in Ackroyd and Crowdy's (1990) classic ethnographic study,[33] Tracy and Scott show how discursive techniques designed to recalibrate dirt into a badge of masculine honour are mobilized by the firefighters they interviewed. Being covered in excrement or blood, rather than being cleaned up, is displayed with pride as a sign of male homosociality, as well as a gender and class-based affirmation of the capacity to 'handle' dirt, as Nathan referred to it when talking about interviewing candidates for jobs in the sex shop he managed.

In *refocusing*, the third of Ashforth and Kreiner's categories, attention is shifted away from the stigmatized features of the work and towards elements that are less tainted or not at all. Hence, 'whereas reframing actively transforms the stigmatized properties of dirty work and recalibrating magnifies their redeeming qualities, refocusing actively *overlooks* the stigmatized properties'[34]. Stewart alluded to this when he explained that when he tells people about where he works, in a gay sex shop on Old Compton Street in Soho, he tries to focus their attention on the 'lifestyle' aspect of the store: 'It's not that I try to hide it ... It's just I try and focus more on the stuff we have upstairs [clothing and books] than maybe downstairs [sex toys and accessories, including BDSM equipment].'

Notable examples of the deployment of these kinds of techniques can be found in studies of nursing and care work emphasizing the ways in which healthcare professionals dignify the dirty aspects of their work through a transformative emphasis on quality of care and on the deployment of specialist knowledge and skill (Bolton, 2005[35]; Chiapetta-Swanson, 2005[36]; Stacey, 2005[37]). Godin's (2000) research on mental health nurses emphasizes how the latter endeavour to associate themselves 'with the clean work of caring, rather than with the dirty work of coercive control'[38]. And in her study of the ways in which gynaecology nurses manage the more difficult or potentially 'distasteful' aspects of their work (e.g. dealing with terminations, miscarriages, cancer, sexually transmitted diseases, incontinence), for instance, Bolton (2005) cites the nurses' emphasis on the 'special' nature of their jobs, actively celebrating their status as knowledgeable, highly skilled and caring workers:

Gynaecology nurses acknowledge and accept the stigma attached to their work. Their association with dirty work is used as a means of emphasizing difference. *The very reasons why their work may be classified as tainted are used to justify and verify its value. They become the celebrated 'other'* in relation to ... socially structured notions of 'good work'.[39]

In addition to their skills and knowledge, the nurses in Bolton's study affirmed the 'special' status of their work through the value they placed on collegial bonds. One of the staff nurses Bolton interviewed, for example, said: 'I think the clinical nurse and the Senior Sister have done a wonderful job of *making people aware of the basic humanity of the situation*',[40] going on to explain that the specific, embodied and intimate nature of gynaecology nursing 'creates a distinctive occupational community' connected, in part, by 'a strong sense of otherness'.[41] This recognition-based sense of community enabled the women to reframe the stigma they perceived to be attached to the more 'dirty' aspects of their work as collectively ennobling.

In many ways, men and women working in Soho's sex shops engage in similar techniques, evoking the specialist nature of their skills and understanding, and the capacity of their expertise as emotional, aesthetic and sexualized labourers, to deflect associations of their work with sleaze. Echoing Jason's mission to reframe the associations of his shop with 'sex, not sleaze', Julie emphasized the advice and support given to customers by her and her colleagues. As she put it,

When somebody comes into the store and is actually quite shy and not very blasé about what they're looking for or what [they] want ... and they ask your opinion and you work out what it is they need or want to try ... and people go out with a good feeling, *there's no sleaziness about it* [emphasis added].

Others connected the emotional skills deployed to the ethos that characterizes the contemporary retail sex industry in Soho. Toby explained the significance of a non-judgemental ethos:

[People care] that you don't make them feel awkward. That you're not blasé with them because, like, with our shop it is something very intimate. It's really intimate, and you have to kind of appreciate that people aren't always 100 per cent comfortable with talking about their sexuality, which is fair enough. Like, I never ever judge. *That's one thing that this shop and working here has taught me – you never judge anyone* [emphasis added].

Toby's sentiment here echoes that of Stacey Denekamp in *Sex Shop Education*, in her account of working in a sex shop in the United States. Here she notes the 'special' nature of sex shops as non-judgemental environments in which those who work are generally 'open' to difference:

A sex shop is one of the few places … where you can openly discuss different things we like, or ask about things we are curious about, without being judged or laughed at. *They're pretty special places when you stop to think about it.*[42]

In their ethnographic study of refuse collectors and street cleaners, Hughes et al. (2017) are cautious of this celebratory approach, however, emphasizing how esteem-enhancing strategies that draw primarily on the symbolic can be both supported and undermined by the physicality of 'dirt' and how relations of power are rooted in subordinating material conditions. Their study shows how the symbolic and material are fundamentally intertwined in perceptions and experiences of dirty work, suggesting that a neglect of the latter might lead to a false optimism regarding workers' ennobling capacities.[43]

Echoing elements of both perspectives, several of the people I interviewed refocused the work they do to emphasize the importance of the advice and guidance they give to customers: 'People have got a lot invested in it [sex], and a lot of people aren't very comfortable coming in, so to get out of them what they want is hard,' Toby said. 'It's an important part of what we do, because you've got to understand what they want. You've got to be able to read them'.

In addition to the three strategies of reframing, recalibrating and refocusing identified by Ashforth and Kreiner (1999) and discussed thus far, a further technique deployed by dirty workers is *distancing*. Grandy (2008) explains how this works in her study of exotic dancers, who, she argues, project onto clients the disgust they perceive to be associated with their work in order to distance themselves from it. Dancers do this 'to minimize the stigma associated with their own identities and [to] position themselves in a more favourable light to others'. This results in a complex hierarchy of projections through which dancers categorize their motivations for dancing, the type of dancing they do and the type of clubs in which they work in order to 'rationalize the work they perform and manage their spoiled identities'.[44] Sanders, in her studies of sex workers, notes similar techniques involving organizing perceived taints and their associated risks hierarchically by sector or setting, such as between street-based sex workers and those who work indoors, in massage parlours and brothels, for instance.

Another important way for workers to collectively deflect the taints associated with their work and place of work draws from governmental discourses of 'upscaling'. Jason hints at how shop owners and managers do this with reference to his design aesthetic, as does Shirley in her evocation of 'freshness' in the store she manages.

In his account of the contested spaces of commercial sex, Hubbard (2004a, 2004b) describes the spatial interplay between 'clean-up' strate-gies and tactical behaviours designed to challenge and resist such strate-gies in the regulation and urban governance of the sex industry.[45] Documenting how clean-up strategies largely involve a combination of urban gentrification, heavy policing and the displacement of vice, Hubbard argues that the introduction of licensing controls for premises associated with commercial sex have served to regulate the sex industry through the 'upscaling' of sex-related businesses (Hubbard, 2004a, 2004b; Hubbard et al., 2009), a process that has cleaned up the sector overall. In particular, this draws attention to the ways in which premises licensing, as a 'field of governance', provides a flexible (and also revenue-generating) mechanism through which the state is able to reconcile the demand for adult entertainment with urban regeneration.

What accounts such as Hubbard's emphasize is that licensing, as a microcosm of the management and regulation of the space and place itself, constitutes a site of struggle, in which 'different constituencies fight to have their understanding of what is appropriate ... legitimated'.[46] What they also highlight is the significance of community as the site of this contestation, and this is particularly important in understanding how these struggles are played out in Soho as a situated, collective mechanism for coping with the symbolic and material dimensions of 'dirt'.

While it is all too easy to romanticize Soho, it is important to recognise the extent to which, in order to share some of the pleasures as well as cope with some of the difficulties, those employed there, including in its sex shops, largely see themselves as constituting a working community. At the risk of homogenization, it seems fair to say that this sense of community relates not just to those who work in the sex shops but to their connections with other workers in Soho (e.g. sex workers), with residents and also with customers, based on a perceived, shared understanding of sexual openness. As Michael summed it up, those who work in the shops often feel a sense of connection to customers, based on a shared feeling of being 'comfortable' in somewhere perceived to be outside of the 'norm'. Echoing Denekamp's reference to sex shops as 'special places', Michael recalled his experiences of finding a 'connection' to customers that provided a sense of mutual comfort:

> Sometimes I'll be outside having a cigarette and [a couple will be deliberating whether to come in or not] … I think it's lovely. I think it's really nice, because they're having a laugh, and you can see they're on a date and stuff like that, and it's not [the norm] really … If you can start talking and you try to make them a little bit more comfortable, the next thing you know they're in there for half an hour having a good old chinwag with you, telling you about themselves, and you realize you have a lot in common, and *you, they feel comfortable in there – the shop and the place, I mean* [emphasis added].

Michael and others explained the friendships built up with customers based on mutual understanding: 'There's two customers … They used to come in and they used to [look at mainstream porn DVDs] and I said, "You're not really into straight stuff, are you?" It's just … I came out with it and they said, "Well, actually, yeah" [affirming Michael's sense that "straight stuff" was not what they were "into"]. I went, "Well, you know, don't worry. You know me. Don't feel nervous about it. Just grab what you really want to grab."'

Korczynski relates the formation of what he calls, drawing on Hochschild (1983), communities of coping to the 'structure of workers' social situation',[47] and the accounts discussed here suggest that Soho, the place itself, is an important dimension of this social situation. For those employed in its many sex shops, the place itself is both an important source of the various taints with which their work is associated (as Nathan put it, 'it's because of what and *where* we are') and, at the same time, a working community in which 'everyone looks after each other's backs', as Julie describes it. Summing up her sense of Soho as a place to work, Julie explained how, in her experience, it is both 'dangerous' and 'a little community':

> Even though Soho has got an image of being … Don't get me wrong – it's still dangerous in parts and our shop in particular, because we're open 'til 11 o'clock, we do see sort of the after-hours and things that go on there … But, believe it or not, it is like a little community, and everybody knows each other and everyone actually looks after each other and it's all connected. It is like a little niche, sort of like within itself, and I find if anybody says, "Oh, Soho's still got this image. Isn't it a bit rough?" it's like, "No, it's probably one of the safest places" … *Everybody, especially the businesses, everybody practically knows each other and everyone looks after each other's back, so it is a little community* [emphasis added].

Jason evokes this sense of Soho as a working community that has 'each others' backs' when he talked about the homeless people, who sleep outside the front door of his shop on Old Compton Street, as an important part of the community:

Nobody should be homeless in this day and age, it's disgusting, but they are and you build up a rapport with them. *You get to know them and work with them because they'll look out for you. They'll look out for the shop* ... They'll tell you if there are pickpocketers, if there are people doing dodgy shit going around. They'll warn you. You know, if a shop's been raided down the street ... that kind of 'come in and rush in and rush out and grab stuff off the rails', they'll tell you. They'll come in and say, 'Oh, you know such and such got robbed. Be careful.' So, you know, treat everybody how you want to be treated. That's what we do [emphasis added].

Here Jason evokes the place itself as both a significant source of the 'dodgy shit' that is routinely encountered by those who live and work in Soho, including in its shop doorways, *at the same time* as constituting an important resource on which workers are able to draw in order to cope with the degrading or debilitating effects of this and of the multiple taints with which their sector and place of work is associated.

But Soho itself is more than simply a mechanism for coping with the business of taint. As we will discuss, the 'dirt' with which both the shops and the area are associated is also an important source of *attraction* for those who work in Soho, many of whom described an abject sense of being simultaneously repulsed and fascinated by their work and their place of work. Toby made explicit reference to this when he described his attraction to Soho as a workplace as being in large part precisely because of its 'dirty' associations, recognizing and 'glamorizing' the various taints by which the area is characterized:

A lot of people have their view on Soho and some people see it as disgusting and they don't want to be here, but there's some people who see it as really exciting and glamorous. You know, the idea of being in the middle of all the clubs, with all the sex and that, that really appeals [to me] ... I kind of like the fact that I'm surrounded by all the sort of old sex cinemas and the old dirty porn shops ... There's this kind of weird atmosphere ... Like you feel you can't shock anyone in Soho, and I'll tell you what – working here for a year, literally, I've seen everything.

Dirt and Desire: From Dirty Work to Abject Labour

As historian Judith Summers has put it, 'Soho may not always be pleasant, but it is never dull,'[48] and for Toby and many others like him the very attraction of the place, the sector and the job itself is precisely its 'dirt'. Hughes himself hints at the allure of dirty work when he notes, in somewhat passing fashion, how 'dirty work may be *an intimate part of the very activity which gives an occupation its charisma*'[49]. But it is the concept of abjection, associated most closely with the work of Julia Kristeva (1982), that conveys in a more nuanced way the *simultaneous* attraction and repulsion that characterizes the way in which most of the people I spoke to seem to feel about their work, and particularly their place of work, and the transgression of boundaries associated with their sector and setting of employment.

Julie echoed the sentiments of many others when she described her need to 'do something different': 'I need variety, to be doing something a little bit different … and I think I've captured that working here … There's always something going on, so there's always an atmosphere, always a buzz.' Toby similarly said that the setting is what he enjoys most about the job: 'it's all the different people that you meet in there [the shop] because of where we are. It's always buzzing. Because I mean … Because of where we are. We're in the middle of everything.' Michael also said that working in Soho was the main attraction for him: 'It's the actual area. It's the area definitely … and the shops round it and the different people, the looks.' Stewart also evoked his attraction to Soho's 'buzz':

I've always loved Soho ever since I came to London … You know, you get the weird, the wacky and the wonderful. You know, literally everybody's thrown in together and, like I said, generally, 95 per cent of the time, or probably more than that, to be honest with you, everyone fits together fine. I mean you get the odd drunk and you get the odd bit of trouble, but, like, overall … And there's just a buzz about the place. I mean you get the different times of the year. I particularly like the first day that the sun comes out and actually, like, decent sunshine … and then lo and behold everybody suddenly appears … and people stroll on the streets. *I've always liked the vibe here. I mean, I've always liked it and felt like I belong* [emphasis added].

This sense of recognition-based belonging was also a strong theme in Mark's narrative on working in Soho, in a community that he describes as a 'surrogate family':

This is kind of a second home because this is where I spent most of my time when I first came to London. So I know it like the back of my hand, and there's just something very comforting about it, especially with it being the gay village. *You kind of feel safe here because there are others like you around, you know. So there's a kind of recognition* … I grew up in a tiny village in the middle of nowhere in the countryside. You know, *there's a sense of belonging here that I've never had before.* It's like a surrogate family, I suppose. You know, it kind of empowers you because 'Well, this is my street, you know,' and I don't mean that in an egotistical and arrogant way but, like I said, you know, I've been here for twenty years now and it feels like a second home [emphasis added].

Toby went into considerable detail on this, reflecting on his fascination with working somewhere that he experiences as both 'disgusting' and 'really exciting', evoking a similar sense of belonging to that described by Mark, Stewart and others when he says, 'I feel more at home here than where I live.' Toby and Mark both suggest that they experience Soho as a community of outsiders, one that appears (albeit in something of an inverted way) to embody Bataille's understanding of abjection as a process that 'establishes the foundations of collective existence'.[50] Toby explained his feelings about this at some length:

I like the idea of working somewhere that's ... You know, you see things every day that people don't expect to see. Especially where I work as well, it's outside of the norm ... You come to work and you make friends with the addicts and the prostitutes ... Because of where I work ... we do quite good deals for the prostitutes and stuff ... I think that's the interesting part of it. You know, *you get to meet ... the sort of people you wouldn't really want to meet in an ideal world ...* and they're really interesting. They've got stories to tell. You can't trust them as far as you'd throw them, but to chat to they're interesting ... Soho's always been the place. Even when I was a kid I loved [it] ... There's just something about it. I really like the place ... That's another thing about Soho – I always keep a watch in case you miss something! There's so much to watch. I love it ... *I feel more at home here than I do where I live.* Because it's so intimate. *It's quite a small area. Because all the shops know each other, we all look after each other.* But at the same time you've got people coming here to find ... you know, like you've got people coming in to ask for kiddie porn and stuff because it's Soho. So you've got that side of it as well ... Yeah, you do get stuff like that, but then it wakes you up and it gives you stories to tell. *It's living life, isn't it?* [emphasis added].

Echoing Toby's enthusiasm and apparently knowing (rather than naïve) identification with Soho, Davina describes similarly how much she loved working there, as a place with which she identifies and which she finds 'inspirational':

It's similar to my own universe of interest. I'm very much into fashion, I'm especially into [antique] lingerie ... I'm a collector of it and I'm also into performance art ... It's a similar universe to me. It's an inspirational place to work in. Yes, it's seedy and it has an edge but that's what makes it exciting. It's what makes it what it is.

What these reflections convey is a sense of connection not simply to their work and place of work but notably to the taints with which both are associated; theirs is an abject identification shaped by a simultaneous attraction and repulsion, a 'temptation and condemnation', to borrow from Kristeva. This goes beyond the taint management and coping techniques described earlier in the chapter, or simply having 'mixed feelings' about their work, but evokes a sense of their work as *abject labour* and of Soho as an abject work place. The latter involves a simultaneous compulsion and repulsion – a charged fascination – with the various taints with which their work and, in this case, their place of work is associated, now and in the past. As Michael explained to me:

I've read a lot of literature about Soho going back to the 1960s, you know, when it was all like proper rogues and villains … the naughty stuff and the prostitution. I think it's so interesting up here. Very … It has opened up a lot of thoughts for me, a lot of doors and opportunities. You can always meet people here and it's good. It's really, really good … I like working here because you can go for a little wander, meet people, buy a couple of records. People come here from all over and they're specifically saying, 'Let's go to Soho. Let's spend a few days in Soho' … You're going to see things here that you're not going to get anywhere else, and it's always been like that.

Davina also evoked the area's sense of community and history when describing Soho as a place to work:

There is something about Soho that makes it … an interesting place to work, *not 'nice', but interesting*.

['In what sense?'] Soho is still *a very particular place*. It's nice to sort of have the energy and vibe of Soho … People in the coffee shops … they can give you really good stories about how Soho used to be. *That continuity gives you a sense of Soho as like, a big family, a community … That's the feel of the place* [emphasis added].

In a similar way, Stewart also explained his enjoyment of the combination of 'madness' and 'sights' he routinely encounters during his working life in Soho:

I mean I'm not going to lie and say that I don't keep thinking, 'Surely there should be something more important in my life than … ' But I like the madness of it. I mean you don't get a madder place in this country – and we get them all in here. I mean that in the nicest possible way, but we certainly get some of the sights of Soho coming in!

Comparing the sense of recognition-based belonging that he associates with Soho to the more 'sterile' environment of retail environments elsewhere, Matt also implied that Soho's 'dirt' is one of the reasons he feels so comfortable working there:

I always consider myself at my most comfortable when I'm in and around Soho. I don't feel threatened by anybody. I feel that I can do, be … You know, *I can be me more than anything else*, do you know what I mean? Whereas in the city [central London] it's just a totally different, more sterile atmosphere [emphasis added].

In what is perhaps the most sustained theoretical discussion of abjection to date, namely Kristeva's (1982) *Powers of Horror*, abjection (from the Latin *ab-jicere* meaning 'the state of being cast out') is defined as that which 'disturbs identity, system, order'. It is that which simultaneously 'beseeches, worries and fascinates',[51] threatening lines of demarcation and containment between what is 'pure' and what is 'dangerous', in Douglas' (1966) terms. The potentially transformative or transgressive capacity of abjection lies in what Kristeva describes as 'the powers of horror' – its ability to evoke a fascination with what is perceived as a threat to the established moral order, an allure that seems to characterize the experiences of those who work in Soho's sex shops (as Julie put it, in but one of many possible examples, 'I need to be doing something different . . . and I think I've captured that working here').

Anthropologist Claude Lévi-Strauss argued that 'primitive' cultures deal with strangeness and strangers in a way that differs from more 'civilized' societies. As Linstead has put it, discussing Lévi-Strauss' book *Tristes Tropiques*, 'difference equals danger: strangers are dangerous'.[52] Whereas primitive societies devour, ingest and consume strangeness, absorbing the magical powers of strangers into themselves, more 'civilized' cultures reject them, cast them out, drive them away and exclude them[53]. Contra Lévi-Strauss, Kristeva (1982) contends that these two processes do not proceed in some kind of developmental linearity; rather, they are inseparable, or, as Linstead puts it, 'they are indispensable twin mechanisms of social spacing, in every society and at every level'.[54] Of note here is Linstead's emphasis on abjection as a *spatial* strategy through which our sense of self is shaped, and order inserted into social systems and settings. Drawing from Kristeva, we can see that these entwined approaches to maintaining social order produce a 'remainder' of that 'which is not rejected yet is not acceptable either and which irritates the system'.[55] This is what Kristeva call *the abject*. As she puts it,

It is not lack of cleanliness or health that causes abjection but *what disturbs identity, system, order*. What does not respect borders, positions, rules. The in-between, the ambiguous, the composite . . . Abjection . . . is *immoral, sinister, scheming, and shady* . . . a hatred that smiles.[56]

Crucially, for Kristeva, abjection 'assumes specific shapes and different codings according to the various symbolic systems' in which it is situated.[57] This highlights that abjection must be understood within the specific setting in which it is experienced. The accounts described here suggest, in this respect, an identification with Soho (the place, the sector and its people) that goes beyond simply reframing, recalibrating or refocusing dirty work (Ashforth and Kreiner, 1999) and instead seeks to retain the 'edge' with which their work, and, crucially, their place of work, is associated *at the same time* as being repelled, even repulsed, by many aspects of it. The 'dirt' with which their work and place of work is associated, both material and moral,[58] appeals to those who work in Soho's sex shops. Yet at the same time, at least some aspects of it, as discussed throughout this chapter and this book, make them recoil in horror. This simultaneity involves a fascination that goes beyond mere ambivalence, constituting a complex relationship between attraction and repulsion that is mediated by and materialized through work place and community. This is why, for those who work in Soho's sex shops, Nathan's summation seems a particularly apt way of capturing the complexity of feelings, experiences and identifications that might be described as abject labour in this particular setting: 'it's the best job in the world, and an absolute nightmare, usually in the same day. It's fascinating, really fascinating … but yeah, *there are things about it that I absolutely hate, and sometimes these are the same things that I love about it.*' Reminiscent of themes explored in Stevenson's Jekyll and Hyde (see Chapter 1), Michael further articulated this complexity with reference to Soho's temporal economy, contrasting his sense of attraction to Soho as a 'buzzing' place in the daytime to his experience of it at night as 'sinister':

I love it around here, the buzz, but when it gets dark … I will say this – it gets very, very sinister … Different place in the day, different place at night … I've seen some horrible things. I've seen one slash attack … One man pulled off his belt and was beating one of his prostitutes up. Just random things. The amount of drugs you get offered is crazy … At night, now that's when I don't like it here.

Daniel alluded to similar concerns when he explained to me that they get more than their share of 'dodgy customers', as he put it, 'especially at night – plenty on drugs, drunk etc. You just have to deal with it, and we always have security on the door to stop the wrong sort of people coming in and the stock going out. And we know that police are only a call away. There's always people around if you need them.'

Stephen was well aware of these issues, like Michael and Daniel, and saw them very much as 'part and parcel' of Soho working life: 'You get the touts and the drug people … and a lot of beggars, but that's just part and parcel of Soho. Like the culture, the diversity, the mixture … it's just everyone doing their own thing. You can wear what you want, do what you want. It's fine. It's great.' Echoing Michael's concerns with Soho's night-time economy, others expressed their worries about drug dealers and users being in the shops at night ('purposefully just being wrong … really bad', as Martin put it) and about the increased risk of outbreaks of violence in the shops at night. Mark described how a fight that had broken out between two gangs of men on the street outside his shop had been brought inside. He had used the panic button under the sales counter to call the police who arrived to break things up within five minutes, reflecting 'you do need that security. With being on Old Compton Street with all the bars and restaurants, evening times can be quite a handful . . . Friday and Saturday nights are a nightmare.'

Also of concern was the impact of Soho's commercial popularity as a place for after-work drinking, and for hen and stag parties in particular, turning the area into what Clayton Littlewood, in his book about the shop *Dirty White Boy* that he co-ran on Old Compton Street, described as a 'safari park'.[59] Echoing this view, Mark went on to say: '[T]here are times when you just don't want to be here. It's like Notting Hill Carnival outside sometimes . . . I love Soho for what it is but . . . when it gets manic and packed it's not a nice place to be . . . People can get very loud and leering, shall we say?' Asked in what way, he replied: 'They think that they can just come in and grab things, and grab you. It's really not nice to be here then.'

Understanding these perceptions and experiences as abject recognizes not only the pains but also the pleasures, the dirt and the desire, or what Kristeva calls 'the powers of horror', associated with working in a sex shop, in Soho. This is important because it helps us to begin to tease out interconnections between the meanings attached to particular types of work and the specific locations in which they take place; to think about the work that the men and women do as abject labour, and Soho itself as an abject work place. Not only does doing so help us to understand more about the social materiality of dirty work; it also brings to the fore the importance of place, both as the source of multiple taints and as a sociocultural, inter-subjective resource on which workers draw in order to cope with the negating effects of taint on their working lives and identities. Place in this instance simultaneously accentuates and alleviates the effects of tainted work. More than this, however, shifting our conceptual lens away from dirty work towards a focus on abject labour, and abject work places, enables us to recognize the *simultaneity* of attraction and repulsion – and the sense of fascination that this engenders – for those who undertake dirty work in sectors and settings like this. To paraphrase Kristeva, it enables us to think more about Soho as a workplace characterized by 'the temptation of condemnation' in our understanding of work identities and experiences there.[60]

Further, Soho's abject nature, and its long-standing appeal as both alluring and threatening, makes it a particularly interesting place to consider some of the ways in which gender is simultaneously un/done (Butler, 2004) in and through work in a place, an industry and an occupation often regarded as male dominated and hyper-hegemonic in its orientation. In the following chapter, we consider some of the ways in which working in a Soho sex shop compels gender conformity at the same time as it opens up possibilities for making 'trouble' with gender[61] and for challenging bifurcated, hierarchical ways of categorizing gender, sexuality and subjectivity. For many of the sex shop workers I talked to, this was one of the main attractions of working in Soho: its capacity to enable those who work there to be and do 'something different', as Julie put it.

Before moving on to this theme, it is important to keep in mind, however, that revelling in Soho's metaphorical filth isn't for everyone. Ongoing efforts to clean up concentrations of commercial sex in places like Soho – and the sex industry more generally – can be understood as attempts to regulate abjection. As we now consider, these revolve largely around measures seemingly designed to retain a commercial and civic fascination with a place's 'edge' at the same time as minimizing its more repulsive or horrific associations that are more difficult to contain or control.

Regulating Abject Work Places

Writing in the 1920s, Reckless (1926) suggested that commercial vice is inclined to thrive in zones of transition characterized by high population turnover and a social life that tends towards fluidity, with social and demographic 'flow' providing a degree of urban anonymity.[62] Such features characterize Soho as an abject work place, both now and historically: they are built into its materiality and moral associations and to the ways in which its economy, history and geography interweave. They help us to make sense of its appeal as a place to live, work and consume as well as to understand how and why the sex industry evolved and endures there. These characteristics also contextualize the extent to which Soho constitutes an ongoing challenge for regulatory bodies whose responsibility it is to govern and police the area, and to maintain its commercial potential as a lucrative part of London and as a working and residential community, without over-sanitizing Soho and, in doing so, destroying it. As discussed in Chapters 1 and 2, one of the many things that makes Soho particularly distinctive is the geographic and commercial intensity of its sex industry: it is a classic example of a 'clustered' sex market in this sense.

Ryder (2004) shows how clustering serves to repel other businesses by 'creating a moral atmosphere which discourages other kinds of retailing and entertainment by driving up rent'.[63] Yet, at the same time, it sustains the 'edge' that makes Soho clearly discernible from other similar places in the sector and setting in which it is situated and which underpins what, for many, is its desirability as a working and residential community.

Formal regulation, driven largely by politicians, developers and investors[64] keen to contain what are perceived to be the socially and economically detrimental 'secondary effects' of Soho's sex industry, has typically taken three forms – licensing, community initiatives and local business campaigns, including place marketing such as the 'I Love Soho' initiative. The sex shops have embraced the latter in particular as a way to market the area and the sector's 'edge', with many of the shops displaying this commitment (see Figure 15).

Not surprisingly, these strategies have sometimes worked in unison; at other times they have been at odds, pursuing different agendas and interests. Tying elements of all three together are recent social media and interest groups such as Stephen Fry's 'Save Soho' campaign, triggered largely by the closure of Madame Jojo's and the development of Cross Rail (see Introduction and Chapter 1). Other initiatives – such as the launch of a Soho Society beer to raise funds for community activities and events such as the annual Soho Fair – also bring various community, civic and commercial interests into alignment.

This kind of coalescence contrasts with what seems to be the default mode of regulating commercial sex in the United States, namely zoning. This is a method that was used to 'clean up' the notoriously seedy area of Times Square in central Manhattan and to re-site the sex industry to a less central area designated specifically for commercial sex purposes. As Cook (2005) outlines, in New York City politicians successively and successfully depicted strip clubs and other sex-related businesses as the cause of increased crime.[65] A long history of regulation culminated in the 1995 Adult Entertainment Ordinance, a 'triumph against licentiousness'.[66] Cook alludes to New York's abject nature when she emphasizes that, throughout its illustrious history, it has been a place that has captivated people because *'like sex, it can be exhilarating, exhausting, and dirty'*.[67] The 1995 Ordinance attempted to control and contain the city's associations with 'dirt', managing out 'the presence of the ugly and perverse, and therefore "other", to create a unified system of normalcy and moral social order'.[68]

By way of illustration, Cook (2005) recalls how, in 1997, the then Mayor Rudolph Giuliani held a ceremonious unveiling of Disney's $30 million renovation of the New Amsterdam Theatre. Once the home of the Ziegfeld Follies, the New Amsterdam was fully repackaged for wholesome, family entertainment – a little like some of the bars and restaurants in contemporary Soho. During the 'public relations display', the then CEO of Disney, Michael Eisner, said that he had reservations about associating the Disney brand with Times Square, because of the

Figure 15 'I love Soho' sign on sex shop entrance, Old Compton Street

historical prevalence of adult shops there and the area's notorious associations with the sex industry.

Giuliani commissioned the Department of City Planning (DCP) to conduct an analysis and publish a report on the impact of adult entertainment in and around Times Square. The report, published in 1993, focused on sex shops, topless bars, strip clubs and adult cinemas and concluded that the area's negative associations as somewhere that is 'seedy and dirty' were because of high concentrations of adult entertainment businesses there. The secondary effects of this concentration, including detrimental effects on public health, safety and welfare, were cited as being of particular concern.[69] Further, increased crime rates, depreciation of property values, deterioration of community and the quality of urban life were also referred to.

Zoning regulations amended in 1995 prohibited an adult business from extending or enlarging its existing premises and forbade any existing establishment in New York from converting into an adult business. Sex businesses were also prohibited from being within 500 feet of residential areas, places of worship, schools and each other. Only one adult establishment was permitted within a single zoning area, and signage of sex-related businesses was also regulated. When challenged in a consolidated (class) action brought by Stringfellow's in 1998, the New York Court of Appeals was satisfied that the City's purpose in adopting zoning regulations was not to restrict freedom of speech or expression but rather to protect its citizens, citing the DCP's report as indicative of the extent to which 'negative perceptions of adult businesses resulted in lower investment in the community and deteriorated the social and economic fabric of the surrounding area'.[70] In speeches subsequently, Giuliani has referred to the 'corrosive effects' of the sex industry, citing concentrations of commercial sex as 'destroying communities',[71] vowing to safeguard New York from 'the shadows cast by . . . sex-related businesses'.[72]

While arguably somewhat rose-tinted, Cook (2005) laments the sanitizing effects of this regulatory zoning: 'a once notorious, albeit garish, area that challenged societal restrictions on sexual freedoms, Times Square had been subjugated into a more acceptable, sterile form of expression'.[73] She concludes that the city's unique character and reputation as 'an urban mecca that has historically been tolerant and open' has been thoroughly Disneyfied and 'managed out' through zoning practices. The latter, she argues, invite and respond to the particular interests of powerful social groups such as politicians, investors and developers, to the detriment of the city as a whole and other groups whose voices and influence are less powerful. As a result,

The Times Square district of New York City, once famous for its glamorous sex appeal and decadence, has been transformed into a regular – some would argue hollow – corporate enterprise.[74]

Jason Prior's discussion of the licensing of sex industry premises in inner Sydney offers an alternative perspective on the regulation of abject spaces and settings. He argues that while, on the one hand, planning processes such as those described by Cook reveal ideas about how these establishments 'contaminate and pollute', there are also emerging arguments that sex industry premises such as gay bathhouses can contribute to health and lifestyle opportunities for specific communities within particular city environments. He shows how these more positive discourses have guided the placement and regulation of bathhouses under the auspices of the City of Sydney 'Adult Entertainment and Sex Industry Premises Development Control Plan' (2006).[75] In contrast to the strategies of exclusion described by Cook and others (see Papayanis, 2000; Ryder, 2004), Prior develops a similar perspective to that of Binnie and Skeggs (2004), who highlight the positioning of Manchester's 'Gay Village' within discourses of safety, community and commercialism as part of the city's entrepreneurial emphasis on tourism.[76]

At the risk of oversimplification, and to borrow from Levi-Strauss' analysis of strategic responses to encounters with difference cited earlier, the secondary effects emphasized by Prior and by Binnie and Skeggs highlight a 'co-opting in' rather than a 'zoning out'. While the latter approach is based on a perception that the sex industry pollutes, taints or contaminates through proximity or association, the former involves a slightly different – over-inclusive, entrepreneurial – perspective emphasizing the 'added value' that the sex industry brings to an area. In particular, the gay bathhouses in Darlinghurst in Prior's study were deemed to provide an important social and sexual amenity for the local gay community, offering 'safe opportunities for socializing out of the reach of gay bashers and an environment for the practice of and education about safe sex'[77].

Moving beyond earlier research, Prior's study shows how sex industry premises can contribute to health and lifestyle opportunities within particular locales in which they are clustered, both responding to and advancing changing perceptions of commercial and non-heteronormative sexualities. At the same time, however, it hints at themes developed in Binnie and Skeggs' account of Manchester's Gay Village – that such approaches are vulnerable to commercial (and civic) co-optation, or to an 'over-inclusive' ingestion, in Levi-Strauss's terms.

This is similar to the more market-driven processes of gentrification and feminization that constitute overtly commercial attempts to manage or regulate the industry's abject associations in places like Soho. Crewe and Martin discuss this in their account of 'upscaling', noting how, in contrast to licensed sex shops, 'erotic boutiques' are permitted to have transparent glass shop fronts that allow natural light in, thus rendering them 'spaces of cleanliness and purity, as opposed to [the] darkness and dirtiness' of more traditional sectors and settings such as those associated with several of the remaining shops in Soho.[78] However, as they go on to note, even those that don't require concealed windows such as Agent Provocateur and Coco de Mer cultivate metaphorical 'darkness' stylistically, actively playing with 'dirty' associations. They show how gentrified stores do this through the use of lighting and colour schemes, illustrating how black and red coloured interior designs feature heavily in boutique style, upscaled sex shops, adding an edgy sophistication to the deliberately darkened atmosphere. This sets them apart in both gender and class terms from traditional sex shops *and* from the more accessible, feminized stores such as Ann Summers. As aesthetic assemblages, they contrast markedly with the 'dark, impenetrable traditional sex shops' that are contained, liminal and marginalized and the feminized stores that are permitted to occupy mainstream retail space, 'visible to all, gaily illuminated with soft pink décor and natural light'.[79]

By effectively merchandising abjection in this way, what unites both gentrified and feminized sex shops, apart from their aesthetic contrast with more traditional stores, is that they repackage sex for women – 'from something that is heavily stigmatized to something that is heavily stylized'.[80] In upscaled stores, 'dirt' is not managed out but harnessed in, as designer sex toys are aligned with discourses of good taste and class distinction (Bourdieu, 1984; Skeggs, 1997), marketed as ornaments to be displayed rather than hidden away. Crucially, this branding of designer sex toys and the shops that sell them as tasteful is enacted – and topographically embedded – 'alongside the denotation of other sex toys [and shops] as taste*less*'.[81] Far from being a homogenous retail format, the sex shop is thus 'a varied and stratified concept'; as we move up or down the scale, the semiotics change, and, as an abject setting and workspace, Soho is a microcosm of this.[82]

In this sense, Soho *situates* our understanding of dirty work and its multiplicity of repulsions and attractions. As a workplace, it helps us to engage with the working lives of those who are condemned by its looming temptations, to borrow from Kristeva, and whose experiences of abject labour bring together the multiple taints associated with Soho as a workplace sector and setting that has, throughout its long history, been associated with physical, social and moral taint. Focusing on Soho as an abject work place also brings to the fore its enduring sense of community as well as the various ways in which abjection is subject to attempts to manage, market and regulate it.

Writing in the 1920s, Alec Waugh noted that Soho 'provides an air of intimacy that is to be got nowhere else',[83] and this atmosphere constitutes both the source, and the resources for coping with, the multiple taints with which working there continues to be associated. As we consider in the next chapter, for many of those who work in Soho's sex shops, their simultaneous attraction and repulsion to their workplace sector and setting, revolves – at least in part – around the place's capacity to compel and constrain different ways of being and of doing gender and sexuality.

5   No Place for a Lady?
Un/doing Gender and Sexuality in Soho

Soho has a long history of embracing gender fluidity. One of its more famous eighteenth-century residents was the Chevalier d'Eon, who moved relatively seamlessly between living as a man and as a woman and, in doing so, set the foundations for Soho's subsequent association with sex and gender as categories to be played with.

This discourse of 'playing' is widely used in contemporary Soho, with those who work in its sex shops frequently referring to the products on sale as adult toys to be used in playtimes and spaces. On the one hand, this notion of adult play emphasizes a widespread, historically and geographically grounded set of associations with Soho as London's adult playground, bringing together sex and entertainment in a highly concentrated locale. In doing so, it conveys something of the sexual fluidity and gender multiplicity with which Soho has historically been associated and continues to be so. However, it does so in a way that plays down the hyper-masculine, heteronormative orientation of much of its commercial sex culture and environment. The rhetoric of play also arguably trivializes the labour involved for those whose business is commercial sex, be they sales assistants, sex workers or erotic performers. In this sense, it implicitly renders their objectification and exploitation, not to mention the multiple risks and taints (see Chapter 4) attached to their work, relatively harmless.

As well as a long history of multiplicity, Soho has an equally long and enduring association with sexual appropriation. Its contemporary semiotic landscape, as discussed in Chapter 3, is replete with hyper-heteronormative depictions of sexual objectification, and signage attests to the continued commercial exploitation of the bodies and sexualities of women in particular. The presence of sex workers outside pubs and bars along Old Compton Street is also indicative of the transactional nature of many of the encounters that take place – or at least begin there. And it is no coincidence that the men training as pick-up artists practise the predatory techniques they have learnt in the classroom in field-based 'gaming' exercises in and around Soho's streets and bars.[1] Soho began as a hunting ground and remains so today. Yet it is also a place that attracts those whose sexualities, terms of identification and lifestyles position them as somehow outside of the mainstream, with many of those who live, work and consume in Soho gravitating there as a queer space of belonging and community, as discussed in Chapter 4. The tightly packed crowds taking part in a candlelight vigil on Old Compton Street the day after the mass shooting of LGBTQ people at the Pulse nightclub in Orlando, Florida, in June 2016 and the extent to which Soho remains a focal point for London's annual Pride festivities illustrate the sense of connection that the place provides at a collective level, just as the accounts discussed here of gravitating to and belonging in Soho as a community of outsiders do at a more individual level. As Judith Summers has put it, Soho's 'inherent tolerance has always offered the unconventional, the eccentric, the rebellious and the merely different a chance to be themselves'.[2]

In many ways, but particularly in its gendered and sexual landscape, Soho is a place of extremes. The complexities and contradictions that characterize the ways in which gender and sexuality are 'played out' in Soho make it a fascinating place to study and, seemingly, to work. It is important to consider these lived experiences against the wider backdrop of the gender dynamics of the sex industry, and relative to regulatory patterns of gentrification and feminization, as well as to the lived experiences of working there that are considered here.

Gender Dynamics in the Sex Industry

Hubbard (2004a) highlights the gendered injustices wrought by neoliberal ontologies of sexuality and regulatory policies shaping the contemporary sex industry in his critique of the imperatives underpinning urban gentrification, the pursuit of capital accumulation and a 'reinscription of patriarchal relations' in city centre 'playscapes' like Soho. He cites urban gentrification as demonstrating how the spatial regulation of sexuality is 'a crucial means by which (unequal) gender relations are reproduced'.[3]

Hubbard's critique emphasizes how the burden of displacement wrought by gentrification and neo-liberal policies designed to support capital accumulation falls unevenly on those involved in the commercial sex industry, illustrating this with reference to the banning of advertising for sexual services on the streets in central London – through the placement of cards in phone booths, for instance – as removing one of the methods by which independent sex workers were able to solicit for work, a spatial displacement from which (largely male) pimps and managers directly profited. Hence, while gentrification might be thought of as a process rooted in class politics, Hubbard emphasizes its gendered dimensions, showing how policies designed to remove street-level sex work, as part of wider efforts to clean up commercial sex and the settings in which it is concentrated, are 'no mere side-effect of the reassertion of capital' but are funda-mental in 'the reinscription of a virile masculinity'.[4] Following Hubbard, exposing this mutually constitutive relationship between capitalism and patriarchy fostered by neo-liberal urban policy – and understanding how it relates to evolving constructions and lived experiences of gender – is vital to making sense of the context and consequences of urban regulation and regeneration in places such as Soho in which commercial sex is concentrated in highly reified forms.

In terms of the gendering of sales-service work in a sex shop, 'traditional' sex shops such as those that continue to have a strong asso-ciative and material presence in Soho – largely perceived as 'a no-go area for women'[5] – are widely regarded as spaces of hegemonic masculinity from which women either exclude themselves[6] or should be protected. Yet at the same time (and through a related process), retail work has historically been socially constructed as 'women's work'. In particular, the relatively high demand for emotional labour within sex shops – Malina and Schmidt (1997), for instance note how exploitative pricing strategies in traditional sex shops rely on customers being ashamed and embar-rassed and on female staff to reassure them[7] – genders it as largely feminized. Hence, the gender construction of sales-service work in sex shops is interesting because on the one hand, important elements of the work have traditionally been associated with skills attributed to women in the labour market, particularly in terms of the performance of emotional, aesthetic and sexualized forms of labour discussed in Chapter 3, while on the other hand, sex shops (and particularly those associated with a place like Soho) tend to be perceived as distinctly male preserves, unsuitable 'for a lady' as Richard, one of the participants put it, and replete with male potency, as Hubbard argues.

Richard was the only participant in my study who did not want me to record our interview. However, he was insistent that I interviewed him when I asked, as he wanted to emphasize that there was 'nothing wrong' with his shop. I met him in 2009 when he worked in a now-closed unlicensed shop on Old Compton Street that specialized in spanking and schoolgirl-themed pornographic books, magazines and films (see Figures 16 and 17).

Richard seemed to be relatively ostracized from the rest of the sex shop working community: he made no references to the other shops, except to

Figure 16 Interiors of the shop where Richard worked, Old Compton Street

describe them somewhat disparagingly as 'novelty shops' or 'chains'. As he put it:

We're a specialist shop. We don't have any contact with the other shops. We keep ourselves to ourselves ... Some of the unlicensed shops are not as seedy as they used to be. We make much more money because the licences are so expensive, but they mean you can trade openly without any trouble.

['Meaning?'] We can sell what we want to, without being constantly scrutinized.

Richard's main concern during our discussion was to emphasize that Soho is a male space. He did not understand why, as an academic researcher, I would want to be somewhere like Soho, or what my 'husband was thinking of', 'letting' me do 'a project like this'. What was really interesting about our discussion was the extent to which he emphasized his strongly held view, one that he kept coming back to,

Figure 17 Interiors of the shop where Richard worked, Old Compton Street

namely that 'this is *not a job or a place for a lady*' (emphasis added). As he said: 'Well, some of the customers might like it, I suppose [being served by a woman], but I think it would invite trouble. We don't want or have any trouble'. When I asked Richard about the women in the shops (in the magazines, DVDs and promotional posters), he simply said that they 'weren't real'. I asked him if he meant that they were not *real* women (as in, just representations) or that they weren't real *women* (as in, not 'ladies', as he put it). He said, 'Both,' and we left it at that.

That Soho is seen as a predominantly, potently male space, unsuitable for 'ladies', real or otherwise, suggests that the men who are employed in the industry are perceived, at one level, as hyper-masculine. As Michael put it when explaining why he often gets people trying to give him their phone numbers, 'working here, people assume that you're always up for it, especially the blokes. People think that this must be the best job in the world for the guys, surrounded by sex all day.'

By the same token, those women who work in the sector are largely regarded, particularly by the older men such as Nathan and Richard, as (knowingly) sexually deviant or as (naively) objectified by the industry and by their male co-workers and customers. Nathan echoed Richard's view that the area and the sector was not really suitable for women, framing his concerns largely in terms of a discourse of protective paternalism, one that positioned women as sexually vulnerable in a place, and a sector, full of sexually predatory men. When he says 'it's just a male thing' he seems to be referring simultaneously to commercial sex (specifically porn), companies (shops) like his and Soho itself. Nathan summed up his view that this is 'just the nature of the beast':

You get more women than you used to. I mean it is a male-dominated field . . . It just always has been. Porn is aggressively made for men by men and that's the nature of the beast. More women are getting into it now, directing the making, but it's just always been . . . mainly male . . . from the films to the shops to . . . Most people who own companies like ours are men. It's just a male thing, here I mean.[8]

This perception of Soho as a male-only space has a long history. Indeed books depicting life in nineteenth- and early-twentieth-century Soho such as Stevenson's *Jekyll and Hyde*, Ransome's *Bohemia in London* and Conrad's *The Station Agent* (see Chapter 1) combined to produce a literary myth of male sociality that framed Soho as a largely masculine setting. Other commentators – such as Daniel Farson in the 1950s, and biographers of Paul Raymond and Murray Goldstein, as well as accounts of the vice squad and criminal gangs throughout the second half of the twentieth century – all contributed to sustaining this association.

Women have played a vital part in Soho's cultural and commercial history, but largely as those who are consumed rather than as active consumers. Perhaps this is what Richard was also alluding to when he said that Soho is no place for a lady: women are the objects rather than the subjects of its narrative. Speiser describes how Edwardian Soho was 'the world's largest flesh market, its streets after dark almost entirely given over to sexual commerce'.[9] Despite a contraction of the sex industry in the hundred years or so since then, and the movement of sex workers off the streets and into flats and massage parlours following the introduction of the Street Offences Act (1958), Soho today is not so different from this. Its reputation as a place where women are 'undone' by commercial sex endures, and the transactional nature of women's presence there is widely signified in the area's material and cultural landscape, replete with sexualized displays of women's bodies as objects to be consumed. Feminization strategies increasingly position women as consuming subjects – but these largely reinstate the gendered order there, as they do in the industry more widely, rather than represent a challenge to it.

Feminization techniques have arguably been used both to attract more female customers to Soho's sex shops and to regulate the industry and the area by challenging its hyper-masculine associations with the area's 'seedy' past.[10] Interweaving the normalization and feminization strategies discussed in Chapter 4, Shirley explained her thinking behind the aesthetic 'makeover' of the shop she worked in and which, as manager of the store, she had initiated and overseen:

The pink is to soften it up and . . . hopefully attract female customers. Sex is not a male-dominated area . . . So making it softer and more approachable from our side, it has helped with the number of single females that will walk in . . . whereas they will look at other stores and go, 'I will not walk in there on my own.' It's an image thing. You want women to come in here and be comfortable . . . I had a group of Australian ladies in a couple of weeks ago . . . They'd been dying to have a look because everybody's heard about Soho and it wasn't what they expected and they thought it was going to be male orientated and a bit grotty and . . . they were actually amazed at, you know, the layout and that it was like this. So yeah, it's breaking barriers. It's breaking that image that Soho had twenty or thirty years ago and trying to go, 'Hello world, actually, we're modern retailers!'

Evans et al. (2010) highlight the gendered assumptions that seem to connect Shirley's desire to aesthetically 'soften' the experience in order to provide a commercial space in which women can feel comfortable, in their discussion of female-orientated sex shops such as Ann Summers as 'postfeminist heterotopias'.[11] Echoing Shirley's emphasis on recognizing that sex is 'not a male-dominated area', and reflecting Judith Butler's critique of the 'heterosexual matrix',[12] they argue that, until recently, dominant discourses of gender and sexuality have connected masculinity with agentic sexuality and femininity with passive receptivity. Contemporary shifts in gender relations have somewhat blurred this, they suggest, producing a move away from female deference towards a more active, consumer-orientated, 'up for it' femininity, materialized in the kind of techniques Shirley describes. As Evans et al. put it, 'this re-signification has produced both new femininities centred on discourses of empowerment, liberation and rights to pleasure, and the emergence and mainstreaming of a consumer culture that addresses this new sexually assertive female consumer',[13] but (unlike Shirley) they are cautious about the extent to which this proffers anything akin to 'breaking barriers' or genuinely challenges the heteronormative hegemony that characterizes the commercial sex industry, especially in places like Soho.

A discourse of feminization, such as that alluded to by Shirley, is articulated largely through a consumer-orientated pursuit of pleasure, framed in terms of empowerment, liberation and autonomy. However, commercial in its orientation, this discourse focuses *rhetorically* on women's pleasure and sexual subjectivity, at the same time as it reproduces objectifying imagery of women's sexualized bodies in an industry that remains effectively a 'flesh market', as Speiser (2017) puts it. It does so not by challenging but by reinstating hegemonically heteronormative notions of feminine sexuality, as Shirley suggests in her references to 'softening' the encounter in order to make it more (commercially) appealing to women.

According to Evans et al., stores such as Ann Summers strategically manipulate both the women involved and the relevant legislation and licensing regulations, the latter because their stock consists largely of lingerie and hen-night novelty items.[14] This provides not only financial freedom from the cost of obtaining and maintaining a licence but also fewer limits on location (meaning that stores can be placed on high streets) and the ability to display sexually explicit stock in shop windows, prohibited in licensed stores. In contrast to the hyper-masculinity encoded into the more traditional shops in places like Soho, Ann Summers features

[c]handeliers, pink walls and subtle black and white prints of heterosexual couples and individual women [that] deepen the experiential connotations that distance Ann Summers semiotically from the problematic seedy male sexuality discourse.[15]

Evans et al.'s critique of this is based on their argument that, rather than challenge gender heteronormativity, this juxtaposition of male- and female-orientated sex shops as seedy and safe, respectively, serves to reinforce it, leaving the heterosexual matrix (Butler, 2000) intact and maintaining bifurcated expectations that associate femininity with wholesome, healthy sex and men with 'dirt'. And the women Evans et al. interviewed saw through this, criticizing both the presumption that women desired 'safeness' and that, by implication, men didn't.[16]

Crew and Martin (2017) show how a further, class-based oppositional binary is maintained by the upscaling practices associated with gentrification that Hubbard has written about. Their analysis suggests that such practices interweave class and gendered bifurcations of safety and dirt, showing how this has resulted, in recent years, in the commercial prolif-eration of erotic boutiques designed to contrast with 'perceptions of sex shops as dark, dirty, male-orientated and seedy'.[17] Their discussion of shops such as Agent Provocateur and Coco de Mer emphasizes how the commercialization and commodification of sexuality in these kinds of settings is 'both deeply classed and profoundly gendered'.[18] Reiterating Evans et al.'s critique, they also argue that shops such as Ann Summers connect to discourses of post-feminism insofar as 'via pink stores and products . . . they make claims of sexual empowerment and yet continue to emphasize the female body as sexual object'.[19] Crewe and Martin show how female-orientated sex shops use gendered signifiers such as light, colour and design to create a feminization of sexual consumption in order to produce what they describe as 'the acceptable face of the sex shop sector'.[20] What this means is that – a little like stereotypically gendered sections or stores aimed at young girls, replete with hearts, stars, pink and glitter[21] – the feminization of retail sex effectively 'undoes' women's sexualities in Butler's (2004) terms. In practice, this means that the complexities, multiplicities and contradictions that characterize lived embodied experiences are signified in simplistic, stereotypical ways that serve to reinstate heteronormative ways of being a 'real' woman, to borrow from Richard. Conforming to the terms of the heterosexual matrix (Butler, 1990/2000), this 'realness' is signified as biologically female, culturally feminine, sexually passive and almost ubiquitously pink.

For Crewe and Martin, this semiotic connection illustrates how the use of the colour pink not only genders sexuality in a hegemonically mascu-line, heteronormative way; in doing so, women's sexual agency is infanti-lized. This has a double effect: 'it both de-eroticizes the space in question *whilst at the same* time hinting at an intertwining of sex, childhood and commodification'.[22] In Soho's sexual landscape, this sets the scene, symbolically and spatially, for an adult corollary to the premature sex-ualization of young girls. This is materialized in very traditional shops such as the one where Richard worked – which (and not uniquely in the area), at the time I interviewed him, was packed with schoolgirl–themed pornographic magazines and films – *as well as* in shops claiming to be more female-orientated, feminist even, such as Ann Summers or the shop Shirley worked in. In commercial terms, this semiotic process and the shops in which it is materialized pave the way for women's sexuality to continually re-emerge as both the object and subject of consumption. This is a widespread phenomenon in the retail sex industry that continues to prop up the sector in places like Soho. In this sense, sex shops don't simply 'reveal'[23] different versions of masculinity and femininity: they actively, performatively construct them.

As Crewe and Martin put it, echoing Nathan's description of the retail porn industry as a 'male thing', most traditional sex shops are 'overwhelming masculinized spaces; produced for men, staffed predominantly by men and frequented largely by men'.[24] In contrast, the recurring use of the colour pink in female-orientated stores produces a set of semiotic and affective associations that position stores such as Ann Summers as female-friendly 'safe' spaces. Sh! in London's Hoxton straddles the distinction, mapped out by Crewe and Martin, between 'upscale' boutiques in which women are constructed as sexually knowledgeable, adventurous and skilled and the more accessible, feminized chains marketed at women presumed not to embody or to have the financial means to buy into this level of sexual distinction. But shops like this have no presence in Soho, at least not at the time of writing.

Malina and Schmidt's somewhat idealistic account of Sh! – written in 1997, when sex shops targeting women were still a relatively 'new and ground-breaking phenomenon', evokes the discourse of 'play' referred to at the start of this chapter. Their analysis, and the marketing material produced by the shop itself, positioning this 'playful' discourse as a largely feminist narrative, however, and Malina and Schmidt's account concludes that as a women-only sex shop Sh! offers 'unique opportunities for co-creations of a new service encounter – a female playspace'.[25] The latter suggests the emergence of women-only sex shops such as Sh! as simultaneously driven by 'an aesthetic of hedonistic consumption' concerned to cultivate new sensations and experiences and a feminist desire to create spaces in which women feel safe to experiment with these possibilities. In practice, they argue, this 'opens up scope for the innovative and creative inter-subjective construction of a service reality which may potentially go beyond what has been imagined before'.[26] Yet pink is also at the centre of their analysis of the store's interior: 'clever use of deep pink colour on the walls serves to envelop customers in a warm glow as they enter the shop. Such a drenching ... leaves customers in no doubt that Sh! is a woman's domain.'[27]

In stark contrast to this warm enveloping, and as discussed in Chapter 4, the masculinity associated with traditional sex shops is deemed to be a particularly 'dangerous' version of commercial sex – dirty, degraded and in need of being contained, controlled and concealed from view for fear of cross-contamination, a perception that underpins discursive practices such as zoning. These associations, and the gendered and classed bifurcations on which they depend, continue to dominate the retail sex environment in Soho, particularly its semiotic landscape and the look and feel of

Figure 18 'Traditional' Soho sex shops, Old Compton Street

many of the area's remaining sex shops, with their seemingly dated depictions of women's bodies and sexualities (see Figures 18 and 19).

The latter, and Richard's concerns about Soho being no place for a 'lady', echo views expressed by participants in McDowell and Court's study of the City of London, namely that the City is not a working community to which, beyond a relatively narrow set of hegemonically defined confines, women can ever really 'belong' in any meaningful sense. In the City, 'women are literally out of place'.[28] This same description in many ways also applies to Soho's sex shops, as Richard and many other participants stressed. In a sector and setting that is perceived by many as a 'no-go area for

Figure 19 'Traditional' Soho sex shops, Old Compton Street

women',[29] women are ubiquitous yet also somehow 'out of place', a view that Richard seemed to be alluding to in his reference to 'real women' not belonging there.

'Traditional' sex shops such as those found in Soho are deemed by many to be spaces of hegemonic masculinity from which women either exclude themselves (see Storr, 2003) or from which they should be protected. As noted, Nathan articulated a kind of protective paternalism in relation to women workers, whom he worried about employing, as well as women customers. With regard to the latter, he described his discomfort with women going into sex shops with their children: 'I mean ... I'm no prude, but when I see women walk in there with their kids, that's not right. It's just not right. What are they thinking?' This view may well reflect Soho's ethical code, in which Nathan and others were deeply embedded – one of non-judgemental openness towards all kinds of sexual identities and activities but *only* between consenting adults; involving children in any capacity is 'crossing a line', as Nathan and many others put it. It may also reflect a more implicit perception that only certain kinds of women are overtly sexual (e.g. 'those in the trade'), a view that I also encountered amongst older men working there, or amongst men who had worked there for some time, notably Nathan, Richard and Andy.

With regard to female shop workers, Nathan was particularly paterna-listically cautious about recruiting women to work in the shop he mana-ged on Brewer Street, in the heart of Soho's 'traditional' sex industry and night-time economy. As he put it:

We don't really have that many women really. You might get some turn up [to interviews] but they might be young and naive and you just ... you just think ... I don't know. It's hard to say really. I suppose half the things I say sound like I'm sexist, but ... I don't like this idea of leaving ... A normal shop's maybe not too bad, but say like the shop here – this is open 'til midnight, and I wouldn't feel comfortable with a female going home ... from here at midnight. I wouldn't feel comfortable with that.

So Soho continues to be viewed by many of those who work there as empirically and normatively a predominantly masculine space, one in and from which women need protection. Illustrating this, Nathan explained his concern about a male customer's apparent interest in a female mem-ber of staff in the sex shop where he worked, describing his protective sense of responsibility towards her as an older man, articulated largely with reference to her style of dress. To sum up his account, he was on the shop floor when a (male) customer came in with a big gift bag containing a large teddy bear (hinting at the infantilization of women discussed earlier in the chapter, and echoing his concerns about women's almost childlike naivety). He asked for one of the 'girls' by name, explaining that he was a regular. He was told that she wasn't there and left the gift to be passed on to her. Nathan explained what happened next:

As soon as he went I called the girl out and went, 'What's this?' and she described the bloke ... He'd been coming in every week buying her [small gifts], and I said, 'Well, just stop. Just stop. That's not healthy for you.' She's only young, twenty-one, pretty girl, blonde hair, used to wear high heels, miniskirts. I said, 'Don't dress like that.' Not that you tell someone ... As I say, I'm only forty, but I actually look at her and think, 'God, my daughters are going to be like that in a few years!' I used to say to her, 'You're in the sex industry and you don't want to be dressing like that because it is encouraging men.' Women should be able to wear what they want, but in this day and age? *Not in this industry, and certainly not in this place* [emphasis added].

Yet, at the same time, as noted, retail work is dominated by women and has been socially constructed as 'women's work'. Hence, on the one hand, sex shop work contains elements of sales-service labour traditionally associated with skills attributed to women, particularly in terms of the performance of emotional, aesthetic and sexualized forms of labour (see Chapter 3). Andy hints at this when he says that his shop always tries to organize the staffing schedules so that 'there's always a man and a woman on, purely on the basis that some people will feel more comfortable talking to someone of their own sex, others to a woman' (the implicit assumption here being that the customer is male).

Phoebe expressed similarly gendered assumptions about the emotional labour involved in dealing with male customers in the lingerie store in which she worked when she said, 'Men are lost little lambs in [a lingerie shop] pretty much, so they look to you [female staff] for guidance.' Yet, on the other hand, sex shops characteristically associated with Soho are thought of as largely male preserves, as Andy and Phoebe hint (even in a shop selling lingerie to be worn largely by women, the assumption is that the customer is male, even if he is a 'lost little lamb'). The 'real' shops are widely deemed to be unsuitable 'for a lady', as Richard put it.

As the manager of the store in which she worked, Shirley had other ideas, however, that she articulated with reference to her confidence in dealing with difficult or disruptive customers without resorting to the kind of protective paternalism described by Nathan:

There is a time in retail when, although the saying's the customer's always right, it's not always the case. There are occasions when they are wrong and they are out of order. If somebody comes in here [behaving inappropriately], I will have them off the premises straight away. Believe me, when I get into one of my firm moods, they don't argue with me. *So you don't need to rely on the blokes to back you up here. You can deal with it yourself and I'm more than capable of that* [emphasis added].

Daniel similarly alluded to customers' confidence in the store where he worked on Wardour Street in Soho, compared to the store where he was based previously, in a suburban shopping centre. As he put it, 'here, because of where we are, people don't mind, they're much more confident. It's because of where we are. Women especially are really confident coming in here. They know what they want and what they like.'

The workings of what Butler (1990/2000) describes as the heterosexual matrix mean that men who work in sex shops are often perceived as hyper-sexual: 'working here, people assume you're always up for it', as Michael put it. Women who work in the sector, especially in Soho, tend to be regarded as either sexually deviant or as objectified by the industry and by their male co-workers and customers. This theme emerged particularly when discussing the ways in which men and women present and perform their bodies while working in sex shops. As noted, Nathan in particular had long-standing concerns about employing young women in the shop he managed, referring explicitly to issues of sexual objectification and what he saw as women's vulnerability to male customers blurring bound-aries between retail and sex work. He saw his role as a manager as being to protect women from this, by influencing where in the shop they work (e.g. in the stock room at the back when predatory customers are in the store), by giving advice on how women should dress, and ideally, by not employ-ing them at all as he felt, as did Richard, that the industry in this particular setting was not suitable for women. The problem, as he articulates it in the following example, is not with male customers' behaviour but rather with women's own naivety. Whereas for Shirley it is the predatory custo-mer who is 'wrong' and 'out of order', for Nathan it is the 'girl' who was 'not right' for the sector and setting:

There was one girl, she was very naive … She came to the interview and she'd a skirt and tights and normal shoes and a blouse and looked very presentable, everything well done, had made the effort and that's one of the reasons why I gave her the job … but then literally *within a month I realised she was … not right*. I mean she was wearing miniskirts and little tops and heels, and I saw a bloke and I said [to her, when she was reaching down, exposing her legs], 'Don't do that again' … and then the same bloke came in again and he was going, 'Can I have a look at that on the top shelf?' so then literally she was going like that [reaching up] and literally I was saying, 'Nicola, stop. Just stop!', and I went, 'Get out the back!' and I just went up to this bloke and I said, 'I know what your game is' … He was about fifty, and I went, 'I know what your game is. This isn't the shop you think it is' (*emphasis added*).

Shirley conflated professionalism with a sexual neutralization of women's bodies in a way that echoed men working in the shops (see Chapter 3) when she referred to her own style of dress as a store manager and the expectations she had of how her staff should present themselves at work. In her description, she differentiates between those who work in sex shops ('serving the public') and sex workers in massage parlours and other commercial sex premises:

It's about professionalism … You know, I'm not trying to sell my products based on the fact that I've half a cleavage hanging out. That is completely unprofessional. Wherever you serve the public, you should be dressed accordingly. The only time I would expect to see people with half their tits hanging out is in probably a massage parlour because that's what they're being paid to do ... or on a lap-top dancing table [sic], you know.

Julie used similar language when referring to her desire to look professional in the store where she worked: 'Not showing cleavage or letting it all hang out ... it's all about the image you want to ... portray. It's the image that our particular company does want to portray.' Shirley also evoked the physical rather than aesthetic demands of the job as a significant factor contributing to how she dresses for work:

I re-merchandised this wall this morning, so I've been physically working. There's no point me having a skirt on being up a ladder, hence I wear jeans and I wear flat shoes because, one, it's health and safety – I've got a basement with steep stairs, so I'm not going to totter around in heels. And, two, the fact that I'm on my feet a lot of the day it's comfort as well ... So there's a comfort thing in there, [and] there's a professional image as well.

Shirley and Julie's respective evocations of professionalism provide an important counter, or at least a complement, to discursive references to sex shops as 'play' spaces, emphasizing (as Shirley in particular does), the work involved. Yet discursive references to play remain prevalent within accounts of women's experiences in particular of shopping and working in adult stores. As noted, some commentators have argued that the emergence of female-orientated stores such as Ann Summers or Sh! challenges traditional notions of sex shops as male domains, describing shops that have a strong feminized aesthetic or a female-only admission policy as 'gynocentric playspaces'[30] promoting a 'hedonistic femininity'.[31] Others, however, have reflected more critically on this development, questioning the extent to which a feminized sexual aesthetic or ethos disrupts the sexual objectification of women or provides scope for anything genuinely liberating. Meika Loe's (1999) discussion of Toy Box, an adult store based in Upland, California, explores the dynamics of these two perspectives, considering some of the practical issues they raise for sex shop workers and for the ways in which we understand their work.

Toy Box is a woman-owned and -run sex shop conceived at the end of the 1970s amidst a growing schism within the US women's movement shaped in part by differing views on pornography.[32] Loe outlines, through a relatively rare focus on the perspectives and experiences of workers, how changes in feminist politics between the 1970s and 1990s impacted on Toy Box and how the business negotiated the contrasting imperatives of a political project and profit accumulation. Loe undertook a total of eighty hours of observation at Toy Box, in its administrative offices, two retail outlets and in its mail order department, between December 1996 and June 1997, a methodological approach that provided insight into how the business works on a day-to-day basis, focusing on what makes Toy Box distinct from other male-owned or -orientated sex shops.[33]

Toy Box was formed, Loe argues, as a commercial reaction to what the owner saw as the typical American adult store at the time – 'associated with "lower class" men and "dirtiness" whose goals were penetration-centred and offered little or no sex information'.[34] Run as a sole proprietorship for fifteen years before it converted to a worker-owned cooperative in 1992, the Toy Box vision was to provide an alternative to the hegemonically masculine orientation of the industry in the form of a 'well lit, respectable enterprise' proffering advice and information and above all an orientation towards sexual empowerment in what Loe describes as 'a newly feminized sex world, attentive to women's sexual, informational and emotional needs'.[35] On the back of feminist consciousness-raising groups, women's health collectives and feminist-orientated sex therapy, Toy Box prefigured emerging tenets of post-feminism by framing shopping as the route to emancipation. As Loe sums it up, Toy Box put its own version of pro-sex feminism into practice in the marketplace, the result being a retail format that materialized its professed vision in two ways: first, through a product range that decentred penetration, emphasizing a playful, polymorphous sexual pleasure; and, second, in the form of a workplace structure that brought women's sexual knowledge, expertise and experience to the fore. Predating Apple's 'genius bars', Toy Box described its shop-floor workers as 'sexperts' who drew on their own sexual know-how and creativity to empower customers and to advise on safe sex practices (in a very similar vein to workers in Soho's sex shops – see Chapters 3 and 4). Loe explains how, by 'speaking a language that is taboo', Toy Box sexperts strove to create a physical and discursive space intended to raise awareness and boost customers' sexual understanding and confidence. In this sense, 'the business [was] premised around creating an alternative sexual space' for customers, particularly women.

This was not entirely unproblematic, however. As Loe also explains, the discursive openness raised issues that would be familiar to anyone who works in a sex shop in Soho: what to do about (mostly) predatory male customers who are stimulated by conversations and interactions with sex shop staff and who use the shops as spaces for direct sexual gratification. Feminization techniques are designed to discourage these kinds of customers, but they remained a perpetual issue at Toy Box, as they do in Soho, thwarting its attempts to be politically and commercially open, a tactic that, in practice, put workers in a relatively vulnerable position whilst purporting to 'empower' women.

This problem recurs in Soho, for men and women, and it is something that those who work there are constantly aware of. As Toby described it:

You get people coming on to you [all the time]. It doesn't matter if you're a boy or a girl, if you're sixteen or sixty. You know, everyone gets that. I mean you have to deal with it . . . It's the wrong shop and the wrong area to work in if you don't like that sort of attention. It really is. Like, I don't know anyone who [can walk] through Soho . . . and not have any trouble – anyone bug them, you know, follow them – you know, it's part of the job and especially . . . You're dealing with people who first of all are really desperate. They want some sort of release, or they've just come into get their little kick from looking at stuff, and you get people pulling their trousers down.

As noted earlier, the twin processes of feminization and gentrification that are repositioning sectors of the retail sex industry and giving rise to stores such as those described by Loe, and shops such as Sh! in London, are dependent upon a residual Other for their market and geographical differentiation – that is, a contrasting sector that continues to be perceived as dirty and dangerous because of its residual gender and class associations and/or because of its location. This role arguably continues to be filled by shops in Soho – and by the place itself.

At one level, this means that it would be very easy to contrast Soho as an anachronistic, phallocentric space with the more contemporary gynocentric or gentrified environments of other sex shops or settings. Yet, along with the idea that Soho is (only now?) becoming increasingly sanitized, that would be an oversimplification that would fail to do justice to the complexity and multiplicity that characterizes the place itself and its sex industry. In the main, and increasingly so, Soho's sex shops elide simple categorization, as Sanders-McDonagh and Peyrefitte (2018) emphasize in their analysis of Soho as a queer constellation shaped by sexual diversity. Yet it would also be remiss not to acknowledge the residual, hyper-heteronormative and hegemonically masculine nature of several of the remaining shops, signified perhaps most notably through their semiotic landscape and product range in particular.

In a fascinating account of city life, Harvey Molotch (2013) argues that goods on display in urban environments are 'instruments' – whether publically or privately consumed – through which urban life is made possible. Just as their production was the outcome of human endeavour, differentially undertaken by individuals and groups, so their consumption (commercially and perceptually) impacts upon social relations, including people's beliefs, actions and ways of relating to one another. These objects, as he puts it, 'are no less a part of urbanism as a way of life than are any other element'.[36] The almost uncanny, phallic ubiquity of sexual displays that constitutes the semiotic landscape of Soho's retail sex environment persists as a defining feature of the place and the sector, with penis-shaped 'toys' a feature of the product range in all of its sex shops.

Yet, as has been noted already, Soho is nothing if not complex and contradictory: theses about the area's concurrent sanitization and emergence as a queer constellation appear to attest to this. The area's historical associations, geographical positioning as an urban village and distinctive materiality, not to mention Soho's long-established reputation as a community of outsiders, all mean that, while the commercial sex industry there continues to 'undo' those men and women who are caught up in it, it also constitutes a space in which sexual objectification, exploitation and constraint can potentially be 'undone'. While self-avowedly feminist shops do not have an obvious presence there, at least not as yet, there are certainly signs that Soho's traditional sex shops are becoming increasingly anachronistic tourist attractions, under threat from development and commercial pressures, not to mention licensing enforcement, as the sector evolves into something that materializes less misogynistic ways of being, and of doing gender and sexuality. It is easy to lament Soho's growing commercialization and sanitization, losing sight of the historical waves of 'clean-up' campaigns that have long since punctuated the area's civic narrative, and, in doing so, underplaying the positive impact that community efforts have had on 'opening up' the place and its commercial sex industry, to borrow from Jason's phrasing.

This means that, in a complex and relatively compact assemblage of artefacts and associations, alongside a landscape composed of sexual objectification and hyper-masculine heteronormativity if not outright misogyny, those who work, live and consume (in) contemporary Soho increasingly also recognize many important aspects of the place that reflect its history as an eclectic community of outsiders offering those who don't feel as if they belong elsewhere a chance to be 'at home'. As discussed in Chapter 1, now and historically, as well as being a site of sexual exploitation *in extremis* – a 'flesh market', as Speiser describes it – Soho has also been a place in which gendered sexuality might be 'undone' (Butler, 2004). This means that the men and women who work there also see in Soho a place where the gender conventions that result in the presumption that men's sexuality is dirty and dangerous, and women's is – or ought to be – 'safe' and pink, might be unravelled in order to be done differently: this is a significant part of the 'edge' that attracts them to working in Soho and the possibilities it opens up.

Un/doing Sex and Gender Hegemonies in Soho

As Judith Summers has put it, Soho's 'inherent tolerance has always offered the unconventional, the eccentric, the rebellious and the merely different a chance to be themselves'.[37] The area's well-established reputation as an oasis of Otherness means that it has, throughout its history, been a socially, culturally and politically important place in which alternative ways of doing gender and sexuality might be possible and those who live outside of normative conventions might find recognition. In this sense, it is also a setting that provides some scope for challenging the normative expectations and exploitative associations considered so far in this chapter, one in which other ways of being and of relating to one another, socially and sexually, might flourish.

Over recent decades, developments in academic thinking and in social and cultural representations mean that a traditional conception of men and women as belonging to fixed, pre-social gender categories has been superseded or at least supplemented by a more performative way of thinking about gender as a process that is enacted within everyday social interactions and which is continually renegotiated. Such an approach highlights that gender is less 'a property' possessed by individuals or a category according to which men and women can be classified in binary, hierarchical terms. Instead, this performative approach emphasizes that gender is a *verb* – an ongoing fluid process enacted within social relations. Further, this approach emphasizes that this 'doing' of gender does not happen in a social vacuum: it is situated within the materiality, the combined history and geography, of particular social contexts, locations and settings, and is enacted within and through these assemblages.

In thinking about gender in this way, feminist writers such as Judith Butler play on the idea that, just as gender is always a process of doing, so too is it simultaneously an undoing. This refers both to the way in which we are 'unravelled' by the need to perform coherent, recognizable gender identities, yet at the same time the performative nature of these means that they can be 'undone' in order for gender to be re-enacted differently; in other words, just as we effectively create ourselves, so we can recreate ourselves. To illustrate how this 'un/doing' is undertaken performatively, Butler references drag artists who reveal, she argues, the extent to which all gender performances are citational enactments undertaken in the hope of being recognized by an appreciative audience; drag is therefore a performative metaphor she uses to refer to social interaction, or intersubjective recognition. It emphasizes that gender is not simply a free-floating performance but must be undertaken in such a way as to be accorded recognition of oneself as socially viable or, as she puts it, culturally intelligible.

It is on the recitation of gender norms over time that Butler focuses much of her attention, considering how citational practices frame social constructions as somehow pre-social or essential so that what is performed comes to be understood as naturally given. But gender performativities are also enacted within specific settings and places – they are socially and culturally situated, so that the normative expectations that shape gender performativity can and do change in different locales. Soho is an interesting example of one such setting, perhaps a 'heterotopia' in this sense, in which the place's 'anything goes' ethos contributes to the perception, widespread amongst many of those who work there, that the place opens up infinite possibilities for the performance and experience of gender and sexuality.

Arguably, in this sense, it is not just workers in Soho that un/do gender but the place itself. As discussed, the social materiality of the setting is heavily encoded with heteronormative, gendered imagery *at the same time* as it opens up the possibility for this to be challenged. The area's burgeoning shops, bars, restaurants; its history and geography; and the 'anything goes' ethos that shapes Soho as a working community all hint at this.

Of the many themes that recurred in the discussions I had with men and women working in Soho's sex shops throughout my years of research, it was this sense of Soho as being a place where 'anything can happen' that stood out as being a constant reference point, particularly for younger participants. Mark emphasized this when he described one of his favourite aspects of working there:

You know, the best thing for me is that we have straight guys that walk down here [into the basement sex shop], and because … most of the products we sell are aimed at a gay market, you know, the straight guys that do come down here, sometimes their faces fall, and they kind of run out all shocked and a bit hurt. You know, their pride's a bit dented because they've just been seen in a gay lifestyle shop. But you do get plenty – some straight, some gay, some whatever, men, women, couples – that come down and think, 'Oh, this is interesting. I haven't thought about this before.' And then they start chatting and exploring. It opens people up, do you know what I mean?
['In what sense?'] In every sense!
['When you say "it"?']
The place, the shop, the street … the whole thing [emphasis added].

If, as work settings, places 'do gender' rather than simply have it done to them, Soho is clearly a heavily masculine space, one that materializes the heterosexual matrix as Butler (1990/2000) outlines it. Yet, at the same time, it shows both the consequences of this for 'unravelling' those subject to its normative ethos *as well as* providing the material setting for this normativity to be challenged, opening up the possibility to be Other, to exist as a recognition-based erotic community, as Mark implies.

Soho has a long history of making 'trouble' with fixed identity categories, including those shaping gender and sexuality. From the Chevalier d'Eon to Madame Jojo's renowned drag queens, diverse ways of being have always 'taken place' there. In contemporary Soho, this is perhaps most obviously apparent in and around Old Compton Street, with its presence of lifestyle stores orientated towards gay male customers; a proliferation of bars, restaurants and clubs such as GAY put out the 'welcome' mat and rainbow flags fly year round, rather than being largely reserved for Pride, as they tend to be in other places. Arguably this process has begun to challenge the heteronormative parameters of the hegemonically 'male thing' described by Nathan.

Suggesting this in their queer reading of Soho's retail sex industry, Erin Sanders-McDonagh and Magali Peyrefitte argue that the 'deviant' and transgressive history of the locale means that Soho's sex shops are able to transcend gendered and sexual boundaries. They focus on the importance of Soho as a setting that has historically celebrated queerness, a history that has enabled a coalescence of sex shops located in close proximity to one another to cater for diverse clientele. Rather than reifying normative sexual scripts, or infantilizing women, they argue that Soho's sexual community problematizes categorization, eliding the classification of women as sexual agents who are simultaneously sexually objectified, ostensibly disrupting hegemonic gender regimes in a place that, in their view, constitutes a 'queer constellation'[38] as a result, one that problematizes the classification of sex shops according to binary constructs.

Potentially signalling, or at least hinting at, an undoing of gender in Butler's terms, this contrasts with Crewe and Martin's (2016) account of sex shops as 'overwhelmingly masculine spaces; produced for men, staffed predominantly by men and frequented largely by men'[39], and resonates instead with the view that this heteronormative male dominance is giving way to a commercial sexual culture and economy that is more fluid – or at least might do so in the future.

While the focus here is on sex shops as commercial settings, it is important to explore the extent to which Soho exists as – or might become – a queer constellation 'beyond consumption', however, and to think about what this might mean for gender and sexuality outside of the commercial exchange of goods and services if we are to posit Soho as a working erotic community that somehow exists beyond the narrow confines of merely transactional relations. As noted, Soho's many sex shops are important sites of advice and support for men and women, including those in the LGBTQ and other communities. For Soho to be a queer constellation in a meaningful way, therefore, means moving beyond simply orientating its sex shops to a range of sexual interests and points of identification and towards materializing the ethos of openness that characterizes Soho as a working community. As an example of this, my observational research emphasized the extent to which the shops are often used not just as sources of advice or support but simply as social reference points, as part of the wider community, and as a 'hub' around which its ethos revolves. Jason (one of the co-owners of a gay lifestyle store on Old Compton Street) touched on this when he described the importance of the setting to the store's orientation in a place that, as he puts it, 'opens the door' for people to feel part of something:

[Soho is] a village and I think that's really important . . . It's a village in the centre of a really big city, and its got all walks of life and I think that, you know, if you've got any attitudes or issues like racism or homophobia or any bigotry . . . there's no point in you being in Soho. I think . . . because Soho's grown up with an emphasis on the sex industry . . . then obviously the gay market has kind of come along and claimed it for their own as well. So I guess, you know, when you start from that point, you're already . . . opening up the door for people that . . . aren't afraid to be different or people who are, you know, doing what they do and not ashamed of it. I think that filters through to the general population in the area who are here because they find they're all part of it.

Jason's emphasis on Soho as a place that is not simply open to difference but proactively welcomes it contrasts markedly with Richard's assertion that it is 'no place for a lady'. The persistence of hyper-masculine heteronormativity in the aesthetics and product ranges of the shops there, and in the sector's semiotic landscape, combined with the abject nature of the work undertaken, and of the place itself, raise the question of what it is that attracts those who work in Soho's sex shops to the sector and the setting and to their sense of Soho as a working community.

Echoing Jason, and Mark's emphasis on recognition cited earlier, participants such as Michael talked on a number of occasions about the ways in which those who 'do something different' with gender and sexuality – that is, those who perform their gendered and sexual selves, and relate to others, in ways that deviate from the terms of cultural intelligibility established by the heterosexual matrix (Butler, 2000) – seem to 'get a lot of courage' from Soho:

Lots of people round here wear clothes that I would not have the courage to wear – you know, like huge leopard skin fake-fur coats and really, really tight black jeans and loads of lipstick; and ... I think, 'I'd love to have the courage to wear that because it does look really good and it works around here'. I mean if [where he lives in East London] had that sort of person walking down the road, you'd have people pointing and laughing, but here it's the other way 'round, and people [who are] like that rule here ... I think it's great and this is the only stretch ... where you actually see men [and men] and women [and women] walking hand in hand and kissing and I think that's really great ... It's almost like it gives people ... Some people get a lot of courage from around here. I really do believe that.

['Have you felt that yourself?'] Oh yeah. Definitely. It's opened me up!

For Stewart it was precisely its gendered and sexual multiplicity that attracted him to Soho, and it is this that sustains his fascination with the place and its people:

We get everything and everyone in here [the shop where he works]. All walks of life. I love the madness of it all, absolutely love it ... We get them all in here. Glamour girls and macho men and *everything* in between, and I mean everything. What's not to love?

Workers such as Michael and Stewart were less interested in the business side of the sex industry than they were in the meanings attached to their own work experiences in what they saw as a relatively radical work environment which enabled them to be sexually fluid, to talk about sex in a mutually open and supportive environment, and to have what they regarded as a relatively significant degree of flexibility and autonomy. In this sense, their views echo those of some of the women interviewed by Loe (1999). One of the 'sexperts' Loe talked to, Liza, explained:

I had an idea about work that was essentially exploitative, and here was a place [Toy Box] where everyone was intelligent and interesting and had a lot of auton-omy, and the boss listened to the workers' ideas. The job just really matched with my critical ideals.[40]

Emphasizing the importance of what she calls 'the scenography of pro-duction' – the relationship between gender performativity, materiality and signification – Butler's (2004) analysis of gender as a perpetual process of 'un/doing' highlights both the agentive capacity of the subject and the constraints that compel and/or restrict particular performances. In her discussion of the latter, she focuses specifically on the dialectical interplay between 'what it might mean to undo restrictively normative conceptions of sexual and gendered life' and the matrices of cultural intelligibility that shape the hegemonic performance of gender in ways that will be accorded recognition according to the terms of the hetero-sexual matrix.[41] The latter involves a process that Butler describes as 'becoming undone',[42] denoting the ways in which the complexity of lived subjectivity becomes conflated, unravelled so to speak, in the construction of a self that is compelled or constrained in particular ways in order to become socially acceptable. The basis of her critique is that this perpetual process of un/doing 'imposes a model of coherent gendered life that demeans the complex ways in which gendered lives are crafted and lived'[43]; to put it simply, the terms of reference, as the conditions of recognition of oneself as a viable social being, mean that the 'everything in between' so admired by Stewart becomes a simple either/or.

What abject labour, performed and experienced in places like Soho, potentially opens up (to borrow from Michael) is the possibility of reinstating and resignifying some of this complexity, reclaiming 'the sheer madness of it all', as Stewart put it. The opportunity to 'do something different', as Julie described her work, provides a sense of being able to challenge, even in a relatively minor way, the terms of the heterosexual matrix or 'presumptive heterosexuality' as Butler has put it in her more recent writing.[44] The possibilities associated with being able to 'make trouble' with gender, to borrow from Butler (1990/2000), in part at least explain the attraction of abject labour and of Soho as a working community for those who seek not to clean up their work, or their place of work, but to revel in Soho's 'edgy' reputation and possibilities to be and do things differently. But those who work there, as noted, are also reflexively aware of the risks attached to this – not simply to the impact of periodic attempts to sanitize Soho but also to themselves as workers in an environment that can be violent, predatory and, on occasion, repulsive. As well as a discourse of play, therefore, reference was frequently made to the significance of safety, not as a way of articulating the protective paternalism to which Nathan referred, or as an essentialist taming of women's sexuality through a 'feminization' of the sector and setting, but as a collective, community endeavour characterized by mutual respect and security for those working in Soho's commercial sex industry. In this sense, men and women working in the sex shops frequently identified with those working in nearby hostess bars and clubs and in the many massage parlours and flats from which sex workers operated: at the risk of romanticizing, this was not simply or instrumentally as part of a clustered market but as an important component of what they perceived as a working community in which, as Julie summed it up, 'everyone's got each others' backs'. For men and women working in the shops, the safety and security of Soho's sex workers, and their vulnerability to risk, was a particular concern.

Safe Sex: Redoing Gender/Regulating Risk

Sanders and Campbell's (2007) account of sex workers' vulnerability to violence emphasizes the importance of location and setting in shaping the risks involved. The sex workers, receptionists and managers of brothels they interviewed reported experiencing a range of nuisance behaviours and violations from clients '*because of the precarious nature of the environment as a clandestine and unregulated industry*'.[45] A little like sex shop workers in Soho, the risks to which the sex workers in their study were subject included robbery, making physical threats, using offensive language or (more specifically for the sex workers) demanding sexual services beyond what has been agreed and paid for.

Comparing the experiences of those who work on the street and those who work from indoor sex work venues, of which there are many in Soho, Sanders and Campbell argue that the vulnerabilities surrounding work-based hazards are 'dependent on the environment in which sex is sold'.[46] They highlight some of the protection strategies that indoor workers and managers develop to maintain both physical safety (security cameras and other technologies such as panic buttons, for instance) and a sense of self that is separate from sex work (e.g. through the use of shared, coded humour and separate names for work and life outside of work – see also Sanders 2004). The non-negotiable use of condoms is a pertinent example of sex workers' need to protect their sexual health and maintain a distinction between commercial sex and intimacy in their non-working lives. Customers who disrespect this are perceived and experienced as particularly threatening, evoking a sense of 'disgust'. As one of Sanders and Campbell's participants described it, referring to a customer who removed his condom part way through sex: 'I don't do nothing without and I really felt like he'd raped me, he'd defiled me'.[47]

Attuned to the regularity with which this particular violation and others occurs, sex workers are highly sensitive to customers' mannerisms and the tone of interactions, becoming skilled in what O'Neill and Barbaret call 'gentling' – using verbal and body language to calm anxiety, and to smooth over potential conflict and threat.[48] This enables sex workers to take some individual and collective control and to assume a shared responsibility for their safety and security, deploying 'collective emotional labour' as a community-based coping mechanism[49] and tactical deployment of their skills in gentling. Sanders and Campbell emphasize the significance of this in sex work when they note that 'the everyday culture of *the collective working environment . . . promotes a certain degree of altruism in a competitive business*'.[50] To support this, and to build it into the social material environment of sex work, they argue that it is possible to go a considerable way towards 'designing out' vulnerability in sex work, not only through physical and organizational measures but also through building a culture of mutual respect within the commercial sex industry. Doing so would involve, at least in part, promoting mechanisms through which working communities can be sustained, by developing policies, as well as licensing and legislative measures that promote the employment and human rights of those who work in commercial sex, they argue.

As one of the primary mechanisms for regulating sex shops, this suggests that legislation and licensing could make an important contribution to the management of vulnerability for the men and women who work in places like Soho. Some feminists argue that stringent regulation of the sex industry results in the increased persecution of sex workers in particular, targeting poor women and immigrant workers whose lives are already precarious. Others suggest that carefully crafted and respectfully, collectively enforced regulation could help to protect those working in the sex industry. Much of the focus of this discussion has been on sex workers, to the extent that relatively limited consideration has been given to those working in the retail side of the commercial sex industry and who (albeit in different ways) see themselves as part of the working communities in which sex workers – and others employed in sex venues and other 'adult entertainment' or sex establishment premises – operate.

Recognizing this would involve something of a shift in orientation, with licensing becoming premised upon a desire to build respect into the regulation of commercial sex rather than simply to contain and control dirt or to generate revenue. Campaigners for the rights of sex workers highlight the importance of a 'sex as work' agenda to securing safer working conditions within the industry, shifting from a 'discourse of disposability' that incites violence and disrespect to a right-based orientation.[51] What Michael, Julie and others suggest through the ways in which they articulate their sense of Soho as a working community is that this discourse of recognition and rights, one that is already in existence within debates on the licensing and regulation of sex work, be extended to the whole commercial sex community.

To recap on issues covered in Chapter 2, the regulation of sex shops, including those in Soho, focuses largely on the rights and responsibilities of licence holders, namely those who own and/or manage shops, and is designed largely to protect the rights of those who consume there and (arguably to a lesser degree) local residents and other workers. Yet licensing could, and arguably should, make a contribution to protecting the rights of those working across the full spectrum of commercial sex. To date, regulation seems to have been largely driven by a desire, typically on the part of local governments, developers and investors, to contain the 'secondary effects' of the sex industry. Such was the case in the Times Square area of New York (Cook, 2005). Cook argues that 'protectionist notions of women and children serve as justification for the moral condemnation of the sex business',[52] with commercial and controlling interests being thinly disguised under a pro-feminist veneer. And such is the case in Soho, in which the interests of regulatory and legislative bodies, commercial developers, property owners and consumers are frequently prioritized over the rights of those who work there, including the right to workplace safety and security, free from the risk of violence and exploitation.

Maintaining Soho's vibrancy and viability as a residential and working community, not beyond but because of its 'edge', represents an ongoing challenge for those who live and work there. For many, Soho is a place where gender hegemony can be 'undone', but the place seems to be at perpetual risk of becoming undone itself, and, without sustainable support for the rights of those who live and work there, this remains a significant problem. Understanding Soho as a working community and regulating the licensed environment in a way that recognizes the rights of those working in the commercial sex industry there, rather than focusing on protecting Soho from them, could be an important step towards securing the area and the sector's intertwined future. Soho's sex shops are more than simply places to buy things: they have almost come full circle to being seen as part of 'old' Soho that needs to be protected from corporate overdevelopment and sanitization. Without them, Soho risks losing a significant component of what it is about the place that continually opens up the possibility of being Other.

Conclusion
Rhythm Is Our Business

The preceding chapters have argued that Soho's distinctive history and location, its architectural character and its spatial layout dynamically combine to make it the workplace that it is. Its rhythms are less a pause in the flows of traffic, people and capital in the spaces that surround it and more a change of tempo – its constant resurgence and reinvention characteristic of its past, present and, no doubt, its future. The grand commercial thoroughfares of Oxford Street and Regent Street and the theatre districts of Leicester Square and Shaftesbury Avenue have, throughout their existence, backed onto Soho's narrow streets and alleyways. The latter have provided the sites of production for these commercial front stages, and they have endured as an escape from their conventional pleasures and performative pressures. The rush of public transport that surrounds Soho has never cut through its streets, many of which remain largely pedestrian or relatively inaccessible to fast-moving traffic. Soho's proximity to the palaces of Westminster and Whitehall, to the clubs of St James's and Pall Mall, and to the Inns of Court and the Old Bailey means that it has long since been a playground for those privileged enough to afford it. It has also been a haven for those deemed not to fit in anywhere else throughout its history. As Frank Mort has described it, Soho's geographical closeness to London's sites of legal, political and commercial power 'generated social and sexual meanings that were enormously fluid, ... played out in the social spaces of everyday metropolitan life'.[1]

The area's organizational geography and colourful past combine to shape Soho into a place of largely commercial sexual encounter. This has been made possible by its narrow streets, courts and alleys that have, throughout its history, housed small-scale industries, workshops and labouring families, at the same time (and often in the same spaces) that they have sheltered cruising, soliciting, spectating and sexual exchanges of all kinds. The material fabric of Soho's built environment has given rise to the meanings with which it has come to be associated, and vice versa. Its distinctive urban landscape 'was and still is porous and multilayered'.[2] This is what has fascinated cultural historians and urban geographers and what has attracted people to Soho since its earliest days as a royal hunting ground. It is what entices men and women to work in its sex shops and what keeps customers visiting those shops, even (perhaps especially) when much of what is on sale in those shops could be acquired more cheaply and easily, not to mention discreetly, online. The practically limitless capacity of capitalism to commercially exploit desire creates and sustains a seemingly inexhaustible sexual marketplace that the active preservation of Soho as a distinctive workplace sector and setting continues to serve. But Soho is more than simply, cynically, capital's playground; it is a thriving community, an urban village and a place where those who do not, or cannot, conform to what or who society expects them to be can find a sense of recognition and belonging, a place to be and 'do' themselves.

In the last three decades or so, Soho has undergone a considerable transformation shaped by a combination of licensing regulation, local community initiatives, and entrepreneurial activity, particularly the expansion of companies specializing in new media and communication technologies. Premises deemed suitable for sex-related businesses continue to command inflated rents, a process that has effectively squeezed out many local traders not directly connected with the sex industry, and even many of those that are, but who are not protected by the shelter of a multinational corporate brand, favourable redevelopment opportunities, or cashing in on the area's LGBTQ market. Yet even though much of the material that is sold in Soho's many sex shops can now be bought online, sex shops continue to thrive; what attracts their many customers is 'the lure of the local'[3] – it is the place itself that draws people to Soho, at the same time as arguably tainting those who shop and work there with the stigma of the area and sector's enduring global reputation for sleaze.

In the final third of the twentieth century, Soho went through what Hutton describes as a rather 'ugly phase'.[4] From the end of the 1950s to the early 1990s, what was being done to Soho, and in the name of Soho, was particularly unattractive. But with a sense of optimism that characterizes both historical accounts and the spirit of the place itself, Hutton sees this as simply a 'hiccup in its long history', noting how, before too long, Soho's working and residential communities mobilized under the auspices of the Soho Society supporting the kind of revivification that has kept Soho going for centuries. Today, Soho's sex shops are limited in number and are tightly regulated and licensed, but the dialectical interplay between Soho as a sector and as a setting means that the area's sex industry retains a distinctive character as what seems to be a surprisingly tight-knit working community. Those shops that are thriving best are situated on its main thoroughfares; they are the shops that have rein-vented themselves as 'lifestyle stores' and which are well integrated into Soho life. No less explicit for it, they have themselves undergone a kind of 'coming out', materializing a changing ethos of openness and experimen-tation which seems to have moved on from the more 'traditional' shops that appear to be struggling to maintain a presence and a market. How long the latter will be sustainable remains to be seen. In the decade or so that I have been researching Soho, the retail landscape has changed considerably in a relatively short period of time. An extract from one of my field notes, made on a Sunday afternoon in April 2018, gives a feel for this:

Massive development work contracted largely by Soho Estates is being under-taken throughout Soho, especially along Old Compton Street and Berwick Street/ Walker's Court. There is also a major Crossrail development on the North side. Berwick Street Market has changed beyond recognition – it now sells street food primarily and is a lunchtime destination for office workers in the area. It is busy but not vibrant in the way that it has been, even during the time in which I have been studying Soho.

The remaining sex shop on Walker's Court feels out of place and time. Contractors walk around it like it is an architectural dig or a protected colony of newts on a building site. They seem to treat it with care and respect, like a relic, but don't seem to know what to make of it.

Soho is busy and lively, packed with bars and restaurants. The shops seem to have come full circle – they now feel like part of 'old Soho', a dimension of its historical 'edge' that local workers and residents are keen to protect, but the rent situation means that the sex industry pushed up rents which are now forcing small, local businesses out (including, in a 'what goes around come around' kind of logic', many of the shops).

Many of the remaining shops are either 'high-street' brands catering to women, focusing on online retail, or are specialist (largely gay lifestyle) stores. In compar-ison, the 'traditional' stores feel anachronistic. The combined effects of gentrifica-tion, sanitization, rent and rate increases and a creeping 'mainstreaming', as well as a strong corporate presence, can be felt and heard in the constant drilling and digging (the constant noise and vibration must be awful for those working and living in the vicinity, especially of the Walker's Court development). 'Work in progress' signs are everywhere, and this seems poignantly apt for the whole place.

The shops seem to be a bit of a tourist attraction – groups of international school and college students take photos and point, but many people are regularly leaving with large carriers bags (they are not just browsing or experiencing the shops but shopping in them). I still find this surprising. Why is this? Why do people shop there where everything seems so dated and overpriced, and when they could just buy online??

By comparison to the shops in and around Walker's Court, the atmosphere in the 'high-street' shops (all those outside of Greene and Walker's Court) is welcoming, bright and lively – sales staff are busy providing guidance and directions and are chatting with customers.

During the decade or so in which I have been studying Soho, increasing gender multiplicity and sexual fluidity, social awareness of everyone's rights to live free from sexual violence, oppression and exploitation and changing consumer practices facilitated by advancing media technologies, combined with licensing regulations and enforcement, all seem to have had a considerable impact on Soho's commercial sex industry. Against this backdrop, many aspects of Soho are thriving or, at the very least, enduring. Its material and cultural infrastructures are continually threatened by building works and property development, however (as reflected on in my field notes entry), and many commentators are increasingly concerned about sanitization. In his book *Soho Society*, Bernie Katz (a frontman of the Groucho Club and self-styled 'Prince of Soho') refers to the area as 'a very naughty and honourable place'. Yet even he, with a knowing self-irony, acknowledges the growing presence of high-profile members' clubs and steady gentrification.[5] A notable example is the international chain of members' clubs, Soho House.

As I sit working on final edits to the book, the second ambulance of the (still early) morning rushes past the café window on Old Compton Street. News is circulated via a community chat group warning local workers not to approach drug dealers, as a man who asked them to move on from outside his front door was stabbed. And the woman on the table next to me, having spent some time telling everyone within ear shot how much she loves the 'crowd' in Soho, proudly announces that she has reached a decision – she is having the crushed avocado and quinoa for brunch, along with the orange juice, but only if the waiter can assure her that the latter is freshly pressed, not chilled. For me, these juxtapositions sum up working life in contemporary Soho – precarious in its pretensions and often pretentious in its precarity. Again though, this is nothing new, and had I been writing *Soho at Work* in the eighteenth, nineteenth or twentieth century, much the same could probably have been written in the Conclusion.

Current threats of over-development are met, however, with fierce opposition from those who seek to maintain the distinctive local character of the area in the face of a growing corporate presence.[6] Soho champions such as the actor, writer and presenter Stephen Fry have joined forces to defend Soho's spirit, particularly in the face of the Crossrail development. For Fry (and many others), 'Soho is not just a metropolitan enclave ... [I]t is a focus, a magnet for the young, creative and open-minded.'[7]

The discussions emerging from these clashing interests and imperatives signify complex intersections between capital, commerce and community; arguably Soho's sex industry is at the heart of these intersections as both a cause and consequence of the area's (simultaneously) warm embrace and exploitative nature. Struggles over Soho's redevelopment have become an important discursive focal point for articulating differing views on the character and role of Soho's sex shops during a period in its colourful and compelling history when it is negotiating transformations in its built environment and social fabric.

In this sense, Soho continues to intrigue – academics, writers and artists still seem to be fascinated by it, and it is a magnet for consumers, theatregoers and revellers with a thriving night-time economy. Something about it remains 'edgy' and enticing, generous and seductive. As Hutton evocatively puts it, like a good wine it has aged well, and it should be savoured, not abused; his latter point seems to be aimed particularly at those who claim to be 'saving' Soho but in the process risk killing it off all together.

Soho's much-written-about urban renaissance since the 1990s has been the result of rebranding, redevelopment and a deliberate promotion of the area's cosmopolitan ambience. None of this is new: this combination takes on different orientations and different forms, mobilizing around different discourses, at various points throughout Soho's narrative. Throughout this history Soho has been known as a place in which appetites of various kinds could be, if not satisfied, at least indulged or whetted. As Mort has put it, 'food, sex and night-time entertainment are regularly rebranded'.[8] Embedded in the area's compressed urban space is a distillation of excess which means that, while successive generations of publicists have reinvented Soho, their reference points are always grounded in the area's distinctive geography, history, economy and culture: 'the resourceful recycling of the district's distinctive urban myths is an important part of Soho's claim to cultural authority'.[9] The combined processes of making, living *and working* history are an important part of the psycho-geographies of city life, as many London literary figures have argued. But Soho does not lend itself to the strolling demeanour of the flâneur; the vibrancy of Soho life is to be found in its bars, restaurants, cafés, clubs and shops, as well as in its courts, alleyways and dead ends; it is not a place to see and be seen but rather a place to hide, as Stevenson so eloquently captured in his positioning of Dr Jekyll's ill-fated alter ego as one of the area's more infamous residents. Soho's essence is in its intimate social and commercial spaces and the sex industry has always been, and remains, a vital part of that.

In contemporary Soho, chic boutique shops, restaurants and hotels coexist alongside high levels of social deprivation. A sense of estrangement and dislocation is intermingled with spaces housing communal allotments, and the 'village' primary school that has been on its current site in Great Windmill Street since 1872.[10] Drug users and dealers, trafficked sex workers and homeless people from across the world are as much a part of what makes Soho the place it is today as are the exclusive members' clubs, five-star restaurants, chain-store coffee shops and global corporations that dominate its post-production film and media industry. Much of the area's night-time economy is fuelled by stag and hen nights, by excessive alcohol and drug use, and by anti-social behaviour; these remain significant features of Soho's after-hours nightlife, causing noise and nuisance to the area's working and residential population.

But Soho's cosmopolitan pleasures, its lure, continue to rely on its dangerous and transgressive associations, historical and contemporary, including their abject manifestations in what makes Soho, even today, an often discomforting place. As Mort emphasizes, perhaps nowhere more than Soho (in contemporary London at least) reveals how pleasure and danger are a part of the ongoing appeal of city life.

Soho is complex and contradictory, and it is nothing if not phoenix-like, capable of rising from its own ashes more colourful and flamboyant than ever before. Poet Laureate John Dryden, one of its many famous inhabitants, noted this with reference to the city as a whole; more recently, London biographer Peter Ackroyd has argued that London is defined by a 'magical energy' that enables it to continually revivify itself.[11]

Of all the many and varied regions of London, Soho is the one that has perhaps preserved its appearance the most. As Ackroyd goes on to note, 'in Soho every street is a memorial'.[12] But Soho is no living or working museum: conviviality and community have always been at the heart of the place, and the proliferation of places to eat, drink and be merry does not sound its death knell but yet another chapter in its long and continually evolving history. A pattern of 'deliquescence and renewal' is at the heart of Soho life.[13] To borrow from Benjamin, Soho deserves a stereoscopic approach so as not to fall into short-sighted, historically dislocated proclamations of its contemporary demise, as in reality there is not one Soho but many, and 'going downhill' has often been the area's descriptor, if not its wry ambition. Soho consists of lives lived in parallel, sometimes intertwining – as in the case of the working community described here – but sometimes these are in conflict or are living or looking past each other. This is part, but only part, of what makes it so fascinating and, presumably, for those seek to control, regulate and develop it, so frustrating.

Ultimately, as Speiser has argued, 'Soho belongs to the people who work there'.[14] For Michael, there will always be something distinctively, even anachronistically, 'Soho' that the sex industry plays a part in: 'There is something about this place. I can't put my finger on it. It's tacky, and seedy, and a bit of a time warp. But it is really lively and different things at different times of the day, on different days.' Julie expressed a similar feeling that she also found difficult to put into words: 'Soho is a special kind of place ... It's, it's hard to say what and why that is. I've found myself very drawn to it in some ways. It captures something that I'm looking for. But I can't see myself here forever.' Asked why not, she replied, 'The hours, getting here – it's not somewhere you can work for long ... The place is changing, but it always does. Where doesn't?'

Evoking similar sentiments to Michael and Julie, and referring specifically to the area's enduring legacy, Speiser notes how 'Soho's streets, its businesses, its world of entertainment as well as its people, and [its] unique mix of all of these ... explains why Soho is as fascinating today as it was 200 years ago'.[15] Somehow, as he describes it, Soho has retained its global reputation as a potentially dangerous place. Speiser also laments, however:

There is much talk of the decline of the area's character due to gentrification, redevelopment and rising rents, as well as the fear that this will lead to the exodus of the remaining traditional businesses and the colourful communities.[16]

But the strong impression that accounts such as Speiser's gives – and which the men and women who work in Soho emphasize – is that the marks that Soho's history have left on the place are hard to erase. Try as the planners and developers might, Soho is one of the few places in London to retain a distinctive character that connects its history, geography, culture and economy. Concerns over Soho's decline go back to at least the eighteenth century, if not earlier. Whether from bombs, brands or bulldozers, the story so far suggests that Soho thrives most when under pressure.[17] Although the shadow of redevelopment is constantly cast over contemporary Soho, with the Walker's Court and Berwick Street Market area being re-modelled at the time of writing, Soho will somehow, in some form, prevail.

Echoing the views of sex shop workers discussed here, and despite what he describes as a tidal wave of gentrification and globalization hitting the area since the 1990s, long-term resident and film producer Colin Vaines concludes his interview-based recollections on six decades of Soho life by emphasizing the area's enduring character as a working and residential community:

Soho has always been a village and historically it's been a village full of low-lifers and high-lifers, romantics and realists, drunks and dreamers, sex workers and bar workers – every walk of life is represented. But one thing binds us together – a ferocious loyalty to the place. Even though the alleyway on which I live could accurately be described as 'dodgy', it still feels the safest place I've ever called home. People have always looked out for each other in Soho, and if a girlfriend was ever bothered by a random guy as she was unlocking the door to my house, you could bet that a local dealer, working girl or strip-club caller would be at her side like a shot, checking that she was OK.[18]

With all of this in mind, and to return to where *Soho at Work* began, the book's attempts to map out an ethnographic, organizational geography have tried to highlight the importance of place to understanding how, and why, *where* work takes place matters. Matter here is taken to refer to a simultaneous, intertwined process of rendering something material and meaningful, and the emphasis has been on this 'mattering' as a process, not a fixed entity or pause in a spatial or historical flow. As Dan Farson and many others have put it, 'it is not in the nature of Soho to be static'.[19] Most decades and centuries have been described as Soho's 'heyday' or 'Golden Age', and no doubt others will be again; those same years have also most likely been cited as its 'decline' and downfall, and, again, no doubt others will be in the future. It is less the 'changing face' of Soho that I have tried to convey here, therefore, and more its continuities: what is fascinating to me about Soho, rather than simplistic ruptures with the past, are its cultural and commercial (not to mention culinary) palimpsest-like[20] overlays and evolutions.

When, in November 2014, the burlesque club Madame Jojo's[21] closed its doors, many actors, writers and presenters collectively and publically mobilized to prevent the area's further demise.[22] Since the 1980s the area has undergone a considerable social and commercial transformation. Its fate seems uncertain, but then it always has. Its chequered history, combined with its reputation as a bohemian place to live, work and consume, means that Soho will always retain an edge that makes it unique. As more businesses are squeezed out by the longer-term impact of online trading, inflated rents and licensing costs, not to mention corporate development, and as mass public transport arrives on its doorstep for the first time in its history, Soho *is* in danger of losing itself as we currently know it.

Yet a strong sense of community can be found just under the surface of Soho's private clubs, ubiquitous coffee chains, family-friendly restaurants and 'traditional' sex shops. As Stephen Fry puts it in his introduction to Bernie Katz's photographic account, *Soho Society*, beneath the two public faces of corporate sanitization and sleaze is a private soul of kindness, warmth and connection.[23] Throughout its history, Soho has flourished most when it has been threatened – this is what makes it distinctive, and this is what is likely to ensure its survival. The sex shops, once viewed as the scourge of Soho, seem to have come full circle and are now regarded rather more affectionately by some as an important part of Soho's distinctive assemblages and associations with dirt and desire. The area's place memories, meanings and materialities are encoded into its semiotic landscape and are embedded in the fabric of its streets and shops. The more this is cut out, or cut away, the more Soho's character as a place of 'backstreet industry and below-stairs debauchery'[24] will be eroded. But for now, at least, a reputation for commercial sex that reaches way beyond the particularities of its setting and which draws together the area's complex and colourful history, geography, politics and economy means that Soho's sex shops, at this particular point in time, remain an important part of an erotic working community that is distinctive, even unique, in the way in which it intertwines place and pleasure. For good or ill, and there is plenty of both, and for how much longer, it is difficult to say – but, to give the last word to Nathan, who had worked there for over twenty years at the time I first interviewed him in Soho in 2008, 'there really is nowhere like it, and there probably never will be again'.

Participants

NATHAN was forty when I first met him in 2008, when he was working as an area manager in the south-east of England for a large UK-based chain of licensed sex shops. I interviewed him several times in the Soho branch on Brewer Street for which he had overall responsibility. He told me that he was married with two daughters and that he had worked in and around Soho for over twenty years, eight of which were for his current employer. He had been employed initially as a store manager (in Soho) and had worked his way up to being an area manager. Previously, he was a builder; he had sought a career change because he said that his wife was fed up with him coming home dirty. The irony of this was not lost on him, as he was well aware of the various 'taints' with which sex shops, and Soho, were associated.

MICHAEL was in his mid-thirties and was working in the shop (where Nathan was a manager) for twenty hours a week while training to be a tree surgeon when I met him in 2008. I interviewed him several times, hung out in the shop where he worked and got to know him well enough for him to take me to other shops and introduce me to sex shop workers there who, in turn, helped me to build a snowball sample through other participants. Between interviews and for some months after we last met in person, Michael and I kept in touch by email, and he regularly sent me updates on changes in Soho or in the store where he worked. I walked around Soho and looked in other shops with Michael several times, and we discussed some of the photographs that I had taken and that we took together. Michael had worked in Soho for about eight months when I first met him, although he had worked for the company (in a branch in outer London) for four years. He had been asking for a transfer to Soho 'for ages' and he was 'ecstatic' when he was offered a job there. Some of our interviews took place in the store, before, after or during observations, in local cafés and often on a bench in Soho Square when he was given breaks to come and talk to me, when the shop was relatively quiet or over his lunchtimes.

DAVINA and PHOEBE both worked in a specialist lingerie store on Old Compton Street. I interviewed them two or three times, always together. Their own personal style was a much closer reflection of the items sold in the shop than was the case with other participants. Both women were in their late twenties when I met them in 2009. I interviewed them in the store where they worked and also undertook observational research there, chatting to them during quiet periods. My contact with them lasted for only two years, until the shop they worked in closed and reopened shortly afterwards as a branch of Hotel Chocolat.

ANDY worked in Soho in a 'traditional' sex shop, selling mostly pornographic DVDs, situated near Walker's Court. When I first met him in 2009, he had worked in Soho for about ten years, in various licensed and unlicensed stores, about five years of which were spent in the shop where I interviewed him. I interviewed him several times since our first meeting, and he invariably cleaned his nails out with a rusty Stanley knife blade while we talked. His 'Old' Soho attitude was an intriguing counter to younger, less-experienced participants such as Michael, Toby, Phoebe and Davina. During all our meetings, interviews and briefer chats, hardcore porn films played on the screens. Although the store was still trading, I rarely noticed customers coming in when I was there. I quickly realized that this was most likely because the predominantly male customer base (surmised from what Andy told me and from the product range) most likely found my presence off-putting, and so I tried to maintain Andy's participation while minimizing the amount of time I spent in the store during periods when he might otherwise have been busy with customers.

TOBY was the youngest participant, aged only nineteen when I met him in 2008, although he looked younger. He had worked in the licensed store on Brewer Street (managed by Shirley) for about twelve months when I first interviewed him. We met several times until around 2012 when he moved on and we lost touch. Along with Michael, Toby was perhaps the most enthusiastic about the job and the area (and the study). I interviewed him in the shop where he worked and in a local café, and we kept in touch by email in between these discussions as (like Michael) he updated me on Soho news and issues that arose that he thought might be of interest.

MARK worked part-time in a gay lifestyle store on Old Compton Street (the one co-owned by Jason). I first met him while he was working a rotational shift in the licensed sex shop in the basement, but he worked both 'upstairs' and 'downstairs' in the store. Jason was Mark's former partner, although he had remained good friends with (and was now an employee of) Jason and his new partner. Mark also worked part-time in a bar in Soho. He was in his forties and had worked in the store since it had opened seven months earlier, and in fact he had helped with the fitting and preparations for the opening, although he had not been directly involved with the design. I interviewed Mark in the shop, with hard-core gay porn films showing on the screens next to the counter where we talked. The shop was usually quite busy, and so we often broke off the discussions and picked up again during quieter periods, so that (as was most often the case throughout the research period), interview and observational methods blended into one.

STEWART was in his thirties and worked in a well-known gay lifestyle store, also on Old Compton Street when I met him. He worked mostly in the licensed sex shop in the basement, which is where I interviewed him several times between 2008 and 2013. His colleague MATT often joined us. During our first interview, for example, Matt joined in the conversation about two-thirds of the way into an hour and a half-long interview, as the store upstairs was quiet and he came downstairs to take part in the discussion and share his own thoughts. Matt had worked in the same store as Stewart for two years but had also worked part-time, often casually to provide cover when needed, in various sex shops in Soho. Stewart had worked in the shop for about three years when I first interviewed him. Matt was not formally employed by the store but was a 'local' (a regular customer) and so often helped out as and when the store was busy or short-staffed. He also wrote regular reviews of products on sale there for a blog he edited. Matt and I exchanged several emails between interviews, and he also kept me updated on any issues he thought were relevant to our discussions.

SHIRLEY was a particularly fascinating person to talk to. In her mid-fifties, she had been headhunted by a recruitment agency to manage the Soho branch of a chain of licensed shops. The shop she worked in was a 'mainstream' sex shop – it was not a sex boutique, or a feminized store, but nor was it one of Soho's 'traditional' sex shops. Located on Brewer Street, one of Soho's main thoroughfares, Shirley had made efforts to make the shop 'clean and bright' since her appointment and had installed a scented air conditioning system so that the shop always smelt fresh (see Chapters 3 and 4 for details). When I first met Shirley in 2009, she had only been in post for about six weeks. I interviewed her several times over the next five years or so until she moved away and I lost contact with her. She was usually busy, and so she often chatted to me at the counter in between serving customers or working with colleagues, giving me opportunities to interweave interview and observational techniques, as I tended to in most stores when the opportunity to do so arose. I sometimes helped Shirley unpack products and remove outer packaging as she restocked shelving, giving us a chance to talk about the products and store layout. Shirley was also keen to 'walk and talk' me around the store, explaining issues such as design concepts and display methods and encouraging me to take photographs of points of interest that she thought might be relevant to the study, in order to convey what it felt like to work in a sex shop.

JULIE was in her late twenties when I first interviewed her. With a first degree in Marketing, she said that her ambition was always to work in retail but to 'do something different', and she explained that she felt she had achieved that working in Soho (see Chapter 4). She had worked in the Soho branch of a well-known chain of feminized, high-street sex shops, situated on one of Soho's main thoroughfares, for about eight years when I first met her. Prior to that, she had worked in other branches of sex shops owned by the same chain, situated in other parts of London. Other participants, notably Andy and Richard, described the shop that Julie worked in, disparagingly, as a 'novelty store'. The products on sale were clearly aimed at a female customer-base, and the decor was dominated by pink and silver, with the product range consisting largely of lingerie and sex toys. The shop sold very few DVDs and no magazines, contrasting with the more 'traditional' shops that participants such as Nathan, Michael, Andy and Richard worked in. Julie had taken two periods of paid maternity leave during the eight years she had worked there, and had returned to working at the Soho branch following both periods of leave. I regularly visited the store where Julie worked to undertake observational research and to conduct interviews with her. Again, we sometimes unpacked stock together while we chatted, breaking off during periods when the store became busy. With Julie and other participants, I only conducted interviews during quiet days/times and (within the parameters of my own work and family commitments) tried to vary the periods when I undertook observational work to understand as much as I could about the breadth of participants' experiences.

RICHARD was semi-retired and in his mid-sixties. He told me that he had previously worked as a self-employed farmer before getting a part-time job, working three days a week, in Soho. The sex shop where he worked was a specialist store, located at the Charing Cross Road end of Old Compton Street, selling mostly schoolgirl- and spanking-themed films and magazines. The shop closed in 2011, and I lost contact with Richard. He was the only participant who preferred me not to record our interviews, although he was very keen to be interviewed, partly, it seemed, to emphasize that there was 'nothing wrong' with the shop or 'the business'. Richard emphasized the first time I interviewed him that Soho's retail sex industry was 'no job or place for a lady' (see Chapter 5 for details), and he was somewhat bemused by my presence there and by the study.

JASON was one of the most interesting people I got to know. He co-owned and managed the gay lifestyle store, which incorporated a licensed sex shop in the basement, in which Mark worked. He described himself as the 'creative director' behind the design concept (see Chapters 3 and 4), which had a loft-style feel to it, with reclaimed wooden floors and shelving and heavy industrial-style metalwork. The shop stocked specialist club, sports and underwear apparel upstairs, including its own branded clothing, and DVDs, books, BDSM equipment, and tools for 'medical play' in a locked cabinet in the basement. Jason was in his mid-thirties when I first met him in early 2011. He had a first degree in art and design and a master's degree in design from Central St Martin's, and he had invested his capital and expertise in the design of the store. The shop had a strikingly different aesthetic to all of the other sex shops in Soho, with the upstairs part of the store feeling more like a well-appointed wine bar and the downstairs having the ambience of a fashionable gentleman's outfitters, with heavy wood and velvet, rich leather and soft lighting. The product range included heavy-duty restraints designed for those for whom bondage was 'a lifestyle not a game', as Jason put it, and a variety of scalpels and other specialist cutting equipment, but the design aesthetic actually made the whole shop feel very cosy. I interviewed Jason several times in the small office at the back of the shop that he and his partner shared with their red setter dog, often over mugs of tea and lengthy discussions about the shop, the industry and the area. We exchanged regular emails for about two years, until Jason and his partner sold the lease and moved their entire business online.

STEPHEN was in his early twenties when I met him in 2009. He had worked in the licensed shop on Brewer Street for just over twelve months, having recently completed an MA in Fine Arts. He had been unable to find work in his chosen area so took the job when he saw a card in the window advertising for staff because, like many other participants, the flexible hours allowed him to combine earning some money with further-ing his career. He was also undertaking some voluntary work and, because he thought his parents and family would be disappointed with where he was working, told them that he worked in a book shop (see Chapter 4). He explained to me with much amusement that this was not strictly a 'lie', as the store he worked in did stock quite a lot of books, albeit it mostly picture ones. We met several times and conducted interviews in the traditional sex shop, selling predominantly pornographic DVDs, maga-zines and a few sex toys (and books), where he worked, as well as on benches or in local cafés during his breaks.

PAM worked in a traditional sex shop in Walker's Court. She was in her mid-fifties and had previously worked in a hostess club for about fifteen years. She had been in her current part-time job for about four years when I first interviewed her in 2016. The shop she worked in sold mainly hard-core DVDs and a few sex toys to an almost exclusively male customer base. The design aesthetic of the store was very dated, reminiscent of photographs of Soho sex shops in the 1970s, and it looked as if the store hadn't been refurbished for some years. I interviewed Pam twice and undertook some observational research in the shop she worked in, which was always very quiet during the time I was there.

MARTIN was in his mid-thirties and worked in the Soho branch of a national chain of sex shops on Brewer Street, when I first interviewed him in 2017. He had worked in the shop for about six years and was very happy for me to spend time in the shop, helping to unpack stock or fold packaging, while we chatted. Again, this meant that our interviews often blended into observational sessions that covered different periods in the working day and week.

DANIEL was in his mid-thirties and was the manager of the same branch of the feminized chain store on Wardour Street where Julie worked (although Julie had left before Daniel started there and he did not know her). He also managed one other branch of the same store, located on nearby Oxford Street. I first met him early in 2017, only a month or so after he had been transferred from another branch based in an outer London shopping centre. Daniel told me that had been asking for some time to be transferred to Soho when the opportunity came up. He explained that this was because it was easier for him to get to but also because he wanted to work somewhere that he felt was 'the heart of the sex industry'. Daniel was a really interesting person to talk to – he felt that the store was very 'vanilla' but that it was an important complement to the more specialist stores in Soho so that the whole area maintained some vibrancy and variety in terms of the range of products and shops that make up its retail sex industry. On a couple of occasions, I helped Daniel unpack stock and fold packaging, and he generously offered me a job several times during these sessions; although I was unable to take up the opportunity for practical reasons, the offers were certainly appreciated.

Notes

PREFACE: WORKING SOHO

1. Sherwell, A. (1901), *Life in West London: A Study and a Contrast*, London: Methuen, cited in Speiser, P. (2017), *Soho: The Heart of Bohemian London*, London: The British Library, p. 25.
2. The poet and editor of *Poetry London*, Tambimuttu originally referred to 'Sohoitis' in correspondence with fellow poet Julian McLaren-Ross. His words – 'If you get Sohoitis ... you will stay there always, day and night and get no work done ever' – are widely quoted in Soho lore and are cited in the opening of Judith Summers' (1989) *Soho: A History of London's Most Colourful Neighbourhood* to give a sense of the destructive magnetism of the place. 'Soho', Tambimuttu wrote, is a word that denotes both a warning and a place of safety. See also Glinert, E. (2007), *West End Chronicles*, London: Allen Lane, p. 157.
3. Hutton, M. (2012), *The Story of Soho: The Windmill Years 1932–1964*, Stroud: Amberley, p. 8.
4. Ibid., p. 14.
5. When I began the study in 2008, most participants worked in shops licensed by Westminster City Council, but some worked in the few remaining unlicensed shops. By the time I completed the research, in 2017 to 2018, all of the shops were licensed, and all of the previously unlicensed stores had either ceased trading or applied for licences.
6. Speiser (2017), p. 7.
7. Mort, F. (2010), *Capital Affairs: London and the Making of the Permissive Society*, London: Yale University Press, p. 11.
8. Walkowitz, J. (2012), *Nights Out: Life in Cosmopolitan London*, London: Yale University Press, p. 3.

INTRODUCTION

1. Summers, J. (1989), *Soho: A History of London's Most Colourful Neighbourhood*, London: Bloomsbury, p. 2.
2. Glinert, E. (2007), *West End Chronicles: 300 Years of Glamour and Excess in the Heart of London*, London: Penguin, p. xi.
3. Walkowitz, J. (2012), *Nights Out: Life in Cosmopolitan London*, London: Yale University Press, p. 6.
4. Richardson, N. (2000), *Dog Days in Soho*, London: Orion, p. 57.

5. Hutton, M. (2012), *The Story of Soho: The Windmill Years 1932–1964*, Stroud: Amberley, p. 7.
6. The term 'sex industry' began to emerge in the 1980s, referring to the recognition of commercial sex as 'a multi-billion dollar global industry featuring high salaries, a large workforce, brisk competition, and sales conventions' – D'Emilio, J., and E. B. Freedman (1988), *Intimate Matters*, New York: Harper & Row, p. 328.
7. Ackroyd, P. (2001), *London: The Biography*, London: Verso, p. 370.
8. Summers (1989), p. 5.
9. Walkowitz (2012), p. 286.
10. Crerar, P. (2017), 'Give 24-hour clubs and music venues a break, says night czar', *Evening Standard*, 7 November, p. 19.
11. Speiser, P. (2017), *London: The Heart of Bohemian London*, London: The British Library, p. 8.
12. Walkowitz (2012), p. 3.
13. Ibid.
14. Farson, D. (1987), *Soho in the Fifties*, London: Michael Joseph, p. 3.
15. Earliest references to Soho as a distinct place can be found from the mid-sixteenth century onwards, but most written references seem to be from the 1630s. Cardwell, J. H., H. B. Freeman, G.C. Wilton and other contributors (1898), *Two Centuries of Soho: Its Institutions, Firms and Amusements*, London: Truslove and Hanson [BiblioLife edition] describes how a map published in the reign of Elizabeth I shows that the district of Soho was then 'quite in the open country' but that the name of Soho or 'So-hoe!' (to give it the punctuation of a hunting cry) was applied to this district at least as early as 1632, when the name is listed in the Rate Books in the parish of St Martin's. Wheatley and Cunningham's (1891, cited in Cardwell et al. [1898]) 'London, Past and Present' records that in 1634 there is to be found a grant for the lease of a 'watercourse of spring water coming and rising from a place called So-howe'. In 1636, people were living at the 'Brick-kilns, near Sohoe'. In the burial register of St Paul's, Covent Garden, is the following entry: '1660. Dec. 16. A pr'sh child from Soeho'. The district called Soho Fields was rapidly built upon from the time of the Restoration to the end of the seventeenth century, according to Cardwell et al. (1898, pp. 1–2). By the time Rimbaud wrote his 'Soho and its Associations' in 1686, Soho had become 'the most fashionable quarter of London' (cited in Caldwell et al., 1989, p. 6).
16. Waugh, A. (1920), 'Round about Soho', in St. J. Adcock (ed.) (1926), *Wonderful London: Volume One*, London: The Fleetaway House, pp. 129–36, 129.
17. Part of Henry VIII's formal break from the Roman Catholic church, the dissolution of the English monasteries was brought about by the Act of Supremacy in 1534, followed in quick succession by Acts of Suppression in 1536 and 1539 which dissolved small and larger monasteries respectively, with their wealth being retained by the Crown. Shaped by a complex set of political and religious factors driven by the succession crisis, as well as greed, this process left the poor with virtually nowhere to turn until the introduction of the Elizabethan Poor Laws that placed the onus of parishes such as St Giles in this part of London to make provision for the area's poor.

18. Willey, R. (2009, first published 1870), *Brewer's Dictionary of London Phrase and Fable*, London: Chambers.
19. Stephen Fry, speaking on ITV News on 10 February 2017.
20. Summers (1989), p. 2.
21. Richardson (2000), p. 61.
22. Summers (1989), p. 2.
23. Farson (1987), p. 4.
24. In Spesier (2017), p. 7.
25. Summers (1989), pp. 2–3.
26. Ibid., p. 5.
27. Ibid., p. 6.
28. Walkowitz (2012), p. 6.
29. Ibid., p. 21.
30. Engels, F. (2009; first published 1845), *The Conditions of the Working Class in England*, Oxford: Oxford University Press, p. 40.
31. Ibid., p. 40.
32. Summers (1989), p. 123.
33. Sherwell, A. (1892), *Life in West London*, cited in Walkowitz (2012), pp. 25–6.
34. Waugh (1920).
35. Cited in Summers (1989), p. 158.
36. Ibid., p. 159.
37. There is some dispute as to whether Old Compton Street is named after Bishop Henry Compton, as Summers (1989) suggests, or after Sir Francis Compton, who built the street in the reign of Charles I, as Cardwell et al. (1898) claim.
38. Summers (1989), p. 159.
39. Ibid., p. 172.
40. Walkowitz (2012), p. 3.
41. Walkowitz (2012), p. 6.
42. Shadwell, T. (2018), 'Soho residents and businesses are upset about a new sex shop opening', *Get West London*, 11 June.
43. Sheppard, O., and J. Prynn (2018), 'Oh Mrs Henderson! Lapdancing club that survived Blitz and inspired film faces closure after sting by women's rights groups', *Evening Standard*, 10 January, p. 3.
44. Hemley, M. (2018), 'Soho's Windmill Theatre loses operating license', *The Stage*, 12 January 2018.
45. Clark, P. (2014), 'The slow death of Soho: Farewell to London's sleazy heartland', *The Guardian*, 24 November.
46. See Ellis-Peterson, H. (2014), 'Madame Jojo's, legendary Soho nightclub forced to close', *The Guardian*, 24 November, and Tyler, M. (2014), 'Sleazy or sanitized, London's Soho thrives most when under threat', *The Conversation*, 2 December. See also www.savesoho.com. At the time of writing, the redevelopment of Walker's Court/Berwick Street includes plans to re-open Madame Jojo's under the auspices of the new Soho Estates complex.
47. For full details of the letter, sent to then London Mayor Boris Johnson, as well the list of signatories who marched through Soho in November 2014

protesting the closure, see www.thisiscabaret.com/benedict-cumberbatch-stephen-fry-eddie-izzard-join-madame-jojos-campaign.

48. 'Stephen Fry signs Save Soho open letter to government', BBC News, 24 January 2015.
49. See Oldfield, S. (2015), 'I took my Grandma to Soho's felt sex shop', *SWLondoner*, 15 October.
50. De Certeau, M. (2011; first published 1984), *The Practice of Everyday Life*, Berkeley: University of California Press, p. 92.

SOHO

1. Hutton, M. (2012), *The Story of Soho: The Windmill Years 1932–1964*, Stroud: Amberley, p. 207.
2. Massey, D. (2002), 'Living in Wythenshawe', in I. Borden (ed.), *The Unknown City: Contesting Architecture and Social Space*, Cambridge, MA: MIT Press, pp. 458–75.
3. Fry, S. (2008), 'Foreword', in B. Katz, *Soho Society*, London: Quartet, p. 11.
4. For a fascinating interview and photo-based account of Soho's recent history, as well as personal reflections on Soho as a working and residential community, see Vaines, C. (2015), 'Soho stories: Celebrating six decades of sex, drugs and Rock'n'Roll', *The Observer*, 17 May.
5. Hutton (2012), p. 157.
6. See, among others, Summers, J. (1989), *Soho: A History of London's Most Colourful Neighbourhood*, London: Bloomsbury.
7. Monmouth House is believed to be the first major building to be erected between the royal palaces and the southern edge of the Forest of Middlesex – see Glinert, E. (2007), *West End Chronicles*, London: Allen Lane, p. 31.
8. Speiser, P. (2017), *Soho: The Heart of Bohemian London*, London: The British Library, p. 8.
9. Ibid., p. 14.
10. 'Rookery' is a nineteenth-century term used to describe densely populated housing in slum areas marked by particularly high levels of deprivation and disease. Beames shows the extent to which London's rookeries were overcrowded, poorly ventilated and unhygienic. Many families lived within a small, single room in tenement buildings. By squeezing dozens of people into one building, corrupt landlords gained high financial returns.
11. Beames, T. (1850), *The Rookeries of London: Past, Present and Prospective*, London: The British Library (online), p. 7.
12. Ackroyd, P. (2001), *London: A Biography*, London: Verso, p. 138.
13. Beames (1850), p. 5.
14. Dickens' handwritten notes for the Preface to the 1850 edition of *Oliver Twist*, The British Library (online).
15. Hutton (2012), p. 15.
16. Black, G. (1994), *Living up West: Jewish Life in London's West End*, London: The Museum of Jewish Life, p. 13.

17. Tames, R., and S. Tames (2009), *Covent Garden and Soho*, London: Historical Publications, pp. 96–7.
18. Cardwell, J. H., H. B. Freeman, G.C. Wilton and other contributors (1898), *Two Centuries of Soho: Its Institutions, Firms and Amusements*, London: Truslove and Hanson (BiblioLife edition).
19. Ibid., p. 131.
20. Walter Berlant (1898), Preface to Cardwell et al., p. vii.
21. Cardwell et al. (1898), p. 65.
22. Ibid., p. 69.
23. Ibid., p. 114.
24. Ibid., p. 91.
25. Ibid., pp. 93–4.
26. Cox, P., and A. Hobley (2014), *Shopgirls: The True Story of Life Behind the Counter*, London: Hutchinson.
27. Ibid., p. 95.
28. Ibid., p. 142.
29. Ibid., p. 142.
30. Ibid., p. iv.
31. Ibid., p. 292.
32. Walkowitz, J. (2012), *Nights Out: Life in Cosmopolitan London*, London: Yale University Press.
33. See Walkowitz, J. (2013), 'The Emergence of Cosmopolitan Soho', in G. Bridge and S. Watson (eds.), *The New Blackwell Companion to the City*, Oxford: Blackwell, pp. 419–30.
34. Speiser (2017), p. 21.
35. Walkowitz (2012), p. 33.
36. Ibid.
37. Ransome, A. (1907), *Bohemia in London*, London: Chapman and Hall, p. 10.
38. Walkowitz (2012), p. 35.
39. Ibid., p. 38.
40. Ibid.
41. Ibid., p. 37.
42. Stevenson, R. L. (2012; first published 1886), *Strange Case of Dr Jekyll and Mr Hyde*, London: Penguin, p. 22.
43. Ibid., p. 34.
44. Speiser (2017), p. 98.
45. Mort, F. (2010), *Capital Affairs: London and the Making of the Permissive Society*, London: Yale University Press, p. 213.
46. Crisp, Q. (1968), *The Naked Civil Servant*, London: Jonathan Cape.
47. In March 2017, the National Trust curated a series of events commemorating fifty years since the partial decriminalization of homosexuality via the Sexual Offences Act 1967. In partnership with the National Archives, events included walking tours of historically important LGBTQ clubs and venues in and around Soho, culminating in a visit to a re-creation of The Caravan club. This important project emphasized the ways in which queer

spaces, settings and places 'matter' insofar as they intertwine meanings and materialities that endure.

48. Mort (2010), p. 113.
49. Arnold, C. (2010), *City of Sin: London and Its Vices*, London: Simon and Schuster, p. 212.
50. Speiser (2017), p. 68.
51. Ackroyd (2001, p. 520) notes the importance of Regent Street to Nash's demarcation of poor and wealthy areas in London's West End, in effect 'cutting off the rich from the sight and odours of the poor'. In designing Regent Street, Nash himself declared his wish to create a physical barrier 'between the Streets and Squares occupied by the Nobility and Gentry' and 'the narrow Streets and meaner houses occupied by . . . the trading part of the community'.
52. Speiser (2017), p. 144.
53. For photographs of Soho as a working community, including the Berwick Street market, see www.ibtimes.co.uk/save-soho-fascinating-old-photos-vibrant-heart-londons-west-end-over-years-1495269.
54. Speiser (2017), p. 147.
55. Ibid., p. 72.
56. Black (1994), p. 57, emphasis added.
57. A Yiddish term meaning 'landsman', used mainly to refer to people who come from the same area or who identify themselves as part of the same community.
58. Black (1994), p. 59.
59. Ibid., p. 19.
60. Speiser (2017), p. 62.
61. Ibid., p. 21.
62. Mort (2010), p. 249.
63. Douglas, M. (2002; first published 1966), *Purity and Danger: An Analysis of Concepts of Pollution and Taboo*, London: Routledge.
64. Walkowitz cites an article in the *Manchester Guardian*, for instance, pondering whether the Plan spelt the 'fin de Soho'.
65. Fabian, R. (1954), *London after Dark*, New York: British Book Centre. Fabian's moralistic account reserves particular venom for the 'Street Girls of Soho'. The latter he variously describes as lazy, vain, frigid and insincere. In an account that has a very different tone to those of the people who lived and worked in Soho in the 1950s, Fabian's view of street girls as the 'bad apples' of Soho presumes that 'they taint any flesh they touch' (p. 67). A similar tone is adopted in Arnold L. Miller's (1961) film *West End Jungle*. Both 'prurient and sensationalist', according to Barney Ashton's viewing notes written to accompany the 2009 release, the latter claims to offer a 'definitive insight into the seedy reality and cunning artifice of the sex workers of early '60s Soho' (release notes).
66. Walkowitz (2012), p. 291.
67. Walkowitz (2012), p. 291.
68. As Mort (2010, p. 224) notes, Fabian was one of a number of the area's biographers to have claimed a privileged insight into Soho's underworld on

account of personal involvement. Other examples include Cardwell's *Two Centuries* and Farson's *Soho in the Fifties*.

69. For photographs of the Fair in the 1950s, including of the famous Waiters' Race, see a British Film Institute (BFI) project: www.bfi.org.uk/news-opinion/news-bfi/features/20-colour-snapshots-vibrant-soho-60-years-ago.

70. Mort (2010), p. 291.

71. Ibid., p. 197.

72. Ibid., p. 198.

73. See www.britishpathe.com/video/alls-fair-in-soho.

74. Mort (2010), p. 200.

75. Glinert (2007), p. 219, emphasis added.

76. Summers (1989), p. 190.

77. Farson, D. (1987), *Soho in the Fifties*, London: Harper Collins, p. 7.

78. Melly, G. (1987), 'Introduction' to Farson, pp. xi, xii.

79. Farson (1987), p. 7.

80. Speiser (2017), p. 131.

81. See, for example, Peppiatt, M. (2015), *Francis Bacon in Your Blood: A Memoir*, London: Bloomsbury.

82. Glinert (2007), p. 142.

83. Ibid., p. 219.

84. Porter, R. (2000), *London: A Social History*, London: Penguin, p. 443, cited in Speiser (2017), p. 132.

85. Stansell, C. (2000), *American Moderns: Bohemian New York and the Creation of a New Century*, New York: Owl Books, p. 43, cited in Mort (2010), p. 202.

86. Stansell (2000), p. 43.

87. Speiser (2017), p. 163.

88. Summers (1989), p. 193.

89. This specific phrasing seems to owe a reference point to Alec Waugh's reflections on his first encounters with Soho in 1917, recalling his impression of 'a place . . . where anything might happen' (Waugh, 1920, p. 136) – see Waugh, A. (1920), 'Round about Soho', in St. John Adcock (ed.), *Wonderful London: Volume One*, London: The Fleetway House, pp. 129–36.

90. Ibid., p. 293.

91. Hutton (2012), p. 112.

92. Mort (2010), p. 222.

93. Hutton (2012), p. 112, emphasis added.

94. Ibid., p. 117.

95. Ibid., p. 119.

96. Ibid., p. 121.

97. Ibid., p. 127.

98. Speiser (2017), p. 8.

99. Mort (2010).

100. Summers (1989), pp. 206–21.

101. Vaines, C. (2015), 'Soho stories: Celebrating six decades of sex, drugs and Rock'n'Roll', *The Observer*, 17 May.

102. Glinert (2007), p. 114.

103. The sex cinemas that grew up in this area, close to the more 'legitimate' cinematic area of Leicester Square, were similar in style and setting to the 'grinder houses' that proliferated in and around Times Square, New York, during the Great Depression. Also close to the mainstream theatre district, these sex theatres showed nudist and sexually explicit films and served as meeting places for anonymous sexual encounters – see Kleinfield, N. R. (1998), 'It's not easy to push sex into the shadows', *New York Times*, 1 March 1998, p. 29.

104. This concentration of the commercial sex industry in Soho mirrors a similar development in New York's Times Square, an area that became 'notorious as the nation's retail sex capital'. The sex industry dominated there during the 1970s in particular, with an estimated 100 strip clubs, topless bars and sex shops. Show World, a multistorey sex emporium, 'became a landmark of the sex industry' – see Cook, J. (2005) 'Shaken from Her Pedestal: A Decade of New York City's Sex Industry under Siege', *City University of New York Law Review* 9(1), pp. 121–59, 125.

105. Farson (1987), p. 67.

106. Arnold (2010, pp. 326–7) describes how 'Megan', a Soho-based sex worker of some twenty-five years, says, 'It's a little village here and we couldn't work in a better place ... The community supports us.' In 2009, when the Metropolitan Police tried to close a brothel on Dean Street, the decision was overturned following lobbying by the English Collective of Prostitutes (ECP) and local residents who supported them, the latter maintaining that the sex workers were an integral part of Soho's working community.

107. See Goldstein, M. (2005), *Naked Jungle: Soho Stripped Bare*, London: Silverback.

108. Farson (1987), p. 211.

109. As Glinert (2007, p. 195) emphasizes, however, crime may have become more organized in the 1950s, but it was certainly not new. In the 1920s, for instance, 'Soho was dedicated to money laundering, illegal gambling in cellar *speilers*, pimping, violence and racketeering'. Much of the profit from these activities went straight into the pockets of the infamous Sabini brothers.

110. Ibid., p. 208.

111. Hutton (2012), p. 202.

112. Mort (2010), p. 214.

113. Tomkinson, M. (1982), *The Pornbrokers: The Rise of the Soho Sex Barons*, London: Virgin Books.

114. Mort (2010), p. 216.

115. 'Clipping' means 'obtaining money through deception by the apparent offer of sexual services or entertainment. This may involve the simple deception of receiving money and sending victims to addresses where no such offer is available, the supply of non-alcoholic drinks at inflated prices and the charging of fees for hostess services when not requested. In some instances, it is associated with luring victims to places where they are robbed' – Westminster City Council (2012), *Sex Entertainment Venues Statement of Licensing Policy*, London: Westminster, p. 27.

116. Hutton (2012), pp. 205–6.
117. Mort (2010), p. 278.
118. Hutton (2012), p. 207.
119. Mort (2010), p. 269.
120. Truman, K. (2016), 'Raymond Revuebar', *Soho Journal* 7 (Winter 2016), p. 30.
121. Mort (2010), p. 278.
122. Ibid.
123. In an interview with Summers (1989), p. 220.
124. Theodore, N., J. Peck and N. Brenner (2013), 'Neoliberal Urbanism: Cities and the Rule of Markets', in Bridge and Watson, p. 25.
125. Arnold (2010), p. 323.
126. Arnold (2010), p. 300.
127. This was an important example of the complex and multilayered nature of Soho's working community and of the centrality of commercial sex to that community. In October 2013, Soho sex workers and supporters protested after women working in a flat in Romilly Street were threatened with eviction following a police crackdown. Letters were sent to Soho Estates, threatening them with prosecution for allowing their premises to be used as a brothel. They in turn threatened the leaseholders with losing their lease for allowing 'immoral activities'. Protesters believed that the evictions were to make way for a major hotel and luxury residential development. The English Collective of Prostitutes initiated legal action against this method of closing working flats – if established brothel closure law was followed, police would have to produce evidence that a crime was being committed on the premises. Tracy, one of the women working in the Romilly Street flat, commented: 'We will all lose our livelihoods. I've been working in Soho for thirty-three years, first as a working woman and now as a receptionist. We are not criminals. We are mothers and grandmothers supporting families.' Leyla, also from Romilly Street, said: 'I have four children back in Thailand who would not survive without the money I send them. Their lives were turned upside down by the recent floods. I don't have the option to give up this job ... If I am evicted it is likely I will end up on the street and be less safe.' And Cari Mitchell, speaking on behalf of the ECP, commented: 'Soho is one of the safest places for women to work. What justification is there for the police to pour time and resources into getting women thrown out on the street? The police claim that they are saving victims of trafficking, but that isn't true. They've not come forward with any evidence that women are being forced, coerced or trafficked.' Mitchell went on to emphasize that local residents and businesses have always supported sex workers in Soho. Thousands signed a petition against previous evictions. Many of the protesters expressed fears that gentrification was behind attempts to close these flats and others, and that 'if sex workers are forced out it will lead the way for other small and unique businesses and bars to be drowned out by major construction, chain stores and corporations', concluded Mitchell (email exchange – 7 October 2013 with Cari Mitchell, English Collective of Prostitutes [ECP] – ecp@prostitutescollective.net). More raids followed under the auspices of the

Metropolitan Police's 'Operation Lanhydrock', which closed an estimated fifty premises from which sex workers were operating between April and October 2015. At the same time, several planning applications were submitted to Westminster City Council for large hotel/commercial developments.

128. English Collective of Prostitutes (ECP) (2014), *The Soho Raids: What Really Happened,* cited in E. Sanders-McDonagh, M. Peyrefitte and M. Ryalls (2016), 'Sanitising the City: Exploring Hegemonic Gentrification in London's Soho', *Sociological Research Online* 21(3), p. 3.

129. Sanders-McDonagh, Peyrefitte and Ryalls (2016), p. 3.

130. Waugh (1920), p. 130.

131. Summers (1989), p. 222.

132. Glinert (2007), p. ix.

133. Ibid., p. 220.

134. Crisp (1968), p. 199.

135. Bevan, R. (2017), 'Soho gets its heart back', *Evening Standard,* 3 August 2017, p. 34–5.

136. Businesses not connected to the sex industry cross-reference Soho's commercial associations with sex (e.g. names that feature on its retail landscape include Strip fitness wear, Nudie Jeans repair shop, Feel hair salon and Snogg frozen yoghurt bar).

137. The everyday lives of Soho residents were documented in an exhibition, *Over the Threshold,* held at the Photographer's Gallery in May 2011. The exhibition depicted a thriving and diverse residential community and aimed to make visible the everyday lives of people who live in an area of central London associated largely with work and consumption, and particularly with commercial sex in all its many forms.

138. Glinert (2007), pp. 229–30.

139. Summers (1989), p. 232.

PUTTING WORK IN ITS PLACE

1. McDowell, L. (1997), *Capital Culture: Gender at Work in the City,* London: Wiley, p. 5.

2. Gieryn, T. F. (2000), 'A Space for Place in Sociology', *Annual Review of Sociology* 26, pp. 463–96, 465.

3. This way of conceptualizing work place is reflected in Louise Nash's study of the City of London that emphasizes the symbolic and material significance of place to understanding the lived experiences of power relations within organizational life – see Nash, L. (2018), 'Gendered Places: Place, Performativity and Flânerie in the City of London', *Gender, Work and Organization* 25(6), pp. 601–20.

4. Ropo, A., and R. Höykinpuro (2017), 'Narrating Organizational Spaces', *Journal of Organizational Change Management* 30(3), pp. 357–66, 359.

5. See Cresswell, T. (2004), *Place: A Short Introduction,* Oxford: Blackwell.

6. Tuan, Y-F. (1977), *Place and Space,* Minneapolis: University of Minnesota Press, p. 6, emphasis added.

7. Simmel, G. (1964), 'The Metropolis and Mental Life', in K. Wolff (ed.), *The Sociology of Georg Simmel*, New York: The Free Press of Glencoe, p. 19.
8. Waugh, A. (1920), 'Round about Soho', in St J. Adcock (ed.), *Wonderful London: Volume One*, London: The Fleetaway House, pp. 129–36, 136.
9. Bachelard, G. (1994; first published 1958), *The Poetics of Space*, London: Verso.
10. See Nash's (2018) study of the City of London for a methodological example of the application of Lefebvre's writing on rhythmanalysis to the study of a particular work place and setting, emphasizing the symbolic and material significance of place to understanding the lived experiences of power relations within working life. See also Lyon, D. (2018), *What is Rhythmanalysis?*, London: Bloomsbury, for a further application of immersive approaches to studying work places.
11. Simmel (1964).
12. Others argue the reverse – Dale and Burrell (2008) suggest, for instance, that 'a bounded and specified "place" of work is disappearing', both physically and psychically – Dale, K., and G. Burrell (2008), *The Spaces of Organization and the Organization of Space: Power, Identity and Materiality at Work*, London: Palgrave, p. 116.
13. Mort, F. (1998), 'Cityscapes, Consumption, Masculinities and the Mapping of London since 1950', *Urban Studies* 35(5–6), pp. 889–907, 889.
14. Crewe, L., and A. Martin (2017), 'Sex and the City: Branding, Gender and the Commodification of Sex Consumption in Contemporary Retailing', *Urban Studies* 54(3), pp. 582–99, 595, emphasis added.
15. Gieryn (2000), p. 465.
16. Escobar, A. (2001), 'Culture Sits in Places: Reflections on Globalism and Subaltern Strategies of Localization', *Political Geography* 20(2), pp. 139–74, 139, emphasis added.
17. Gieryn (2000), p. 467, emphasis in original.
18. See Urry, J. (2013), 'City Life and the Senses', in G. Bridge and S. Watson (eds.), *The New Blackwell Companion to the City*, Oxford: Blackwell, pp. 347–56.
19. See Massey, D. (1997), 'A Global Sense of Place', in T. Barnes and D. Gregory (eds.), *Reading Human Geography*, London: Arnold, pp. 315–53.
20. Reynolds, T. (2006), *Blood, Sweat and Tea*, London: Harper Collins.
21. Derrida, J. (1994), *Specters of Marx*, London: Routledge, p. 83.
22. Mort, F. (2013), 'Modernity and Gaslight: Victorian London in the 1950s and 1960s', in G. Bridge and S. Watson (eds.), *The New Blackwell Companion to the City*, Oxford: Blackwell, p. 434.
23. Benjamin (1999, p. 83) describes the network of narrow streets in Paris as harbouring 'lairs of love' (not nests), and a similar point might be made about Soho's geographies of commercial sex.
24. Simmel (1964), p. 11.
25. Baldry, C. (1999), 'Space – The Final Frontier', *Sociology* 33(3), pp. 535–53, 535.

26. Lefebvre, H. (1991), *The Social Production of Space*, Oxford: Blackwell, p. 410, emphasis added.
27. Soja, E. (1989), *Postmodern Geographies*, London: Haymarket.
28. Lefebvre, H. (2000) *Everyday Life in the Modern World*. London: Athalone Press, p. 20.
29. Lefebvre, H. (2009) *Rhythmanalysis: Space, Time and Everyday Life*. London: Bloomsbury, page 29.
30. Benjamin, W. (1970) *One Way Street and Other Writings*. Trans. E. Jephcott and K. Shorter. London: Verso.
31. See Benjamin (1999), p. ix. In contrast to the Parisian Arcades in Benjamin's account, Soho might be thought of as a kind of 'dialectical hinterland', a place that is simultaneously destructive and creative, and which depends upon being located in the shadowlands of London's consumer economy in order to maintain the cultural (and commercial) viability of this dialectic.
32. Buck-Morss, S. (1989), *The Dialectics of Seeing*, Cambridge, MA: MIT Press, pp. 293, 3.
33. Featherstone, M. (1998), 'The Flaneur, the City and Virtual Public Life', *Urban Studies* 35(5–6), pp. 909–25.
34. Soja, E. (1996), *Thirdspace: Journeys to Los Angeles and Other Real-and-Imagined Places*, Hoboken, NJ: Wiley-Blackwell; De Certeau, M. (1984), *The Practice of Everyday Life*, Berkeley: University of California Press.
35. Hancock, P. (2006), 'The Spatial and Temporal Mediation of Social Change', *Journal of Organizational Change Management* 19(5), pp. 619–39, 621.
36. Dale and Burrell (2008).
37. Ibid., p. 39.
38. Ibid., p. 48.
39. Fleming, P., and A. Spicer (2004), '"You Can Check Out Anytime But You Can Never Leave": Spatial Boundaries in a High Commitment Organization', *Human Relations* 57(1), pp. 75–94.
40. See Hancock, P. and M. Tyler (eds.) (2009), *The Management of Everyday Life*, Palgrave: Macmillan.
41. O'Neill, R. (2018), *Seduction: Men, Masculinity and Mediated Intimacy*, Cambridge: Polity.
42. See Hancock and Tyler (2009) for a discussion.
43. Taylor, S., and A. Spicer (2007), 'Time for Space: A Narrative Review of Research on Organizational Spaces', *International Journal of Management Reviews* 9(4), pp. 325–46, 331.
44. Felstead, A., N. Jewson and S. Walters (2005), *Changing Places of Work*, London: Palgrave.
45. Tyler, M. (2011), 'Tainted Love: From Dirty Work to Abject Labour in Soho's Retail Sex Industry', *Human Relations* 64(11), pp. 1477–1500, p. 1481.
46. Soja, E. (1980), 'The Socio-Spatial Dialectic', *Annals of the Association of American Geographers* 70(2), pp. 207–25. See also Soja (1989).
47. Sanders-McDonagh, E. and M. Peyrefitte (2018), 'Immoral Geographies and Soho's Sex Shops: Exploring Spaces of Sexual Diversity in London', *Gender, Place and Culture* 25(3), pp. 351–67.

48. Courpasson, D., F. Dany and R. Delbridge (2016), 'Politics of Place: The Meaningfulness of Resisting Places', *Human Relations* 70(2), pp. 237–59, p. 238.

49. Iedema, R., D. Long and K. Carroll (2012), 'Corridor Communication, Spatial Design and Patient Safety: Enacting and Managing Complexities', in A. Van Marrewijk and D. Yanow (eds.), *Organizational Spaces: Rematerializing the Workaday World*, Cheltenham: Edward Elgar, pp. 41–57.

50. Casey, E. (1993), *Getting Back into Place: Toward a Renewed Understanding of the Place-World*, Bloomington: Indiana University Press.

51. Cresswell (2004), p. 7.

52. See, for a discussion, Creswell (2004); Massey (1997); and Tuan (1977).

53. Lippard, L. (1997), *The Lure of the Local*, New York: The New Press.

54. Courpasson, Dany and Delbridge (2016), p. 238.

55. Casey (1993), p. xiii.

56. Shortt, H. (2014), 'Liminality, Space and the Importance of "Transitory Dwelling Places" at Work', *Human Relations* 68(4), pp. 633–58.

57. Collins, A. (2004), 'Sexual Dissidence, Enterprise and Assimilation: Bedfellows in Urban Regeneration', *Urban Studies* 41(9), pp. 1789–806, 1789.

58. Hubbard, P. (2004a), 'Revenge and Injustice in the Neoliberal City: Uncovering Masculinist Agendas', *Antipode* 36(4): pp. 665–80, 665.

59. Ibid., p. 666.

60. See Hubbard, P. (2004b), 'Cleansing the Metropolis: Sex Work and the Politics of Zero Tolerance', *Urban Studies* 41(9), pp. 1687–702.

61. Smith, N. (1996), *The New Urban Frontier: Gentrification and the Revanchist City*, London: Routledge. For Smith, gentrification is not simply the development of an urban landscape that reflects middle-class culture and capital but a more sinister 'policy of revenge'.

62. Papayanis, M. (2000), 'Sex and the Revanchist City: Zoning Out Pornography in New York', *Environment and Planning D: Society and Space* 18(3), pp. 341–53.

63. Ravo, N. (1994), 'Zoning Out Sex-Oriented Businesses', *The New York Times*, 6 March, p. 11.

64. Cameron, S. (2004), 'Space, Risk and Opportunity: The Evolution of Paid Sex Markets', *Urban Studies* 41(9), pp. 1643–657, 1649.

65. Berlant, L., and M. Warner (1998), 'Sex in Public', *Critical Inquiry* 24 (Winter), pp. 547–66.

66. The photographic-ethnographer Alessandrini Gregoire's blog contrasts the industrial landscape before and after the gentrification of New York's Chelsea and Meatpacking District – see Storm, C. (2015), 'Step Back 25 Years Into the Gritty Days of New York City's Meat Packing District', *Business Insider UK*, 28 May.

67. Hubbard (2004a), p. 671.

68. Hubbard, P., R. Matthews and J. Scoular (2009), 'Legal Geographies – Controlling Sexually Oriented Businesses: Law, Licensing and the Geographies of a Controversial Land Use', *Urban Geography* 30(2), pp. 185–205, 185.

69. Ibid., p. 186.
70. Hubbard (2004a), p. 666.
71. Houlbrook, M. (2005), *Queer London*. Chicago: Chicago University Press, p. 87.
72. Mort (1998), p. 891.
73. Hubbard et al. (2009), p. 193.
74. Fleming, P. (2007), 'Sexuality, Power and Resistance in the Workplace', *Organization Studies* 28(2), pp. 239–56.
75. Burrell, G. (1984), 'Sex and Organizational Analysis', *Organization Studies* 5(2), pp. 97–118, 102.
76. Weber, M. (1968; first published 1925), *Economy and Society: Volume One*, New York: Bedminster Press.
77. Burrell (1984), p. 99.
78. Ibid., p. 102.
79. See Brewis, J. (2005), 'Signing My Life Away? Researching Sex and Organization', *Organization* 12(4), pp. 493–510; Brewis, J., and S. Linstead (2000a), 'The Worst Thing Is the Screwing (1): Consumption and the Management of Identity in Sex Work', *Gender, Work and Organization* 7(2), pp. 84–97; Brewis, J., and S. Linstead (2000b), 'The Worst Thing Is the Screwing (2): Context and Career in Sex Work', *Gender, Work and Organization* 7(3), pp. 168–80; and Brewis, J. and S. Linstead (2003), *Sex, Work and Sex Work: Eroticizing Organization*, London: Routledge.
80. Brewis and Linstead (2003), p. 195.
81. Mort (1998), p. 901.
82. Walkowitz, J. (2012), *Nights Out: Life in Cosmopolitan London*, London: Yale University Press, p. 9.
83. Hubbard, Matthews and Scoular (2009), p. 201.
84. Halford, S. (2004), 'Towards a Sociology of Organizational Space', *Sociological Research Online* 9(1), pp. 1–16, 3.
85. Lefebvre (1991), p. 73.
86. Tyler (2011), p. 1480.
87. Hearn, J. (2014), 'Sexualities, Organizations and Organizational Sexualities: Future Scenarios and the Impact of Socio-Technologies', *Organization* 21(3), pp. 400–20.
88. As Evans et al. (2010) note in their discussion of feminized sex shops as 'postfeminist heterotopias', Foucault's account of heterotopic spaces and settings is relatively brief and underdeveloped but seems to be highly applicable to sex shops or, perhaps more convincingly, the urban locations in which they tend to be situated – see Evans, A., S. Riley and A. Shankar (2010), 'Postfeminist Heterotopias: Negotiating "Safe" and "Seedy" in the British Sex Shop Space', *European Journal of Women's Studies* 17(3), pp. 211–29.
89. Foucault, M. (1986), 'Of Other Spaces', *Diacritics* 16(1), pp. 22–37.
90. Mort (1998), p. 894.
91. Binnie, J. and B. Skeggs (2004), 'Cosmopolitan Knowledge and the Production and Consumption of Sexualized Space: Manchester's Gay Village', *The Sociological Review* 52(1), pp. 39–61, 57.

92. Mort, F. (2010), *Capital Affairs*, London: Yale University Press, p. 23.
93. Mort (1998), p. 894.
94. Low, S. (2013), 'Spatializing Culture: Embodied Space in the City', in Bridge and Watson, p. 469.
95. Sassen, S. (2013), 'Analytic Borderlands: Economy and Culture in the Global City', in Bridge and Watson, p. 211, emphasis added.
96. London biographer Peter Ackroyd makes a similar observation with regard to Fleet Street, an area traditionally associated with newspapers, as an example of 'the city's topographical imperative, whereby the same activity takes place over hundreds of years in the same small area' so that the materiality of the setting, 'its very earth and stones', mutually shape the character and behaviour of those who inhabit it and 'work' the area. Ackroyd illustrates this with reference to the Strand, noting how 'there are certain kinds of activity, or patterns of inheritance, arising from the streets and alleys themselves' – Ackroyd, P. (2001), *London: A Biography*, London: Verso, pp. 401, p. 465.
97. See also Ryder's (2004) discussion of Times Square, New York, in which he argues that proximity to theatres and live entertainment (to which we might add hotels) was the main factor contributing to the area's development as a concentration of sex-related businesses – Ryder, A. (2004), 'The Changing Nature of Adult Entertainment Districts: Between a Rock and a Hard Place or Going from Strength to Strength?', *Urban Studies* 41(9), pp. 1659–86. See also Sagalyn (2001), who argues that, by the 1970s, the industry had identified office workers as its main customer group, with Times Square and the surrounding areas being well placed to attract customers travelling to and from work – Sagalyn, L. B. (2001), *Times Square Roulette*, Cambridge, MA: MIT Press.
98. Mort (1998), p. 897.
99. Ibid., p. 898.
100. Kent, T., and R. Brown (2006), 'Erotic Retailing in the UK (1963–2003): The View from the Marketing Mix', *Journal of Management History* 12(2), pp. 199–211.
101. Manchester, C. (1986), *Sex Shops and the Law*, London: Gower Publishing.
102. Gold, J. (1995), *Good Vibrations*, London: Pavilion Books, p. 201.
103. Kent and Brown (2006), p. 202.
104. Moore, A. (2003), 'A Woman's Touch', *The Observer Magazine*, 20 July, p. 22, cited in Kent and Brown (2006), p. 209.
105. Crewe and Martin (2017), p. 595.
106. Ibid.
107. Binnie and Skeggs (2004), p. 39.
108. Hubbard, Matthews and Scoular (2009), p. 200.

SHOPPING FOR SEX

1. Houlbrook, M. (2005), *Queer London*, Chicago, IL: University of Chicago Press.
2. Hochschild, A. R. (1983), *The Managed Heart: Commercialization of Human Feeling*, Berkeley: University of California Press.

3. Böhme, G. (2003), 'Contribution to the critique of the aesthetic economy', *Thesis Eleven* 73, pp. 71–82, 72.

4. Horkheimer, M., and T. Adorno (1973 [1947]), *Dialectic of Enlightenment*, trans. J. Cumming, London: Allan Lane.

5. Böhme (2003), p. 72, emphasis in original.

6. See Stein, M. (1990), *An Ethnography of an Adult Bookstore: Private Scenes in and Public Places*, Lewiston, NY: Edwin Mellen Press; Tewksbury, R. (1990), 'Patrons of Porn: Research Notes on the Clientele of Adult Bookstores', *Deviant Behaviour* 11, pp. 259–71, and Tewksbury, R. (1993), 'Peep Shows and Perverts: Men and Masculinity in a Adult Bookstore', *Journal of Men's Studies* 2(1), pp. 53–70.

7. See Berkowitz, D. (2006), 'Consuming Eroticism: Gender Performances and Presentations in Pornographic Establishments', *Journal of Contemporary Ethnography* 35(5), pp. 583–606, and Storr, M. (2003), *Latex and Lingerie: Shopping for Pleasure at Ann Summers Parties*, Oxford: Berg.

8. Malina, D., and R. Schmidt (1997), 'It's Business Doing Pleasure with You: *Sh!* A Women's Sex Shop Case', *Marketing Intelligence and Planning* 15 (7), pp. 352–60, 359.

9. Kent, T., and R. Berman Brown (2006), 'Erotic Retailing in the UK (1963–2003): The View from the Marketing Mix', *Journal of Management History* 12(2), pp. 199–211, 201, emphasis added.

10. Thompson, B. (1994), *Soft Core: Moral Crusades against Pornography in Britain and America*, London: Cassell.

11. See Coulmont, B. and P. Hubbard (2010), 'Consuming Sex: Socio-Legal Shifts in the Space and Place of Sex Shops', *Journal of Law and Society* 37(1), pp. 189–209.

12. Ibid.

13. In 1985 and 1982, respectively, this Act was extended to Northern Ireland under the Local Government (Miscellaneous Provisions) (North Ireland) Order 1985 No. 1208 (NI 15) and Scotland under Part III of the Civic Government (Scotland) Act 1982.

14. Local Government (Miscellaneous Provisions) Act 1982, Chapter 3, Schedule 3, 3(c), p. 77 states that the number of Sex Establishments shall be determined by what the authority consider 'is appropriate for that locality', having regard to (i) the character of the relevant locality, (ii) the uses to which any premises in the vicinity are put, (iii) the layout, character or condition of the premises'.

15. Ibid., 4(b)(ii), p. 72.

16. Westminster City Council (2012), *Sex Entertainment Venues Statement of Licensing Policy*, London: Westminster, p. 5.

17. Ibid., p. 6.

18. Ibid., p. 13.

19. Ibid., pp. 15, 18.

20. That those who work in licensed sex shops widely refer to unlicensed stores as 'back street' shops indicates the significance of Soho's geography and layout to the nature and evolution of its sex industry.

21. City of Westminster Council, Licensing Sub-Committee Report, 31 July 2014, 'Application for a New Sex Establishment (Sex Shop) License under the Local Government (Miscellaneous Provisions) Act 1982 for Adult World, 5 Walker's Court, London, W1F 0BT', 4.2.2, emphasis added.

22. Ibid., 4.5.2 and Appendix B3.

23. Ibid., 4.6.2 and Appendix B4.

24. Coulmont and Hubbard (2010), p. 199.

25. Ibid., p. 200.

26. Evans, A., S. Riley and A. Shankar (2010), 'Postfeminist Heterotopias: Negotiating "Safe" and "Seedy" in the British Sex Shop Space', *European Journal of Women's Studies* 17(3), pp. 211–29, p. 216.

27. Edwards, M. (2010), 'Gender, Social Disorganization Theory and the Locations of Sexually Orientated Businesses', *Deviant Behaviour* 31, pp. 135–58, 140.

28. Arnold, C. (2010), *City of Sin: London and Its Vices*, London: Simon and Schuster, pp. 150–1.

29. Mort, F. (2010), *Capital Affairs*, London: Yale University Press, p. 206.

30. Speiser, P. (2017), *Soho: The Heart of Bohemian London*, London: The British Library, p. 15.

31. Mort (2010), p. 208.

32. Simmel, G. (1964), 'The Metropolis and Mental Life', in K. Wolff (ed.), *The Sociology of Georg Simmel*, New York: The Free Press of Glencoe, p. 9.

33. Mort (2010), p. 209.

34. Ryder (2004) argues that it is the increasing ability to purchase goods and services traditionally sold in sex shops online – what he calls the 'trend towards *aspatial retailing and aspatial adult entertainment*' – that has contributed to the commercial decline of the retail sex industry, rather than the regulatory effects of zoning or licensing – see Ryder, A. (2004), 'The Changing Nature of Adult Entertainment Districts: Between a Rock and a Hard Place or Going from Strength to Strength?', *Urban Studies* 41(9), pp. 1659–86, 1682, emphasis added.

35. See Noble, W. (2016), 'Is the Soho Sex Shop Dead?', *The Londonist*, 30 September.

36. Cameron, S. (2004), 'Space, Risk and Opportunity: The Evolution of Paid Sex Markets', *Urban Studies* 41(9), pp. 1643–57, p. 1643.

37. Ibid., p. 1646.

38. Ibid., pp. 1647–8.

39. Ibid., p. 1652.

40. Collins, A. (2004), 'Sexual Dissidence, Enterprise and Assimilation: Bedfellows in Urban Regeneration', *Urban Studies* 41(9), pp. 1789–806, Table 2 'Stages in the Development of Urban Gay Villages in England', p. 1802.

41. Brents, B., and T. Sanders (2010), 'Mainstreaming the Sex Industry: Economic Inclusion and Social Ambivalence', *Journal of Law and Society* 37(1), pp. 40–60, p. 40.

42. Mort (2010), p. 212.
43. See Tomkinson, M. (1982), *The Pornbrokers: The Rise of the Soho Sex Barons*, London: Virgin Books.
44. Farson, D. (1987), *Soho in the Fifties*, London: Michael Joseph, p. 95.
45. White, M., and M. Lutwyche (2009), *Clipped: Inside Soho's Clip Joints*, Birmingham: VHC Publishing, p. 7.
46. Thompson, T. (2004), 'Soho Clip Joints to Be Forced out of Business by Police', *The Observer*, 29 February.
47. Hutton, M. (2012), *The Story of Soho: The Windmill Years 1932–1964*, Stroud: Amberely, p. 128.
48. Ibid., p. 149.
49. Melly, G. (1987), 'Introduction', in Farson, p. xv
50. Farson (1987), p. 161.
51. Ibid., p. 161.
52. Ibid., p. 163.
53. White and Lutwyche (2009), p. 62, emphasis added.
54. Ibid., p. 105, emphasis added.
55. Ibid., p. 108.
56. Ibid., p. 129.
57. Denekamp, S. (2015), *Sex Shop Education*, London: Amazon, p. i.
58. See Ashforth, B., C. Kulik and M. Tomiuk (2008), 'How service agents manage the person-role interface', *Group and Organization Management* 33 (1), pp. 5–45, 15, p. 16.
59. See Hancock, P. (2005), 'Uncovering the Semiotic in Organizational Analysis', *Organization* 12(1), pp. 29–50.
60. Kirkby, D. (1997), *Barmaids: A History of Women's Work in Pubs*, Melbourne: Cambridge University Press, p. 205.
61. Althusser, L. (2001), *Lenin and Philosophy and Other Essays*, London: Monthly Review Press, see especially pp. 117–18.
62. Waring, A., and J. Waring (2009), 'Looking the part: Embodying the discourse of organizational professionalism in the City', *Current Sociology* 57(3), pp. 344–64, p. 348.
63. McDowell, L., and G. Court (1994), 'Performing work: Bodily representations in merchant banks', *Environment and Planning D: Society and Space* 12, pp. 727–50, p. 732.
64. Waring and Waring (2009), p. 361. However, Waring and Waring arguably treat the City as a sector of work rather than a specific place or setting, retiring the significance of the locale, although they acknowledge, however that 'in the global financial centres of London … the values of competition, motivation, success and profitability permeate the workplace and have an impact on how workers are expected to perform and act'.
65. Goffman, E. (1969), *The Presentation of the Self in Everyday Life*, Harmondsworth: Penguin.
66. Sherry, J. (1998), *Servicescapes: The Concepts of Place in Contemporary Markets*, London: McGraw-Hill.

67. See Burrell, G. (1984), 'Sex and Organizational Analysis', *Organization Studies* 5(2), pp. 97–118, and Elias, N. (2000; first published 1939), *The Civilizing Process, Volume One: A History of Manners*, Oxford: Blackwell.

68. See Berkowitz (2006).

69. Gherardi, S. (1995), *Gender, Symbolism and Organizational Cultures*, London: Sage, p. 43.

70. Denekamp (2015), emphasis added.

71. Berkowitz (2006), p. 593.

72. That Nathan pointed out the screens in this way is perhaps an interesting indication of how staff in the sex shops are so used to them that they no longer really 'see' the screens and the films they play, or even really think about them, even though they are present, often in multiple forms, in all of the stores. (To me, it seemed odd that he pointed out something that as an 'outsider' I was acutely aware of, but seen this way his gesture makes more sense.)

73. Crewe, L., and A. Martin (2017), 'Sex and the City: Branding, Gender and the Commodification of Sex Consumption in Contemporary Retailing', *Urban Studies* 54(3), pp. 582–99.

74. Attwood, F. (2005), 'Fashion and Passion: Marketing Sex to Women', *Sexualities* 8(4), pp. 392–406, 392; see also Loe, M. (1999), 'Feminism for Sale: Case-study of a Pro-Sex Feminist Business', *Gender and Society* 13(6).

75. Attwood (2005), p. 393.

76. Gold, J. (1995), *Good Vibrations*, London: Pavilion Books, p. 50.

77. Ibid., p. 51.

78. Ibid., p. 62.

79. Ibid., pp. 113, 176.

80. Williams, D. (1990), 'The Roots of the Garden', *The Journal of Sex Research* 27(3), pp. 461–6, 464–5, cited in Edwards (2010), p. 142.

81. Loe 1999, pp. 712, cited in Edwards (2010), p. 142.

82. Edwards (2010), p. 142.

83. Smith, C. (2007), 'Designed for Pleasure: Style, Indulgence and Accessorized Sex', *European Journal of Cultural Studies* 10(2), pp. 167–84, p. 167.

84. Attwood (2005), p. 394.

85. Smith (2007), p. 169.

86. Storr (2003), p. 212.

87. Attwood (2005), p. 399.

88. Ibid., p. 395.

89. Smith (2007), p. 176.

90. Ibid., p. 167.

91. Williams, R. (1977), *Marxism and Literature*, Oxford: Oxford University Press.

92. Crewe and Martin (2017), p. 585.

93. Smith (2007), p. 177.

94. Ibid., p. 178.
95. Charlotte Semler, co-founder of Myla, refers to her brand as the 'Gucci of sex shops ... the polar opposite of Ann Summers' (cited in Attwood, 2005, p. 399), hinting that the latter is associated with men's consumption preferences, working-class tastes and poor-quality products.
96. Noble, W. (2016), 'Is the Soho Sex Shop dead?', *The Londonist*, 30 September.
97. Brooks-Gordon, B. (2016), *The Price of Sex: Prostitution, Policy and Society*, Cambridge: Polity.
98. Maison Mika (combining French and Japanese terms, for 'House of Beautiful Things') is a sex shop in Singapore established by Trina Yeung with the explicit aim of providing a celebratory sexual space for Asian women in a very male-dominated industry and environment. As well as products and services, the shop provides sex education workshops, driven by the company's commercial mission: 'Your pleasure is our passion'.
99. Smith (2007), p. 179.
100. Bernstein, E. (2007), 'Sex Work for the Middle Classes', *Sexualities* 10(4), pp. 473–88.
101. Bernstein, E. (2001), 'The Meaning of the Purchase: Desire, Demand and the Commerce of Sex', *Ethnography* 2(3), pp. 389–420, p. 389.
102. The apparent rise in 2013 can be attributed to the effect of the Police and Crime Act 2009 that required lap-dancing clubs to apply for new licences.
103. Rhodes, D. (2018), 'Sex Shops and Lap Dancing Clubs in England Fall by a Third', BBC News, 23 February 2018.
104. Westminster City Council (2012), p. 21.
105. Bernstein (2001), p. 411.

IT'S A DIRTY JOB ...

1. Hughes, E. (1952), 'Work and the Self', in J. H. Rohrer and M. Sherif (eds.), *Social Psychology at the Crossroads*, New York: Harper, pp. 313–23.
2. Korczynski, M. (2003), 'Communities of Coping: Collective Emotional Labour in Service Work', *Organization* 10(1), pp. 55–79, p. 58.
3. The R-18 category is a legally restricted classification in Britain that is used primarily for explicit works of consenting sex or strong fetish material involving adults. Films may only be shown to adults in specially licensed cinemas and may be supplied to adults only in licensed sex shops. R-18 films cannot be supplied by mail order, hence Andy's reference to customers coming to Soho to buy them – partly because they can only be bought in licensed shops, or seen in licensed cinemas, but also because (as he emphasizes) 'coming to the place' is part of the consumption experience (source: www.bbfc.co.uk).
4. Following Hughes (1952), sociologists have come to understand dirty work as tasks, occupations and roles that are likely to be perceived as physically, socially or morally disgusting and degrading, engendering feelings of repulsion, disdain and/or pity. Sociologists have particularly emphasized the socially constructed nature of dirty work and the fluidity of definitional

boundaries and meanings, as well as the intersections between dirty work and identity. Recent research has highlighted the fluidity and multiplicity of dirty work, as well as the diversity of dirty workers' experiences and identities. See Simpson, R., N., Slutskaya, P. Lewis and H. Höpfl. (eds.) (2012), *Dirty Work: Concepts and Identities*, London: Palgrave.

5. Douglas, M. (2002), *Purity and Danger: An Analysis of the Concept of Pollution and Taboo*, London: Routledge.

6. Hubbard, P. (2004a), 'Revenge and Injustice in the Neoliberal City: Uncovering Masculinist Agendas', *Antipode* 36(4), pp. 665–86, p. 670.

7. Papayanis, M. (2000), 'Sex and the Revanchist City: Zoning Out Pornography in New York', *Environment and Planning D: Society and Space* 18(3), pp. 341–53.

8. Hubbard (2004a), p. 673.

9. Hubbard, P. (2002), 'Maintaining Family Values? Cleansing the Streets of Sex Advertising', *Area* 34(4), pp. 353–60.

10. Kristeva, J. (1982), *Powers of Horror*, New York: Columbia University Press, p. 5, emphasis added.

11. Hughes (1951), pp. 313–323.

12. Relatively few studies of the workplace draw on Kristeva's (1982) writing on abjection – a notable exception is Linstead's (1997) psychodynamic analysis of the reproduction of dysfunctional cycles of violent masculine behaviours in organizational settings – Linstead, S. (1997), 'Abjection and Organization: Men, Violence, and Management', *Human Relations* 50(9), pp. 1115–45.

13. Ashforth, B., and G. Kreiner (1999), 'How Can You Do It? Dirty Work and the Challenge of Constructing a Positive Identity', *Academy of Management Review* 24(3), pp. 413–34.

14. Warhurst, C., and D. Nickson (2009), 'Who's Got the Look? Emotional, Aesthetic and Sexualized Labour in Interactive Service Work', *Gender, Work and Organization* 16(3), pp. 385–404.

15. See Berkowitz, D. (2006), 'Consuming Eroticism: Gender Performances and Presentations in Pornographic Establishments', *Journal of Contemporary Ethnography* 35(5), pp. 583–606; Stein, M. (1990), *An Ethnography of an Adult Bookstore: Private Scenes in and Public Places*, Lewiston, NY: Edwin Mellen Press; Storr, M. (2003), *Latex and Lingerie: Shopping for Pleasure at Ann Summers Parties*, Oxford: Berg; Tewksbury, R. (1990), 'Patrons of Porn: Research Notes on the Clientele of Adult Bookstores', *Deviant Behaviour* 11, pp. 259–71; and Tewksbury, R. (1993), 'Peep Shows and Perverts: Men and Masculinity in a Adult Bookstore', *Journal of Men's Studies* 2(1), pp. 53–70.

16. Malina and Schmidt (1997) argue that the exploitative pricing strategies deployed in traditional sex shops rely on the sense of stigma experienced by customers, trading on the vulnerability engendered by their embarrassment and feelings of shame – Malina, D., and R. Schmidt (1997), 'It's a Business Doing Pleasure with You: Sh! A Women's Sex Shop Case', *Marketing Intelligence and Planning* 15(7), pp. 352–60, p. 356.

17. Hubbard, P. (2000), 'Desire/Disgust: Mapping the Moral Contours of Heterosexuality', *Progress in Human Geography* 24(2), pp. 191–217, 200.

18. Smith, C. (2007), 'Designed for Pleasure: Style, Indulgence and Accessorized Sex', *European Journal of Cultural Studies* 10(2), pp. 167–84, p. 169.
19. Hughes, J., R. Simpson, N. Slutskaya, A. Simpson, and K. Hughes (2017), 'Beyond the Symbolic: A Relational Approach to Dirty Work through a Study of Refuse Collectors and Street Cleaners', *Work, Employment and Society* 31, pp. 106–22, p. 106.
20. Ashforth, B., and G. Kreiner (2014), 'Dirty Work and Dirtier Work: Differences in Countering Physical, Social and Moral Stigma', *Management and Organization Review*, 10, pp. 81–108, p. 81.
21. Hughes (1952), p. 319.
22. Writing in the late 1950s, Goffman based his analysis of the social construction of 'spoiled identities' on earlier writing on dirty work, noting how many workplace performances and interactions involve concealing work which is 'unclean, semi-legal, cruel, and degrading in other ways' – see Goffman, E. (1959), *The Presentation of Self in Everyday Life*, Harmondsworth: Penguin, p. 53.
23. Hughes (1952), p. 319.
24. Jacqueline Gold, speaking as CEO of Ann Summers, describes first encountering Soho's viewing booths when visiting the shops there as a young woman, recalling how 'they were very seedy ... The worst moments were when the films jammed and all these red-faced men would come out of the booths to complain!' – Gold, J. (1995), *Good Vibrations*, London: Pavilion Books, p. 28.
25. Hughes (1952), p. 319.
26. Sanders, T. (2005), 'It's Just Acting: Sex Workers' Strategies for Capitalizing on Sexuality', *Gender, Work and Organization* 12(4), pp. 319–42.
27. Grandy, G. (2008), 'Managing Spoiled Identities: Dirty Workers' Strategies for a Favourable Sense of Self', *Qualitative Research in Organizations and Management* 3(3), pp. 176–98.
28. These experiences echo the regular encounters with sexually predatory customers described by Stacey Denekamp (2015, p. 46) in her account of working in a US sex shop. As she put it, 'they for some reason think that because of where we work, we are sluts or whores and can be treated with disrespect. Just because I like sex does not mean I want to have sex with everyone. They will hit on us over and over, try to touch us, say really rude things and they think it's funny. It is not funny at all' – Denekamp, S. (2015), *Sex Shop Education*, London: Amazon, p. 19. See also Chapter 3.
29. Kristeva (1982), p. 4.
30. Ashforth and Kreiner (1999), p. 419.
31. Ibid., p. 422.
32. Tracy, S. and C. Scott (2006), 'Sexuality, Masculinity and Taint Management Among Firefighters and Correctional Officers: Getting Down and Dirty with "America's Heroes" and the "Scum of Law Enforcement"', *Management Communication Quarterly* 20(1), pp. 6–38, p. 20.
33. Ackroyd, S., and P. Crowdy (1990), 'Can Culture Be Managed? Working with "Raw" Material: The Case of the English Slaughtermen', *Personnel Review* 19(5), pp. 3–13.

34. Ashforth and Kreiner (1999), p. 423, emphasis added.
35. Bolton, S. (2005), 'Women's Work, Dirty Work: The Gynaecology Nurse as "Other"', *Gender, Work and Organization* 12(2), pp. 169–86, p. 177, emphasis added.
36. Chiappetta-Swanson, C. (2005), 'Dignity and Dirty Work: Nurses' Experiences in Managing Genetic Termination for Fetal Anomaly', *Qualitative Sociology* 28(1), pp. 93–116.
37. Stacey, C. (2005), 'Finding Dignity in Dirty Work: The Constraints and Rewards of Low-Wage Home Care Labour', *Sociology of Health and Illness* 27 (6), pp. 831–54.
38. Godin, P. (2000), 'A Dirty Business: Caring for People Who Are a Nuisance or a Danger', *Journal of Advanced Nursing* 32(6), pp. 1396–402, p. 1396.
39. Bolton (2005), p. 177, emphasis added.
40. Ibid., emphasis added.
41. Ibid., p. 179.
42. Denekamp (2015), p. 19, emphasis added.
43. Hughes, J., R. Simpson and N. Slutskaya (2017), 'Beyond the Symbolic: A Relational Approach to Dirty Work through a Study of Refuse Collectors and Street Cleaners', *Work, Employment and Society* 31(1), pp. 497–510.
44. Grandy (2008), p. 176.
45. Hubbard, P. (2004b), 'Cleansing the Metropolis: Sex Work and the Politics of Zero Tolerance', *Urban Studies* 41(9), pp. 1687–702.
46. Hubbard, P., R. Matthews and J. Scoular (2009), 'Legal Geographies – Controlling Sexually Oriented Businesses: Law, Licensing and the Geographies of a Controversial Land Use', *Urban Geography* 30(2), pp. 185–205, p. 186.
47. Korczynski (2003), p. 55.
48. Summers, J. (1989), Soho: A History of London's Most Colourful Neighbourhood, London: Bloomsbury, p. 2.
49. Hughes (1952), p. 314, emphasis added.
50. Bataille, G. (1970), 'L'abjection et Les Formes Miserables', in *Essais de Sociologie*, Paris: Gallimard, p. 1.
51. Kristeva (1982), p. 1.
52. Linstead (1997), p. 1121.
53. While its anthropological approach and language is dated and by no means unproblematic, Lévi-Strauss' analysis of the social organization of difference has considerable resonance with the lived experiences of dirty work discussed here. As noted however, the ways in which his ideas are articulated are very much of their time.
54. Linstead (1997), p. 1121.
55. Ibid.
56. Kristeva (1982), p. 4, emphasis added.
57. Ibid., p. 68.
58. Simpson, R., N. Slutskaya, P. Lewis and Höpfl, H. (2012), 'Introducing Dirty Work, Concepts and Identities', in R. Simpson, N. Slutskaya, P. Lewis and H. Höpfl (eds.), *Dirty Work: Concepts and Identities*, London: Palgrave, pp. 1–18.

59. Littlewood, C. (2008), *Dirty White Boy: Tales of Soho*, San Francisco, CA: Cleis.
60. Kristeva (1982), p. 5.
61. Butler, J. (2000; first published 1990), *Gender Trouble*, London: Routledge.
62. Reckless, W. C. (1926), 'The Distribution of Commercial Vice in the City: A Sociological Analysis', *Publications of the American Sociological Society* 20, pp. 164–76, 172, cited in Ryder (2004), p. 1664.
63. Ryder, A. (2004), 'The Changing Nature of Adult Entertainment Districts: Between a Rock and a Hard Place or Going from Strength to Strength?', *Urban Studies* 41(9), pp. 1659–86, 1668. See Prior (2008), who also describes the clustering of gay businesses and services in the Oxford Street, Darlinghurst area of Sydney in the later decades of the twentieth century – Prior, J. (2008), 'Planning for Sex in the City: Urban Governance, Planning and the Placement of Sex Industry Premises in Inner Sydney', *Australian Geographer* 39(3), pp. 339–52.
64. Notably Soho Estates – the property development company established by Paul Raymond (see Chapter 1).
65. See also Ryder (2004), who argues that zoning in New York was largely driven by a concern with 'contamination, stigmatization from being associated with adult entertainment by proximity and loss of property values', p. 1663.
66. Cook, J. (2005), 'Shaken from Her Pedestal: A Decade of New York City's Sex Industry under Siege', *City University of New York Law Review* 9(1), pp. 121–59, p. 123.
67. Cook (2005), p. 124, emphasis added.
68. Ibid.
69. 'Primary effects' are the impact that the experience has on viewers when they are watching erotic dancing or viewing pornographic material (Cook, 2005).
70. See Cook (2005), p. 135.
71. Allen, M. (1998), 'Giuliani Tells Sex-Based Shops That the End Is Drawing Near', *New York Times*, 20 July, p. 81, cited in Cook (2005), p. 136.
72. Perez-Peña, R. (2000), 'City Loses Another Round in Fight with Topless Bars', *New York Times.* 5 May, p. 83, cited in Cook (2005), p. 137.
73. Cook (2005), p. 134.
74. Ibid., p. 159.
75. Prior (2008).
76. Binnie, J., and B. Skeggs (2004), 'Cosmopolitan Knowledge and the Production and Consumption of Sexualized Space: Manchester's Gay Village', *The Sociological Review* 52(1), p. 39–61.
77. Prior (2008), p. 348.
78. Crewe, L. and A. Martin (2017), 'Sex and the City: Branding, Gender and the Commodification of Sex Consumption in Contemporary Retailing', *Urban Studies* 54(3), pp. 582–99, p. 587.
79. Ibid., p. 588.
80. Ibid., p. 593.
81. Ibid.
82. Ibid., p. 589.

83. Waugh, A. (1920), 'Round about Soho' in St J. Adcock (ed.), *Wonderful London: Volume One*, London: The Fleetaway House, pp. 129–36, p. 136.

NO PLACE FOR A LADY?

1. O'Neill, R. (2018), *Seduction: Men, Masculinity and Mediated Intimacy*, Cambridge: Polity.
2. Summers, J. (1989), Soho: A History of London's Most Colourful Neighbourhood, London: Bloomsbury, p. 190.
3. Hubbard, P. (2004a), 'Revenge and Injustice in the Neoliberal City: Uncovering Masculinist Agendas', *Antipode* 36(4), pp. 665–86, p. 670.
4. Hubbard (2004a), pp. 678, p. 682.
5. Smith, C. (2007), 'Designed for Pleasure: Style, Indulgence and Accessorized Sex', *European Journal of Cultural Studies* 10(2), pp. 167–84, p. 169.
6. Storr, M. (2003), *Latex and Lingerie: Shopping for Pleasure at Ann Summers Parties*, Oxford: Berg.
7. Malina, D., and R. Schmidt (1997), 'It's Business Doing Pleasure with You: Sh! A Women's Sex Shop Case', *Marketing Intelligence and Planning* 15(7), pp. 352–60, 356.
8. Thank you to Wade Guyitt for noting Nathan's specific phrasing here, in particular the use of the term 'making', suggesting that even when women 'direct the making' of pornographic films, they are still not 'making' it by or for themselves: it is still only men who can produce pornography according to their own desires.
9. Speiser, P. (2017), *Soho: The Heart of Bohemian London*, London: The British Library, p. 18.
10. McCleary and Tewksbury (2010, p. 219) show that female customers are most likely to visit busy sex shops located in high-street areas with a high flow of pedestrian traffic, and those with security guards, interpreting this to indicate that women prefer to visit stores they perceive as 'safe' (see Chapter 2). Their study suggests that women are, perhaps not surprisingly, least likely to visit stores such as those that have private viewing booths. In some of the shops they studied, women were actively discouraged (or even informally prohibited) from entering areas of stores with viewing booths. Staffing differences and differences in product range and/or merchandising do not play a significant role in this, they suggest. Rather, environmental and aesthetic factors such as the degree to which a store is perceived as 'clean' and 'safe' explain gender differences in consumer patterns – see McCleary, R. and R. Tewksbury (2010), 'Female Patrons of Porn', *Deviant Behaviour* 31, pp. 208–23.
11. Evans, A., S. Riley and A. Shankar (2010), 'Postfeminist Heterotopias: Negotiating "Safe" and "Seedy" in the British Sex Shop Space', *European Journal of Women's Studies* 17(3), pp. 211–29.
12. Butler, J. (2000 [1990]), *Gender Trouble*, London: Routledge. Although she has moved away from it in more recent writing, in her early discussions of gender performativity in the 1990 publication of *Gender Trouble* Butler uses the term 'heterosexual matrix' to refer to an ideological schema that positions

sex, gender and sexuality in a normatively linear relationship, so that 'normal' men are male, masculine and (hetero)sexually active and dominant, whereas women are female, feminine and (hetero)sexually relatively inactive and passive. These two linear categories are organized hierarchically in such a way that maintains male/masculine privilege and dominance, governing the terms on which gender viability, or intelligibility, will be recognized. For Butler (1990/2000), making trouble with gender means challenging the parameters, or terms, of this matrix cross-cutting its binary and hierarchical linearity. This is a theme she develops in *Undoing Gender* (Butler, 2004) in which she emphasizes that gender is simultaneously our 'undoing' and, because it is performatively enacted, contains within it the possibilities of being done differently – in a way that challenges, or makes 'trouble' with, the normative constraints of the heterosexual matrix.

13. Evans, Riley and Shankar (2010), p. 211.
14. See also Storr (2003) and Crewe and Martin (2017). The latter argue that the market repositioning pursued by chains such as Ann Summers enables them to bypass legislative regulation and locate themselves very visibly in mainstream retail spaces.
15. Evans, Riley and Shankar (2010), p. 217.
16. Ibid., p. 221.
17. Crewe, L., and A. Martin (2017), 'Sex and the City: Branding, Gender and the Commodification of Sex Consumption in Contemporary Retailing', *Urban Studies* 54(3), pp. 582–99.
18. Ibid., p. 593.
19. Ibid., p. 594.
20. Ibid., p. 585.
21. See Russell, R., and M. Tyler (2002), 'Thank Heaven for Little Girls: Girl Heaven and the Commercialization of Feminine Childhood', *Sociology* 36 (3), pp. 619–37.
22. Crewe and Martin (2017), p. 589.
23. Ibid., p. 591.
24. Ibid., p. 588.
25. Malina and Schmidt (1997), p. 352.
26. Ibid., p. 353.
27. Ibid., p. 356.
28. McDowell, L., and G. Court (1994), 'Performing Work: Bodily Representations in Merchant Banks', *Environment and Planning D: Society and Space* 12, pp. 727–50, p. 729.
29. Smith (2007), p. 169.
30. Malina and Schmidt (1997), p. 352.
31. Smith (2007), p. 167.
32. Loe (1999, p. 709) cites a conference presentation given in 1984 by feminist anthropologist and campaigner Carole Vance, which 'crystallizes' the two sides within feminism with reference to an orientation to a politics of either sexual pleasure or sexual danger – Loe, M. (1999), 'Feminism for Sale: Case Study of a Pro-Sex Feminist Business', *Gender & Society* 13(6), pp. 705–32.
33. Ibid.

34. Ibid., p. 712.
35. Ibid., p. 712.
36. Molotch, H. (2013), 'Objects and the City', in G. Bridge and S. Watson (eds.), *The New Blackwell Companion to the City*, Oxford: Blackwell, p. 77.
37. Summers (1989), p. 190.
38. Sanders-McDonagh, E., and M. Peyrefitte (2018), 'Immoral Geographies and Soho's Sex Shops: Exploring Spaces of Sexual Diversity in London', *Gender, Place and Culture* 25(3), pp. 351–67. See also Sanders-McDonagh, E., and M. Peyrefitte (2016), 'Sanitizing the City: Exploring Hegemonic Gentrification in London's Soho', *Sociological Research Online* 21(3), pp. 1–6, for a contrasting view of Soho as hegemonically gentrified and over-sanitized, rather than a queer constellation.
39. Crewe and Martin (2017), p. 597.
40. Loe (1999), p. 719.
41. Butler, J. (2004) *Undoing Gender*. London: Routledge, p. 1.
42. Ibid., p. 1.
43. Ibid., p. 5.
44. Ibid., p. 186.
45. Sanders, T., and R. Campbell (2007), 'Designing out Vulnerability, Building in Respect: Violence, Safety and Sex Work Policy', *The British Journal of Sociology* 58(1), pp. 1–19, p. 7, emphasis added.
46. Ibid., p. 1.
47. Ibid., p. 9.
48. O'Neill, M., and R. Barbaret (2000), 'Victimization and the Social Organization of Prostitution in England and Spain', in R. Weitzer (ed.), *Sex for Sale*, London: Routledge, cited in Sanders and Campbell (2007), p. 11.
49. See Korczynski, M. (2003), 'Communities of Coping: Collective Emotional Labour in Service Work', *Organization* 10(1), pp. 55–79.
50. Sanders and Campbell (2007), p. 12, emphasis added.
51. Ibid., p. 16.
52. Cook, J. (2005), 'Shaken from Her Pedestal: A Decade of New York City's Sex Industry under Siege', *City University of New York Law Review* 9(1), pp. 121–59, p. 139.

CONCLUSION

1. Mort, F. (2010), *Capital Affairs*, London: Yale University Press, p. 12.
2. Mort (2010), p. 13.
3. Lippard, L. (1997), *The Lure of the Local*, New York: The New Press.
4. Hutton, M. (2012), *The Story of Soho: The Windmill Years 1932–1964*, Stroud: Amberley, p. 218.
5. Katz, B. (2010), *Soho Society*, London: Quartet Books.
6. At its Annual General Meeting (AGM), The Soho Society reported on 26 April 2018 that in 2017 and the first four months of 2018, 452 planning applications had been submitted to Westminster City Council for proposed developed within the Soho area. Other issues that were raised as being of

particular and ongoing concern included rental levels comparable to those in Mayfair and the direct and related pressures for local business and residents. Concerns about air quality were also raised, as was the limited availability of affordable housing in the area. Deliveries to/from bars, restaurants and other commercial places were also noted as a particular problem, exacerbating noise, pollution and traffic congestion. The whole tone of the meeting (that I was invited to attend) was welcoming and lively. In my notes I highlighted that there is clearly a thriving residential community, which is well integrated into local business and wider activities. The Committee and volunteers put a lot of time, energy and expertise into the Society and into maintaining Soho's distinctive character, staving off threats from Westminster City Council, central government and corporate developers. There was a very strong sense of Soho as a village community or, rather, as a series of communities sharing the same space.

7. Stephen Fry, 'Crossrail 2 Threatens Soho's Authentic Soul', speaking on ITV News, 10 February 2017.

8. Mort (2010), p. 357.

9. Ibid.

10. The School's website describes its history: 'Three schools merged to form the current Soho Parish School: St Anne's was founded in 1699, St James's in 1827 and St Peter's in 1872. The School's current location in Great Windmill Street originates from 1872, when it was St Peter's (as carved on the outside walls). Each of these three schools began as charitable foundations dependent on voluntary giving. In the 1870s the School provided regular medical and dental checks, something most people in the parish could not afford at the time. Children were also given free school meals, for many children the only hot food they would eat in a day. As a microcosm of Soho as a whole, the School has been multi-cultural and multi-lingual since its inception – many children came from Jewish families at the beginning of the twentieth century, then Italian, Chinese and Bangladeshi (in roughly chronological order). There are now many other nationalities attending the school' – see www.sohoparish.co.uk/History-of-the-school.

11. Dryden's (1667) poem 'Annus Mirabilis' is cited in Ackroyd, P. (2001), *London: A Biography*, London: Verso, p. 514.

12. Ibid., p. 531.

13. Ibid., p. 549.

14. Speiser, P. (2017), *Soho: The Heart of Bohemian London*, London: The British Library, p. 165.

15. Ibid., p. 165.

16. Ibid., p. 166.

17. Tyler, M. (2014), 'Sleazy or sanitized, London's Soho thrives most when under threat', *The Conversation*, 2 December.

18. Vaines, C. (2015), 'Soho stories: Celebrating six decades of sex, drugs and Rock'n'Roll', *The Observer*, 17 May.

19. Farson, D. (1987), *Soho in the Fifties*, London: Michael Joseph, p. 168.

20. This is a term that Louise Nash uses to describe the historical layering that characterizes the social materiality of the built environment in the City of

London – see Nash, L. (2018), 'Performing Place: A Rhythmanalysis of the City of London', *Organization Studies*, online early, pp. 1–21.

21. Madame Jojo's was famous for its live entertainment, especially its drag performances. Concerns have been raised about the continuing closure of live music and entertainment venues in London and the longer-term implications of this for the creative industries and arts. Reports suggest that between 2007 and 2017, almost half of London's nightclubs and a third of its live music venues closed, a quarter of its pubs and nearly 60 per cent of its LGBTQ venues – Crerar, P. (2017), 'Give 24-hour clubs and music venues a break, says night czar', *Evening Standard*, 7 November 2017, p. 19.

22. As a touching example of the club and the area's continuing cultural importance, singer Héloïse Letissier of Christine and the Queens recently described how she found herself gravitating to Soho and particularly Madame Jojo's when she left Paris for London whilst struggling with depression and anxiety about her sexuality. She recalls how the club's drag queens, drawn to her openness and fragility, nursed her back to health, embracing her in a community that she describes as full of 'trust' and 'generosity' and to whom her band's name is a long-standing tribute and token of her gratitude – Cragg, M. (2016), 'Interview – Christine and the Queens: From Soho drag club to French superstardom', *The Guardian*, 7 January. See also Damien Frost's (2016) *Night Flowers* (London: Merrell) for a photographic account of Soho's drag community.

23. Fry, S. (2008), 'Foreword', in B. Katz, *Soho Society*, London: Quartet, p. 11.

24. Richardson, N. (2000), *Dog Days in Soho: One Man's Adventures in 1950s Bohemia*, London: Phoenix, p. 57.

Index

Note: page numbers followed by 'n' refer to notes